D0081613

The Birth of Big Business
in the United States, 1860–1914

The Birth of
Big Business in
the United States,
1860–1914

Commercial, Extractive, and
Industrial Enterprise

DAVID O. WHITTEN
BESSIE E. WHITTEN

Westport, Connecticut
London

Library of Congress Cataloging-in-Publication Data

Whitten, David O.
   The birth of big business in the United States, 1860–1914 : commercial, extractive, and industrial enterprise / David O. Whitten and Bessie E. Whitten.
      p.   cm.
   Includes bibliographical references and index.
   ISBN 0-313-32395-X (alk. paper)
   1. Industries—United States—History.   2. United States—Economic conditions.   I. Whitten, Bessie E. (Bessie Emrick) II. Title.
HC103.W48 2006
338.0973'09'034—dc22   2005019177

British Library Cataloguing in Publication Data is available.

Library of Congress Catalog Card Number: 2005019177
ISBN: 0-313-32395-X

First published in 2006

Praeger Publishers, 88 Post Road West, Westport, CT 06881
An imprint of Greenwood Publishing Group, Inc.
www.praeger.com

Printed in the United States of America

The paper used in this book complies with the Permanent Paper Standard issued by the National Information Standards Organization (Z39.48-1984).

10 9 8 7 6 5 4 3 2 1

Dedicated to the Crum family,
because we love them

Edward and Barbara
Edward and Teri
David and Katy
Carson
Brandon
Carter
Courtney
Caroline

Contents

Preface

The late twentieth and early twenty-first centuries witnessed portentous changes in business enterprise. Personal computers, cellular telephones, and the World Wide Web symbolize a world of people and institutions wired together to share information and consummate transactions. Sharing the limelight with spectacular advances in market operations is a merger movement of impressive dimensions. Firms ranging from publishing houses to automobile manufacturers are being absorbed by megacorporations. In the member nations of NAFTA—the North American Free Trade Agreement comprising Canada, Mexico, and the United States—and the European Union, in Japan and beyond, consumers at the local level have watched McDonald's restaurants and Wal-Mart SuperCenters transfigure retailing throughout communities and regions. Small businesses, endangered for decades, will either disappear into history or recover as an antidote to the enormity and uniformity of branching retail operations.

The economic changes of the 1990s are rooted in developments during the years following the Civil War. Titans of business emerged in the nineteenth century. Advances in the twentieth and twenty-first centuries are extensions of the business evolution that brought forth the Sherman Antitrust Act in 1890, the law used more than a century later to throttle the gargantuan Microsoft empire. Wal-Mart SuperCenters threaten local grocery stores (outlets that are themselves huge when compared with the mom-and-pop operations their forebears pushed into oblivion), drugstores, floral boutiques, hardware stores, beauty shops, garden centers, and a wide variety of other small businesses in the twenty-first century, much like Sears, A&P, Grants, and Montgomery Ward decimated small businesses a century before.

Large-scale operations, being more productive than small-scale ones, will overwhelm smaller enterprises to the extent that society permits. In a democracy, voters will accept the destruction of small businesses to gain greater outputs and lower prices from firms capitalizing on scale economies. If more goods improve standards of living, consumers are going to encourage concentration of production and distribution in firms capable of the lowest costs. As though to balance the advantages to society of economies of scale, the same forces that guarantee lower costs to immense production and distribution also foster monopoly complete with the power to charge prices higher than those offered by business subject to competition. In the United States these opposing forces have been addressed through antitrust laws and regulation.

If competition means more output and lower prices than monopoly, antitrust laws prevent the concentration of production and distribution in one firm and encourage oligopoly. If monopoly is advantageous to consumers, monopoly is permitted—even encouraged—but regulated to guarantee the greatest output at the lowest cost. Antitrust and regulation promised consumers the best of scale economies until the deregulation boom in the last quarter of the twentieth century.

Between the Civil War and World War I the United States grew into a nation dominated by giant business. The physical expansion of the country combined with development of transportation and communication facilities to create an imposing free market and businesses capable of capitalizing on the accompanying economies of scale. It is not a novel theme, but one widely accepted and presented along with studies of the giant firms that made the United States the industrial titan of the world. This study applies a broader approach to the theme, one that acknowledges the growth of not just business firms but institutions in general. The United States Post Office, for example, is not usually included in studies of communications firms; yet, despite government ownership and operation, the Post Office was taking shape within the same economic environment as the telegraph and telephone companies. It too became a giant in these interwar years.

Americans know the heritage of the Old West. Huge ranches, cowboys, and encroaching sod busters and the conflict between them are the raw materials of national folklore. That segment of history between the Civil War and World War I belongs to the era of conflict that produced American Tobacco, Standard Oil, and United States Steel. Similarly, the giant department stores and mammoth mail-order houses are part and parcel of the industrial growth of America: Mass production cannot be sustained without mass consumption. *The Birth of Big Business in the United States, 1860–1914*, an introductory work for students and general readers, draws together these diverse threads of the American experience, lacing them into the fabric of U.S. business history.

Introduction

Between the Civil War and World War I the size of American enterprise—industrial, commercial, agricultural, and governmental especially—expanded rapidly. In 1860 the United States was a giant country made up of small-scale, local enterprises. In 1914 giants dominated American business, punctuated American farming, and showed signs of spreading throughout the national institutional structure. *The Birth of Big Business in the United States, 1860–1914* is a business history of the period with an emphasis on expanding business enterprise broadly cast to include giants of commerce, manufacturing, and extractive industries. Government projects are included to illuminate the role of business in the developing local and national socioeconomic structure of the era.

Despite ups and downs, the story of the New World has been one of prosperity and growth. What was true for the entire hemisphere was even more true for the United States. The young country had roots in a colonial period built around business activity: the very purpose of the first thrusts of colonization had been profits for investors. The business of colonization suffered early setbacks when undercapitalized colonies struggling in the raw American environment failed to produce sufficient profits for their anxious, impatient investors. Nevertheless, the American colonial era—the seventeenth and eighteenth centuries—was dominated by mercantilism, government-directed economic policy that assigned a pivotal role to colonies.

Motivated by mercantilistic goals, the British Crown provided grants of land to the colonizing companies and then assumed responsibility for defunct colonial ventures. English colonists depended on Crown support as they wrestled a harsh natural environment for survival while battling Native Americans and the Dutch, French, and Spanish. The Crown was an essential part of the colonial economy and society. As long as national government aided and abetted the business life of the colonists, Americans were loyal subjects. When government demanded that goods bound for England or the colonies must travel in ships of the mother country or the colonies, the Americans shared in a prosperous monopoly in shipping. However, when the English government ordered a tariff on French molasses bound for America, making that product more expensive than the otherwise more costly British product, the American colonists simply smuggled in the cheaper French good. Until 1763 American colonists enjoyed the benefits of the British government's participation in the American economy and avoided government intervention that increased costs.

Before 1763 British domestic conflict and competition with other European nations for goods and markets prevented serious enforcement of mercantilistic legislation created to maximize Great Britain's returns from its colonial empire. Minimal enforcement of the trade and navigation code was a fillip to colonial prosperity: Americans observed those laws they found profitable and ignored the rest. American shippers took advantage of the monopoly on shipping, and indigo planters collected the bounty paid by the Crown to subsidize cultivation and processing of the organic blue dyestuff. Those laws costly to the colonials were evaded when possible. By 1763, evasion of such legislation was institutionalized in America.

In the 1660s the British-Americans overwhelmed the Dutch in America and absorbed their commercial holdings. A century later the British and their American allies seized French possessions in North America and laid the groundwork for the American Revolution. As long as mercantilistic policies worked to the benefit of American business enterprise and Crown intervention was ineffective, British subjects in America remained loyal. After 1763, however, the more effective implementation of mercantilistic policies encouraged Americans to regard the cutting of ties with England as necessary for continued American prosperity. The colonies, matured beyond mercantilism, had developed into an economic unity. By the beginning of the War of Independence in 1776 the world had outgrown mercantilism, as evidenced by Adam Smith's *Wealth of Nations*, first published in that year.[1]

The century from the 1760s to the 1860s was one of continued expansion on the American scene. The ties of government were broken with Britain, and a new government was established on the foundations of the Confederation government that had been hastily constructed to manage the war. The constitutional government that came to represent the new political entity proved to be hardly less disruptive than the British counterpart that had been thrown off. Americans living in the western portion of the nation learned in 1794 that a government capable of providing them with the services expected of government could also levy taxes on them and force payment if necessary. The response to the Whiskey Rebellion of 1794 revealed a government more sympathetic to the needs of the young republic than its British predecessor had been but one nonetheless willing and able to intervene in, as well as participate in, the economic affairs of the nation.[2]

The affairs of the United States were stormy prior to 1860, just as they would be beyond that time and down to the present. Prosperity, however, was a common thread joining the ups and downs of the business system. A second war with the British (1812) had strong business overtones, although the commercial sector of the nation opposed the conflict: the isolation from foreign goods during that spell provided a boost for the nation's manufacturing sector. The dreams of Alexander Hamilton approached fruition with the legislation of a system of tariffs to protect the infant industrial enterprises. The hopes of Thomas Jefferson would thrive in the Southern United States, where the profits in agriculture thwarted the development of a business culture to rival the quasi-noble landowning planters. Opposing sections—a business-industrial North and a commercial-agricultural South, both prospering—set the scene for civil war. The roots of confrontation were put down early in U.S. history, matured for half a century, then erupted in armed hostilities.

Business panics and economic fumbling characterized early U.S. growth. The War of 1812 coincided with the demise of the Bank of the United States: Hostilities were accompanied by monetary chaos growing out of a war economy and an unregulated monetary system. The second Bank of the United States, chartered in 1816, paced an orderly return to monetary stability and extensive investments in private and public capital. Social overhead capital in roads, bridges, highways, and canals expanded business horizons in the United States as the nation grew geographically and demographically. Private investment built a world-competitive merchant fleet, textile manufacturing plants, iron works, and smaller craft-based industry.[3]

The U.S. monetary and economic systems collapsed in 1837 in what is arguably the worst panic of the nineteenth century, and perhaps the most serious in the nation's history. Recovery was inhibited by the refusal of political authorities to return to a stable system of money and banking. Patchwork institutional arrangements in the monetary sector, however, stimulated sporadic economic growth until the outbreak of the Civil War. The war with Mexico was taken in stride, causing hardly a ripple on the waters of American prosperity. The final decade-and-a-half before the Civil War witnessed the rise of the railroads. Although iron rails connected most of the populous areas of the nation by the beginning of the war, nothing resembling a unified transportation network had materialized. Entrepreneurs with a vision of the national economy that was growing out of the expanding transportation potential of canals, turnpikes, and railroads fostered the prosperity that would distinguish the future. The nation suffered a financial panic in 1857 as the boom driven by the Compromise of 1850 ran out and uncertainty took its toll on business enterprise in general and investment in particular.

By 1860 the contiguous United States was in place. The gross area of the continental United States was 888,811 square miles in 1790, and the complete 3,022,387 square miles had been acquired by 1860. A labor force to develop and work the continental real estate expanded concomitantly with landmass. Less than four million Americans resided in the United States in 1790, about one-sixth of the population in 1850. Between 1850 and 1860 the population of the nation increased by 35 percent, to the 31,513,000 estimated total on the eve of the Civil War. Just as the nation itself was young, so was the population: in 1860 the median age of the people living in the United States was 19.4 years.

An expanding population and workforce combined with a fertile, mineral-rich, continental political entity produced an expanding and prosperous economy. The number of manufacturing establishments, including hand and neighborhood industries, rose by 14 percent between 1849 and 1859. The value added by manufacturing increased by 84 percent over the same years. Output was already expanding faster than the number of manufacturing establishments, a prelude to the concentration of production that became a dominant feature of business in the years after the Civil War. Increased reliance on non-human energy sources accompanied the rise in industrial output. In 1850 an estimated 8,495,000 total horsepower for all prime movers foreshadowed the coming of machine-age power in abundance: The 1860 estimate was 62 percent larger, but the 1910 estimate would be more than ten times the 1860 estimate. The use of non-human energy sources for industrial production, which had been the mark of the Western world since the Middle Ages, was already showing signs of tremendous increase by the beginning of the Civil War–World War I period.

The prosperity of the 1850s can be gleaned from the import trade. In 1850, $164 million worth of foreign goods entered the United States, a sum that, despite national monetary woes, would more than double by 1860. The prosperity in that last prewar decade originated largely in the expanded markets created by railroads: The twenty-three miles of U.S. railroad track in 1830 had multiplied a hundred times by 1840 and stood at 9,021 in 1850, and then tripled to 30,626 miles by 1860. Much of the original track laid in the United States was imported from abroad, but output from domestic blast furnaces was also used as rail output increased by 120 percent between 1850 and 1860.

As transportation facilities improved, so did communications. The number of daily newspapers published rose from 254 in 1850 to 387 in 1860, an increase of 52 percent. Personal correspondence was facilitated as the federal government, responding to a constitutional provision, established 10,000 new post offices over the 1850s to bring the total to 28,498 in 1860. Public sector employment expanded as the number of federal civilian employees increased from 26,274 in 1851 to 36,672 in 1861. And the money supply kept pace with the economic expansion of the 1850s: currency increased from $285 million in 1850 to $442 million in 1860.[4]

Many of the actors who brought life to the economic stage in the years after the Civil War were already playing in 1860: Forty-nine-year-old Isaac Merritt Singer was enjoying the wealth generated by his sewing machine, a device the Union would put to work to clothe its soldiers in uniforms and shoes; Cornelius Vanderbilt, sixty-six, enlarged an already impressive fortune by exploiting wartime demand for shipping and rail transportation; Daniel Drew, sixty-three, had long since given up droving and the stockyards for railroads and stock exchanges; and Cyrus Hall McCormick, fifty-one, offered farmers his agricultural machinery as a substitute for field hands drafted into the military. Some entrepreneurs would capitalize instead on the postwar economy: Andrew Carnegie was a young man of twenty-five in 1860; John Wanamaker and James J. Hill were twenty-two; and John D. Rockefeller was twenty-one. Others were children: Theodore N. Vail was but a lad of fifteen, and Alexander Graham Bell and his friend Thomas A. Edison were both thirteen; Edward Henry Harriman was twelve; F. W. Woolworth was eight; and James Buchanan (Buck) Duke was a babe of four. Several men who would shape the nation in the years after the war were born during the conflict: Henry Ford and William Randolph Hearst share a birth year, 1863; and Julius Rosenwald had been born a year earlier, 1862. S. S. Kresge barely missed the war, being born in 1867; whereas J. C. Penney, another nineteenth-century retail magnate, did not arrive until 1875.

The American Civil War pitted the industrial Northeast, allied with the agrarian Northwest, against the agricultural South and its peculiar institution of slavery. The South sustained a business culture dominated by plantation agriculture. In the Northeast and the Northwest, extractive industries were producers of raw materials to be processed and marketed for a profit—farming, mining, and fishing were sources of business enterprise. In the South, agriculture was the cultural hub and business was ancillary, for investment opportunities in land and slaves lured capital and entrepreneurial talent away from the competitive pursuits of business.

As the sesquicentennial of the Civil War approaches, the psychological wounds left by that conflict are unmistakable. Although most Americans see slavery as the root of hostilities, a vocal few insist that slavery was not an underlying cause of the war. Alternative explanations for the conflict begin with states' rights and extend to so sublime a reason as tariffs. The battle flag of the defunct Confederacy remains controversial as two states, Georgia and Mississippi, continue to incorporate the emblem in the design of their state flags. In the year 2000 Georgia reduced the disputed emblem from the dominant field to a badge. Nevertheless, Georgians bicker: Some demand removal of the final vestige of the Confederate symbol; others insist on returning it to its former prominence. Mississippians, in turn, voted in 2001 to retain the Confederate fields on their state flag.

South Carolina's state flag, a relic of colonial and Revolutionary heritage, is unencumbered by the Confederate emblem; instead, the full battle flag was flown on the South Carolina statehouse dome. In the twenty-first century South Carolina was forced to remove the contested emblem to end an economic boycott. The organizers and supporters of the embargo accept no revisionist explanations for the Civil War, but neither do they hold the South solely responsible for the deplorable exploitation of human beings. The entire United States prospered at the expense of slave labor, not just the Southern economy. With that in mind, activists continue to press for reparations based on the prosperity of the U.S. slave era and, by extension, the national prosperity in the years since slavery was abolished.

Although the characteristics of modern business enterprise were evident a decade or more before the Civil War, that epochal conflict is used as the starting point for *The Birth of Big Business in the United States, 1860–1914*. Wars, being more military and political culminations than economic ones, do not always serve well as historical dividing lines for economic and business history. Nevertheless, a war represents so traumatic an experience that it alters the societies involved in it. American business may have appeared unchanged in the post–Civil War years, but the death of hundreds of thousands of Americans and the hardship and deprivation endured by the general public warped the social and economic scene.

A period of war that pushes a society to its productive limit will expose the extremes in available technology. Improvements in productive technology can exist in an idle state in an economy under little stress to expand, but the pressures of a war force the society to innovate to its technological capacity and thereby expose the available level of technology. Although wartime demand does not bear evenly on all sectors of an economy and society, it clearly has broad impact. The sewing machine, for example, gave rise to the ready-made clothing industry, but that manufacture required the demand for uniforms to stimulate development that would continue apace in the postwar years. At the far end of the 1860–1914 era, the bright promise of powered flight would be turned to dark uses. Aviation had advanced in fits and starts before World War I, but recognition of the full potential of the heavier-than-air flying machines came with the exigencies of war.

The story of the ready-made clothing industry belongs to the post–Civil War period and of modern aviation to the post–World War I era. That is not to say that the two industries would not have developed without the wars but that they were stimulated by the demands a war places on society. The war between the American states, then, will serve as a starting point here, for it brought to fulfillment the technological machinery of the day. The study ends as American businessmen watch with interest the outbreak of hostilities between the Allies and the Central Powers in the war that was to have ended all wars.

NOTES

1. See Edwin J. Perkins, *The Economy of Colonial America*, 2d ed. (New York: Columbia University Press, 1988).

2. David O. Whitten, "An Economic Inquiry into the Whiskey Rebellion of 1794," *Agricultural History* 49, no. 3 (Summer 1975): 491–504.

3. See Laurence J. Malone, *Opening the West: Federal Internal Improvements Before 1860*, Contributions in Economics and Economic History, no. 196 (Westport, CT: Greenwood Press, 1998).

4. Statistics from U.S. Bureau of the Census, *Historical Statistics of the United States, Colonial Times to 1957* (Washington, DC: U.S. Government Printing Office, 1960).

PART I

Background

CHAPTER 1

American Business in the Civil War

The American Civil War (1861–65) capped decades of dissension between the Southern slaveholding states and the remainder of the United States. Regional differences in America were as old as the colonial era, when British holdings divided by economic interests into the New England, Middle, and Southern colonies. The states that had been created from the British New England and Middle colonies comprised the Northeast. The newly settled states west of the Appalachian Mountains and north of the Mississippi River made up the North-west, and the old Southern colonies, combined with the new states west of Georgia, constituted the South. The sections had often compromised their differences, and, while volatile, the issues contested in 1860–61 were not beyond the give-and-take of the bargaining table. Neither the slaveholding states nor the Union stood to gain much from armed conflict certain to cost dearly in lives and property.

By 1860 the United States was a successful trade bloc in a world dependent more on colonialism than on treaties and political ties to guarantee access to raw materials and markets. In a rapidly developing continental economy unencumbered by national boundaries, clever capitalists exploited general laws of incorporation to amass funds through a stock market accessible to millions of citizens via telegraph wires that eliminated miles between investors and entrepreneurs. Telegraph companies, the first continental businesses, blazed the path for the railroads, the pride of the nineteenth century.

The economic interdependency that twenty-first century optimists rely on to discourage wars was disregarded by Americans in 1860–61. Passion replaced promise, and the Northeast and Northwest, despite political differences, allied to defend the Union against the secession of eleven Southern states into a separate nation. Both Union and Confederacy suffered from the South's defection.

Southern farmers relied on Northeastern businesses to sell their cotton, tobacco, rice, and sugar and to provide the manufactured and luxury goods in demand in the South. Because capital and land in the South were devoted to slave-driven commercial staple-crop agriculture, these states were a market for foodstuffs from the Northwest. The North, for its part, found a profitable business in handling Southern trade. Although the issues separating the sections were grave—slavery, land policy, tariffs, and monetary reform—they were negotiable.

The founders of the Confederacy built their government on the federal model. Southerners experienced in Union politics made use of confiscated buildings and equipment. Drawing on meager state resources and those seized from the Union, the South established an army and a navy for defense against federal forces bent on holding the nation together. The Union, unequipped for war, set about building an invasion force but did not abandon efforts at compromise. Knowing that to attack the peculiar institution would turn a likely war into a certain one, the Lincoln administration avoided the issue of slavery. When hope for compromise disappeared, President Lincoln enunciated emancipation to sustain the drive to save the Union and short-circuit the movement for "peace at any price."

Slavery was more than an issue in contention between North and South; it was an institution around which the Southern society and economy operated. Although the North was not built directly on slave labor, it was dependent on slavery through its interaction with the economy of the South. Slavery was a source of labor in the South and a business operation in human beings. Slave sales were as important as slave labor. Owners sought profits from the employment of chattel labor and from selling slaves when the number owned multiplied through births exceeding deaths. Southern slave owners were shrewd enough to recognize a dim future for slavery if America's first Republican president succeeded in limiting slavery to the existing slave states.

Without expanding markets for chattel labor and sales, slavery would lose its economic viability. What would happen as the South produced more chattels than it could profitably employ? Abraham Lincoln's election forced Americans to assess the future of the nation and decide where slavery would fit into that future. Lincoln did not represent abolition, but he did stand for a realistic evaluation and containment of an institution that had never fit comfortably within the milieu of American constitutional government.

The market system provided a prosperous economy but generated institutions that did not measure up to the national moral code. After all, society establishes moral boundaries and builds governments to maintain them. American Negro slavery was a glaring example of the worst in economic institutions. By 1860 many, if not most, Americans had decided that a market in human beings should no longer be tolerated in the United States.

Seeds of change that would produce business monoliths in the United States were planted before the Civil War. Mobilization accelerated the development of the national economy and stimulated business enterprise. Transportation and communication facilities built to carry out a war between armies on many fronts also turned states and communities into a national market. In the first weeks after Confederate forces bombarded Fort Sumter, authorities sought to establish federal priority over railroads, rivers and canals, and the telegraph. Washington, D.C., had been cut off from the rest of the nation in the early days of war, when rioting protesters destroyed railroad bridges and telegraph lines into the capital to block the movement of troops to the city. The confusion arising from the breakdown in transportation and communications emphasized the need for government control of rail and telegraph facilities. Federal officers, civilian and military, encouraged owners of splintered or competitive private enterprises to create giant cooperative operations that could supply both the military and the home front. The push-pull of business cooperation and competition dictated by the war stimulated the maturation of a national market out of the prewar economy of small local and regional enterprises.

Business and government grew up together in the United States. Unlike Europeans, who had developed an antagonistic attitude toward government, Americans recognized their government as their own creation. Federalism in the United States reflected American business, and the two shared social mores and waxed and waned in the same economic environment. The treatment of private property put to military use at this time illustrates the genius of the business-government nexus.

Railroads were essential to the survival of a society at war. But transportation companies belonged to private citizens free to manage their capital as they saw fit. The war would stimulate maturation of the nascent concept that the rights of property must coexist with the rights of society. U.S. railroad companies had rarely cooperated with each other. How quickly could they learn to work together toward a national goal under the directing hand of government?

The future for rail transportation in the United States was bright in 1861: Tracks were easier, faster, and cheaper to lay than canals were to dig; moreover, canals froze in winter, but tracks could usually be dug out to keep the trains running. Although the first rail systems connecting major cities in the East were in place by 1860, there was no national rail network. Travelers embarked upon long rail trips as a series of smaller excursions. The A&B Railroad offered service from city A to city B. Proceeding to city C meant more than a transfer of trains in city B, for the A&B Railroad neither extended to city C nor connected to the B&C Railroad. In city B the traveler had to find transportation to the B&C terminal, buy a ticket, and wait for the next train. Before standard time zones, train schedules were unreliable, for towns and cities measured time by the sun without regard to the complications created for people traveling eastward or westward.

Railroads, like society in the United States before the war, were local in character but were rapidly introducing a regionalism to life and business as they reduced travel time between cities. Before railroads, only towns and cities convenient to water transportation were accessible regionally, nationally, and internationally. Rail transportation promised increased accessibility to landlocked areas, but unlike rivers, lakes, and oceans, rail lines had to be built and profitably operated to repay the costs of construction and overhead. Traveling or shipping goods long distances became increasingly complicated as the number of railroad companies multiplied because local companies had little incentive to cooperate for larger goals. The economies of scale and profits inherent in a national market would have encouraged cooperation between the companies eventually, but the exigencies of the Civil War accelerated the evolution of a national rail system.

In pursuit of the war, Union authorities had to transport unprecedented numbers of men and animals and tons of materiel rapidly and inexpensively. The available infrastructure did not align with this need. Often, rail lines did not extend into areas where armies were on the march; even if tracks were in place, variant gauges (the distance between the rails) complicated the movement of rolling stock. Trains ran from New York State to Ohio at the beginning of the war, but no one train loaded in New York City could navigate the diverse rails and systems to deliver the goods at the Ohio destination. Army officials faced with the restraints of railroads built and run for local markets struggled to restructure the companies as regional and national operations.

Tracks and equipment belonged to private companies run by men unaccustomed to cooperating with other railroads or to grappling with the complex issues of tariffs and equipment that running a train over multiple lines would involve. If the army confiscated rail companies, how were the owners to be compensated? If lines were extended, who would build them and who would own them? Should civilian train crews and private equipment be exposed to fire? Solutions to transportation problems helped at once to win the war for the Union and to establish precedents for national business operations and business-government cooperation.

The U.S. Army took over railroads in strategic locales. Under army control, railroad owners continued the day-to-day operation of their firms. The army gave the companies objectives but let the civilian officials determine how best to achieve these. Provided they fulfilled the army's needs first, firms could continue to use their resources in private traffic; a train loaded with war goods and soldiers might include civilian goods and private citizens as well. Where there were competing lines, the government apportioned its business between them. Army business was not so different from private enterprise: Each person transported for the government cost the Treasury two cents per mile, and freight rates were discounted at about 10 percent from the regular private rates. The millions of passenger-miles and ton-miles requisitioned by the army proved lucrative for the rail companies.

Railroad companies were not forced to work their men and equipment in dangerous situations. When the threat of enemy fire was great, army engineers used rented or government-owned equipment on tracks that had been leased from private companies, laid by soldiers, or seized from the enemy. Foundries and machine shops were busy filling federal contracts for rails, locomotives, and rolling stock. Army crews repaired rails destroyed by the enemy and extended lines into the South. These men became proficient at repairing bridges, tunnels, and other rail facilities in record time and frequently while under fire. When necessary, soldiers and civilian crews worked together to connect government-owned rails with private tracks.

The Civil War prompted local railroad companies to merge into the regional networks that later became a national system. Congress passed a transcontinental railroad act during the war, and although transcontinental roads were not immediately constructed, legislation offering financial encouragement for private enterprise to connect East and West with iron rails spelled out a future for big business in transportation. Giant postwar railroads evolved from the cooperative bonds between firms and between firms and government; these would be directed by men experienced in managing large cooperative enterprises during the war. By the mid-1860s trains leaving New York ran unobstructed as far as Ohio, and Americans prepared to extend that distance to the Pacific Ocean.

By this time, any doubt that railroads could bind the United States into an economic entity had been erased. Optimism, however, was not enough to overcome the obstacles between postwar America and the national economic unity its citizens anticipated. Railroads in the South lay in ruins. Dissimilar gauges prevented swift, uncomplicated interchange of trains from system to system, and the expense of altering tracks and equipment delayed construction of a uniform-gauge rail system. Moreover, the problems and profits evident in railroading that attracted talented engineers and entrepreneurs also attracted unscrupulous promoters who skimmed profits while adding little to the transportation infrastructure.

The war was a fillip for canal and river transportation as federal expenditures for hauling personnel and materiel were directed to boat rentals, leases, or purchases and to shipbuilding, as well as to navigational improvements to waterways. Federal experience clearing watercourses of debris, both natural and war-related, led to postwar waterways management by the Army Corps of Engineers. The sale of vessels owned and operated by the government at the conclusion of the war stimulated domestic waterborne transportation. But American ocean shipping was not similarly advantaged by the war. Many U.S. vessels were destroyed by Confederate commerce raiders, and large numbers of those remaining were removed to foreign registry to avoid attack. Prewar trends were emphasized: American ocean shipping had been losing ground to other nations before the war and that loss was accelerated by the conflict.

When Confederate forces opened fire on Fort Sumter in Charleston harbor, news of the event was flashed around the nation by a well-developed telegraph system. The twenty-year-old wire communications industry had already progressed beyond the era of small enterprise; regional and national networks transmitted messages between populated areas. Since existing companies were accustomed to cooperating, the war did not affect the telegraph companies as dramatically as it did the railroads; the technology of wire telegraphy presented few obstacles to interfirm exchange of business, and capital requirements were less prohibitive than for railroads and manufacturing. By the end of the war, the telegraph wires that crisscrossed the states and territories had been rationalized into an effective national communications network. Although refinements in business operations and production marked the postwar period, pre-voice wire transmission was essentially in place by 1865.

The Confederacy's first impact on U.S. affairs was political. The stress of secession was both emotional and real: the democratic experiment had run aground, and the Confederate States of America had seized real property and materiel of the United States. The second impact was felt in the private sector. Before a round was fired, U.S. commercial interests were feeling the pain of a divided Union.

Many of the commercial transactions between North and South had been financed on credit. As states seceded from the Union, the probability of Northern business houses making good on accounts receivable from Southern counterparts declined rapidly. Almost 6,000 Northern businesses failed in the first year of the war; the financial loss came to an estimated $178.5 million. Once the war got under way and business adjusted to the altered conditions of the times, the failure rate declined.

The loss of Southern customers for imported and Northern manufactured goods was compensated by the wartime demands of government. The market for cheap ready-to-wear clothing for slaves was replaced by government orders for ready-made uniforms for soldiers and sailors. The wagons and buggies sold to Southerners before the war found a ready military market during the conflict. Comestibles previously sold to the South were purchased by quartermasters to feed thousands of soldiers. Beyond the war-related demand that benefited commercial houses, civilian demand both in Europe and in a North almost untouched by war added to the prosperity of the U.S. merchants.

Business in cotton was the Southern advantage in a war between the sections. Southern politicians expected Northern cotton interests to work against a war; that failing, the dependence of English cotton textile factories on the Southern fiber crop would, they anticipated, guarantee British pressure on the North to allow the Southern states to secede and would ensure foreign aid to the South in the event of armed hostilities. Yet the cotton advantage did not serve the South well, for the North adjusted to the cotton shortage early in the war by using wool extensively. As the war progressed, cotton from liberated areas in the South eased the shortage. In foreign commerce, the cotton tonnage lost to the war was largely replaced by grain shipped abroad to ease shortages there. Bad European crop years were balanced by bumper crops in the United States.

Interior trade also shifted to meet the needs of war. The movement of produce from the Northwest to the East had traditionally been down the Mississippi River and through the port of New Orleans. The railroads had been eroding the traditional route since the 1850s. The closing of the river and the city of New Orleans during hostilities stimulated the shift to rails, and new cities arose to meet the demands of the times. Chicago, for example, became the undisputed meatpacking center of the country and Cleveland advanced in the refining of petroleum, the exciting new extractive industry that developed apace with the war.

War placed a heavy demand on the abundant resources of the American continent, and business met that demand by developing the nation's vast natural resources. Although the mining of precious metals is a romantic tale of risk and reward, the truly rich mineral blessing of the time was petroleum. Less than a year before the outbreak of hostilities, oil was discovered in Pennsylvania. The reaction was immediate and decisive as insightful fortune hunters sank wells and produced millions of barrels of raw petroleum.

The American mind of the early twenty-first century wonders at the attraction of oil in the pre-automobile society of the 1860s. In the days before Thomas Alva Edison's electric globe, the market for illuminants attracted entrepreneurs to whaling for the best lamp oil and to distillation of kerosene from coal for the cheapest. Coal distillation also produced greases and other lubricants essential in a society increasingly dependent on machinery for transportation and manufacturing.

Lamp oil distilled from crude oil sold at prices well below those for whale oil and coal oil, the main illuminants for people without access to a ready supply of gas. Grease and lubricating oils were in demand wherever moving parts rubbed together. Wagon wheels required lubrication, as did the complicated machinery of a locomotive and the train it hauled. Lubricants for these purposes were distilled from petroleum at less cost than from coal; moreover, the quality of petroleum products was superior to organic compounds typically used on farm machinery. Fortunes were amassed in oil long before the automobile became a reality.

The infant oil industry comprised hundreds of producers. Wells sunk at slight cost in a swelling market for oil rendered a large return on a small investment. Refining crude oil was a wasteful, underdeveloped operation in the hands of many people, each one working on a small scale. The oil industry approximated what economists term perfect competition. In the factor market side of the oil industry, there were so many buyers and sellers that no one of them, acting alone, could influence conditions in the market. No single well owner, for example, could expect to change the market price by increasing or decreasing production. Among so many competitors, the actions of any one of them were washed out by the market.

In the product market side of the oil industry, so many sellers dealt with so many buyers that no one seller and no one buyer, acting alone, could influence the market. The oil business includes two sets of sellers and two sets of buyers. Factor market sellers deal in oil or oil-related products like refining services, barrels, and drilling equipment. What they sell is related to oil, but they deal not with ultimate consumers but with producers of goods for further sale. Product market sellers, however, distribute their output to buyers who consume the products for their own satisfaction, not for the creation of another product for further sale. A single seller can work both markets. In the early days of the industry, retailers sold lamp oil to households for personal use (product-market transaction) and to other businesses to produce additional products and services (factor-market transaction). In the twenty-first century, three of the four sectors of the oil industry are dominated by giant corporations; only the ultimate consumer remains without individual market power. The origins of these giant enterprises are evident in the Civil War days, the very infancy of the oil industry.

The large numbers of sellers in the newborn oil industry produced more oil than the market could absorb. Indeed a latent demand for oil products existed, but the oil producers were unable either to coordinate their production of crude oil or to rationalize the construction of refineries and retailing facilities, the development of new petroleum products, or the organization of retail outlets. Early in the Civil War, the market was flooded with the products easiest to manufacture and sell, and the prices of these commodities quickly fell to levels too low to support all the participating firms. As marginal operators disappeared, the stronger ones expanded, and by war's end the industry had been reduced enough that production limitation agreements were possible. Petroleum giants were materializing before the industry was five years old.

The war economy also gave impetus to agriculture. Farmers replaced manpower lost to the war with machinery and, in the process, increased production to meet robust domestic and European demands for foodstuffs. Before the war, farm machinery dealers disseminated information about the availability and capability of laborsaving agricultural equipment. Once farmers began using machinery, they encountered returns to scale that made small operations obsolete. Machinery was expensive, but when its costs were spread over a vast output, costs per unit fell below costs of hand production. Farm size rose as machinery came into general use, and falling production costs gave farmers a choice between mechanizing production or going out of business. The origins of giant agribusiness are rooted in developments of such trends begun in the decades before the war.

Federal agricultural legislation passed during the Civil War benefited farmers for decades after hostilities ended. The U.S. Department of Agriculture was created by Congress during the war. From modest beginnings, the federal department grew to gianthood. In addition to gathering and publishing agricultural data, the department's mission was to seek out and disseminate information on scientific farming. Research and information—the charge of the Department of Agriculture—would eventually be recognized as significant factors of growth in agricultural as well as industrial production.

A second piece of wartime legislation, the Morrill Act of 1862, contributed to American farm prosperity and the growth of large farm units. Also known as the College Land Grant Act, the Morrill Act granted federal support to the states for the creation of agricultural and mechanical colleges. The states received the backing through grants of public lands for development or sale. The land grant colleges were to train young people for technical and farm employment, and to serve as bastions of agricultural research. A close working relationship between the new Department of Agriculture and the land grant colleges provided support for the functions of both in the postwar years.

The Homestead Act was the culmination of a liberal land policy. With the goal of putting public lands into as many private hands as possible, this Civil War law permitted free disposal of 40-acre parcels to Americans willing to live on the land at least five years. The Homestead distribution reinforced the Jeffersonian small-farm ideal without effectively countering the economies of scale that favored large farms. The act put public land into private hands but did not prevent the flow of acre ownership to speculators and agribusiness entrepreneurs: large-scale farming could not be legislated away.

At the same time that crop output was expanding in the North to feed Americans and Europeans, animal husbandry was showing signs of wartime prosperity and trends toward what would be an expanding postwar industry. So heavy were the demands for livestock to be used for meat and labor that the number of domestic animals in the North and South declined over the course of the war. Armies required cavalry mounts and herds of draft horses, pack mules, or oxen to transport supplies, baggage, and ammunition. The demand for meat rose as recognition that diet affected the soldiers' performance forced the Army commissary department to purchase large quantities of meat to feed the troops. Households, too, were demanding more and better meat for home consumption. Although meat preparation in the 1860s was mostly still a local operation, meat packing was taking on regional and national proportions. The developing American taste for canned meat furthered the large-scale packing firms that would flourish in the postwar years as interstate meat-packing houses.

The prosperity of oil and agriculture was typical of extractives during the early 1860s. Lumber was the reliable building material for everything from houses, train cars, bridges, and barracks, to furniture, wagons, machinery, ships, railroad ties, and plank roads. War demand spurred that industry as it did mining. Although wood was used in nearly all construction, iron was coming into its own: More machine parts were of metal, cast-iron bridges were gaining acceptance (Andrew Carnegie founded a cast-iron bridge company during the war years), and the output of weapons was setting new production records. The output in iron and in coal, copper, and salt mining kept pace with war demand, but the extraction of precious metals required no stimulus. The discovery of gold and silver in Western lodes brought forth the men and capital that would establish new levels of wealth in the money metals. The development of economies in extraction, processing, and transportation created bonanza mining operations in the decades beyond the Civil War.

Manufacturing advanced under the pressures of war, as well. Government demand was widespread and more than sufficient to compensate for lost Southern markets. Ordnance and munitions contracts swept along the metals industry, and weapons of iron, brass, and bronze were produced in record quantities. Orders for the iron rails that section gangs needed to repair track and lay new lines kept rolling mills busy and expanding. Iron plate for ships of war was ordered in quantities sufficient to encourage rapid expansion of plate rolling mills. Machine shops turned out locomotives and steam engines for ships and riverboats. Even horseshoe manufacture became a large-scale operation, supplying hundreds of thousands of shoes ordered by the government. The era of the small-scale metalworking shop was cut short by the unprecedented military demand for metal products.

Wagon and cart manufacturers were pressed to keep up with the army's demand for wagons and ambulances. Shipyards were backed up with army, navy, and foreign contracts for boats and ships. Chemical manufacturers found plenty of demand for gunpowder, and drug companies filled orders of all description for military and civilian use. Except for cotton textile manufacturing—which suffered supply shortages early in the war—the textile industry was absorbed in the task of filling orders for uniform material, blankets, tents, and sailcloth, and the myriad other textile goods the nation had already come to regard as necessities for both life and death. The ready-made clothing business filled the orders for uniforms and, in the process, gave impetus to sewing machine manufacturing. The call for leather goods for every variety of military use stimulated that industry. Adaptation of the sewing machine to boot and shoe manufacture allowed production of superior footwear in unprecedented quantities and at prices below prewar levels.

Prosperity, increased use of machinery, and larger-scale production linked manufacturing expansion across the various industries, and these commonalities were themselves interrelated. The prosperity came from the sale of vast quantities of goods produced at a cost diminished by the substitution of machine technology for many hand operations. Large-scale outputs made the use of machines both necessary and possible. Machines carried out some production operations, such as boot and shoe stitching, that could not be completed by hand if the huge demand were to be met. The expense of machinery, however, required very large output levels to reduce the machine cost per unit of output to hand-production costs and below. As the size of requisite output rose, the number of producers market demand could support declined, creating in the Civil War years and later a few giants producing greater output than the combined yields of the hundreds of hand-producers they supplanted.

The expansion of the public sector for military purposes and of the private sector in transportation and communication, commerce, extractives, and manufacturing required a financial base. In fiscal matters, government and business operated in tandem. Local, state, and federal governments in the U.S. market economy engage private firms for financial services. A government payment by treasury check flows through private banks on its route back to the Treasury. The private sector functions most effectively if the government establishes and enforces financial operating rules for participants. Without government aid in requiring banks to redeem their notes in specie and guarantee specie redemption to depositors and underwriters, the private sector wastes time and money sifting through the market in search of sound monetary institutions.

After the Andrew Jackson administration stopped using the second Bank of the United States (BUS) as a fiscal agent, there was no official institutional liaison between the Treasury and the private banking system. The second BUS was unique, a monopoly bank holding the only federal bank charter then extant. Although the majority of BUS stock was privately owned, the bank acted as a fiscal agent for the Treasury and, through size and influence, contributed to the stability of the financial community. A "pet bank" system replaced the BUS with selected state banks, and the Independent Treasury carried out monetary and fiscal operations without recourse to the private monetary sector. The demands of war forced changes, and by 1865 the national monetary structure had been shored up with the National Banking system that continues to operate in the twenty-first century.

The National Banking Act (1863) allowed federal charters for all qualified applicants. The establishment of national banks throughout the country gave the federal government entrance to banking across the states. The high uniform requirements for national banks introduced standards and homogeneity to banking amid the profusion of state banks' divergent rules and regulations. Only federal mints struck coins, but bank notes, the dominant money used in the country, were issued by chartered banks. Banks issuing notes chose their own standards within the broad limits spelled out by laws that varied widely from state to state. Thousands of notes, differentiated by size, color, bank of origin, and value, circulated before the Civil War. Some notes were redeemable in gold or silver (specie) at face value, but others could not be redeemed at all. Between these extremes lay the value of most of the notes. Businesses relied on privately printed catalogues of note values that were sold and updated at regular intervals—an inadequate solution to a strategic business problem. By creating a uniform paper money and higher standards for banking, the federal government alleviated the uncertainty surrounding paper money valuation, but not without creating new monetary difficulties.

The National Banking Act (and amendments) did not require banks to surrender state charters for federal ones but, by levying a face value tax on the state notes, did effect an end to state bank notes in favor of national bank notes. A uniform national currency did not solve the nation's money and banking problems, however. Most banks in the 1860s switched to federal charters to secure access to note-issuing privileges. State banking resurged later in the century when demand deposits and checks gained popularity and bank notes declined in importance.

The new banking legislation and bank notes were central to Union war finance. Paper money issued in the South was based more on promise than on real value. The Confederate dollar waxed and waned on the outcome of battles, seldom trading for—or even near—face value. Northern war finance required a more solid base because the initiative in continuing the war was with the United States: The Confederacy could not quit the field without surrendering its existence, but the United States was free to abandon the war and accept a new nation. Union politicians dared not let war finance dampen national morale. If taxes rose too high or currency value fell too low (inflation) or fluctuated wildly, the national mood might turn against continued hostilities.

The fiscal policies of Secretary of the Treasury Salmon P. Chase enabled the successful prosecution of the war. Chase inherited a department in financial straits from the recession of 1857. The government was not well situated for day-to-day financing, and underwriting a war demanded extreme measures. Chase was equal to the demand. Disregarding the spirit of an independent Treasury, he sought aid from New York banks in floating a war bond issue and petitioned Congress for a legal tender act to provide immediate operating funds. He received both. The banks expected to pay the Treasury for the bonds with their notes; Chase, however, demanded hard money, a move that created a hard-money shortage of such proportions that the banking system stopped redeeming notes. Suspension of hard-money payment for notes had threatened early in the war, but the Treasury's action accelerated the suspension and created friction unnecessarily between the Treasury and the banks. Nevertheless, the banking system stood by Chase and the Union throughout the national crisis, financing bond issues on several occasions.

Chase's legal tender law allowed the Treasury to issue paper money endowed, but for two exceptions, with the legal tender qualities of hard money. This fiat money was not acceptable for the payment of import duties and could not be used to pay interest on federal bonds; nor was the Treasury required to redeem these notes with hard money. Because the only backing for the money was the recently developed green printer's ink on the reverse, the notes were called greenbacks. Greenbacks were analogous to Confederate currency in that both were fiat money: money backed by a promise. Like the Confederate dollar, the value of the greenback rose and fell with the tides of war. A gold exchange opened in New York City to handle speculation in the paper notes. Although some saw betting on the strength of the nation's dollar in time of war akin to treason, speculation reflected the business community's reactions to economic conditions. The Treasury used greenbacks (Congress authorized $450 million in three separate acts) to finance the day-to-day demands of the war. To keep the notes coming back to the Treasury, Congress taxed an extensive list of goods and eventually inaugurated an income tax. Borrowing, however, paid for the bulk of the war effort. The Treasury accepted greenbacks in exchange for certain bonds and credited the deposit of greenbacks at interest. These pseudobanking operations encouraged a regular flow of funds to the Treasury, but the sale of bonds was the lifeblood of Northern war finance.

Chase's treasury introduced two innovations to bond marketing. The National Banking Act provided for government bond sales to national banks. Banks could, while drawing interest, deposit the bonds with the comptroller of the currency in exchange for 90 percent of their value in national bank notes. The notes could then be loaned out for still more interest. When banks make a loan, they can expect some part of that loan to return to the bank in the form of deposits. These new deposits form part of another loan. In this process the banking system expands the money supply. The purchase of a federal bond—a loan—would not represent the same likelihood that funds would return, so banks preferred to make local loans rather than purchase the federal war bonds. Providing notes for bonds on deposit improved the earnings potential of a bond purchase and helped the Treasury borrow funds. As the nineteenth century progressed, greenbacks and national bank notes created monetary difficulties, but for the war finance program, they functioned satisfactorily. Beyond funds for the Treasury, the federal currency supplied the economy with a larger, more homogeneous money supply than was available before the war.

Marketing government bonds to households was another of the Chase treasury's innovations for financing the war. Jay Cooke & Company of Philadelphia contracted with the Treasury to sell government bonds to the general public. Patriotism was harnessed to produce funds for the war effort. Using agents and advertising to encourage Americans to support the war with their dollars, the Cooke company marketed over a billion dollars' worth of federal bonds. The success of public sales of bonds revealed the potential of the national market and made savings bonds a permanent feature of the U.S. financial landscape.

National banks, national bank notes, and savings, aided by taxation and greenbacks, underwrote the war for the Union; yet the socioeconomic impact of these innovations may have been stronger than their financial success. Despite inflation and other money and banking problems that time would reveal, Northern finance procedures strengthened nationalism. The unencumbered movement of people and business through the United States, an essential ingredient for the growth of a great nation, demanded a uniform money and banking system. After the war, the flow of goods from state to state and region to region was less complex as the new monetary system was extended into the South. The Civil War had preserved the Union as a political unit; the financial creations of the war would strengthen the Union as an economic entity.

Fiat money (greenbacks) and government borrowing through bond sales to banks and households fueled inflation. The wholesale price index (1910–14 = 100) increased from 93 in 1860 to 185 in 1865. Price increases faced by consumers were equally harsh. On a base of 1860 = 100, the consumer price index climbed slowly at first, rising from 101 in 1861, to 113 in 1862, to 139 in 1863, and then, gaining momentum in the final war years, vaulting to 176 in 1864 and 175 in 1865.

Inflation reshapes a society by shifting purchasing power from some people to others. Fixed-income recipients see the value of their incomes fall victim to rising prices. Citizens on variable incomes benefit or lose vis-à-vis changes in their incomes and in prices. Business operators are usually able to stay ahead of cost increases by passing them along to buyers of their products. If the market for the seller's output is inelastic—the loss of sales is proportionally smaller than the increase in price—the firm may make more money with the rise in price. In a time of general inflation, when the prices of most goods and services are rising, demand is likely to be inelastic because consumers have nowhere to turn for cheaper alternatives when prices start upward. Some goods may disappear from the market, however, abandoned by buyers forced to sacrifice nonessentials for the sake of essentials.

Wages fell victim to the expanding size of producing units and the declining power of the dollar during the war. Between 1860 and 1865, wages rose 48.6 percent, but consumer prices increased by 75 percent. Workers lost individual bargaining power rapidly, despite their halting efforts at designing tactics to offset the loss through organization and collective bargaining. Labor unions comprised small groups of workers organized at the plant level; national federations of local unions were not unknown but were uncommon. Unions, like small businesses, remained focused on local issues while big businesses controlled employment and production on a regional and national scale.

Men working together formed unions to redress grievances common to their place of employment. These dissociated groups aspired to improve pay and working conditions. Membership was seasonal: In busy summer months, jobs were plentiful and unions less necessary; in slower months, union activity was greater, but its impact was less. A strike during a period of reduced production carried little force, and because even better-timed strikes frequently involved workers at only one or two firms, the impact of a union's victory was slight.

Unions were weak in the courts, where the influence of capital bent decisions toward employers. The availability of substitute labor took the sting out of union-led strikes. During the war years, women were accepted into the labor force in increasing numbers, but their short-term employment made efforts to organize them into unions fruitless. The availability of black labor liberated by the Civil War and willing to work at low wages weakened the unions' efforts, as did the influx of immigrant labor. Women, minorities, and immigrants have never been welcomed into the American labor movement.

Strong antiunion sentiment proved an obstacle to effective unionization in the United States. Americans, a people with agrarian roots, insisted that work—not strikes and riots—generate a good living. Peripatetic agitators and labor unrest made unions a nuisance in the nineteenth century, and not until the twentieth century and the New Deal did American labor catch the tenor of the times and the national sympathy. By then, giant corporations were entrenched bastions of American society. The Civil War had done little for organized labor beyond encouraging the national businesses that were models for national unions and business unionism.

The government-business relationship flourished in the postwar years. The ability of the two institutions to work in harness had been evident before the war, but the pressures of the internal conflict fused the two and established guidelines of cooperation on so grand a scale as to fix in the public mind an appreciation of the role of business in national life. The federal government had relied upon American business to produce the materiel essential to the war. Business had at once delivered the goods for battle and sustained a pronounced prosperity in the nation. The quest for continued national economic success was founded on business enterprise. With few exceptions, business in the nineteenth and twentieth centuries would be given rein to draw the economy to ever higher levels of production and remuneration.

The scale of business-government cooperation was enlarged by the demands of war. Business before the war had been local or regional, unable to overcome the hurdles between small-scale and national operations. The war pushed entrepreneurs to find ways around administrative barriers so that business could equal the national scale of the war. Business enterprise in the postwar years profited from the experience of giant ventures in cooperation with government officials. That a war of so massive a scope had been executed to a victorious conclusion within the basic confines of society was not lost on public or private interests. Beyond the monetary returns and valuable experience, the business sector had earned an intangible yet priceless reward for its wartime efforts: public goodwill.

The wartime division of tasks between business and government was not carefully planned but evolved to carry through jobs at hand. The Civil War was the proving ground for the great democratic experiment. The value of success was inestimable: business and government continued their working relationship after the war, and businessmen and public servants moved back and forth between the private and public sectors. The private-public interaction produced federal subsidies for privately built, owned, and operated national railroads from coast to coast; high tariffs to protect American manufacturers from foreign competition; and court rulings that were tilted in favor of business interests in cases pitting embryonic labor unions against powerful management.

The high position held by the business sector in the government-business nexus reflected the established social view in a democratic nation. The war left Americans more committed than ever to private enterprise. So severe a war and so protracted a period of extreme government influence in the operation of society and the economy could conceivably have warped the social fabric toward stronger government. Some feared a militaristic national character would be a natural result of the intensity of civil war. Americans, though, defied the anticipations of social observers by returning to a prewar lifestyle at the end of hostilities. Colonels and generals, like sergeants and privates, looked for employment in business positions rather than for new wars in which to exercise their military skills. The victors in civil war chose to pursue the bright future of the United States.

The war had a harsh impact on the South, though, leaving it with a heavily damaged infrastructure and little hope of rebuilding—effective, practical reconstruction died with Lincoln. Reviving Southern agriculture depended on working out an accommodation with the newly freed men and women. Political and economic institutions would be reconstructed with little help from the North as the victors quit the field with the victory, leaving the physical and emotional refuse of conflict to transmogrify at nature's speed. The centennial of the Civil War found the South struggling for economic parity with the rest of the nation and the descendants of slaves denied the equality of citizenship guaranteed them by the U.S. Constitution.

The American Civil War did not change the direction of national development, but it increased the rate of advance in transportation, commerce, extractive industries, manufacturing, and finance. Of the important production sectors of the economy, only labor gained no particular advantage from the war. Business prospered in the North and suffered in the South. The Confederate states were left to reconstruct and redefine their status in the Union. The North and the expanding West continued the growth stimulated by the war. The continental dimensions of the conflict and the close working relationship it fostered between business and government left the two institutions with a heritage of harmony that bolstered the influence of government and hastened the emergence of giant institutions.

CHAPTER 2

Giant Business in Communications and Transportation

The giant businesses of the post–World War I United States rose on the foundations of a national economy established in the years after the Civil War. Continental markets that attracted expansion of firms seeking economies of scale emerged in the United States with the advent first of coast-to-coast communications, then of Atlantic-to-Pacific rail connections. U.S. citizens owned the heart of the North American continent but had too few communications and transportation links to capitalize on national economic potential. At the outset of the Civil War, the Pacific coast was weeks away from the national capital in Washington, D.C., but six months later, on October 26, 1861, the transcontinental telegraph line was completed. That wire brought the far-reaching borders of the United States into nearly instant contact with the center of government.[1]

The decades after the Civil War brought the culmination of America's early efforts to create rapid, dependable, high-volume, inexpensive communications and transportation facilities. Cheap transportation had influenced colonial development. As people moved inland along the navigable waterways that cross the Atlantic coastal plain, they built cities linked by water to other colonial population centers and Europe. Beyond the fall line, rivers were unnavigable; settlers lost easy contact with other colonists, and the development of infrastructure was slow and expensive. Americans living far from the smooth-flowing rivers of the East coast and the continent-dividing linkage of the Mississippi, Missouri, and Ohio rivers prospered despite inadequate communications and transportation facilities. Nevertheless, the attraction of the interior and the needs of people already living there stimulated construction of transportation networks.

As early as the mid-1820s, New York State's Erie Canal demonstrated the profitability of opening America's interior landmass to easy, inexpensive ingress and egress. Between 1830 and 1850 the estimated cost of hauling freight from

Buffalo to New York City fell from 19.12 cents per ton-mile to 1.68 cents, a decline of more than 91 percent.[2] Profits recouped construction costs within seven years of the canal's opening. A flurry of canal building followed, as other states tried to improve transportation by emulating the Erie. The Pennsylvania system connected Philadelphia with Pittsburgh via canal over the mountains separating the two cities. Not all the projects were completed, however, and those canals put to use were not always practicable or profitable (the Pennsylvania system would stretch contemporary technology beyond workable limits and fail). Nevertheless, the canal era endowed the country with a useful system of man-made waterways to supplement natural watercourses. The canal connecting Portsmouth and Cleveland is one example; another canal joins Cincinnati and Toledo. The Chesapeake and Ohio Canal, intended to link Baltimore to the Ohio River, was never completed. Several states compromised their finances by backing, underwriting, or guaranteeing canal bonds. The panic of 1837 forced some states to fall behind in their canal obligations; Mississippi repudiated its debt, but most states resorted to less extreme measures and eventually paid off their encumbrances.[3]

Canal expansion was a fillip for steamboat companies operating on American rivers and the Great Lakes. Steam power for lake ships and riverboats had been harnessed early in the nineteenth century to haul inland products over the traditional route to New Orleans, an embarkation point for coastal vessels destined for other U.S. cities and for ocean ships bound for Europe. Each waterway maintained its own peculiar form of carrier. Canal barges were drawn along by draft animals walking tow paths along the banks—water roiled by power-driven vessels would have eroded the dirt banks of the canals. River steamboats were constructed with flat bottoms and several above-water decks for passengers and freight. These unwieldy structures looked more like floating hotels than ships but served their purpose with distinction. Lake steamers, however, were more like ocean-going keel steamers than like the flat-bottomed canal barges and riverboats. American inland water carrying parallelled American ocean carrying and declined during the years between the Civil War and World War I as all forms of inland water transportation felt the sting of the more versatile steam-powered locomotive hauling rolling stock along iron rails.

Before steamboats plied inland waters, farmers along the Ohio and other waterways linked to the Mississippi River loaded agricultural products onto barges and flatboats for the voyage down the father of waters to New Orleans, a journey of three to six weeks. Usually a small shelter was constructed in the middle of the craft to protect travelers and goods from sun and rain. Often entire families set off to market, stopping along the way to sell to farmers who looked to visitors from upstream for foodstuffs while they exploited a comparative advantage in cotton, sugar, or rice.

Rafters watched for farmers' signs along the shore advertising to buy mules, corn, tobacco, cloth, coffee, pork, etc. Once the flatboaters' goods were marketed, the raft itself was sold as lumber (often the last buyer would have purchased the raft as part of the deal). If the flatboat reached New Orleans with goods unsold, the family might sell them there or continue downstream to the sugar plantations south of the city. After the raft and its contents had been marketed, the family began the long trek home along the Natchez Trace.

The cost of rafting downstream was small. The craft was constructed from abundant timbers on the farm when the hired hands and family had no crop work (low opportunity cost). The trip was no more dangerous than the downstream voyage on a steamboat; food was prepared on board, and the travelers could stop whenever they pleased and stay as long as they liked. The advent of steamboats on the river offered the flatboaters the option of rafting to New Orleans for nearly nothing and returning on the steamboat instead of walking. Steamboats reduced the cost of the rafters' return trip by eliminating the weeks-long walk from New Orleans to Ohio or other points north. Steamboats made flatboats more economically attractive.[4]

Before railroads improved the movement of goods and people, societies found water travel easier, cheaper, and faster than land travel. Major streets in the older Eastern cities were paved with stones and brick, but city back streets, principle thoroughfares in frontier towns, and rural roads everywhere punished walkers, horseback riders, and carriage and wagon drivers. In dry weather, choking dust shrouded even the best dirt roads, and autumn rains turned the dust to quagmires: wheels seized in mud so firmly that teams of horses pulled wagon and carriage frames off their axles. Freezing temperatures transformed the muddy tracks into icy furrows that shattered wagons and carriages and felled horses, mules, and walkers. Spring thaws again reduced the roads to mud that dried into hard ruts that invited scraping during the warm season. These conditions prevailed throughout rural America, disappearing into history only in the decades after World War II. In the twenty-first century, tortuous road conditions bedevil only sportsmen and adventurers who shun the pavement.[5]

Plank roads were a short-run solution to the difficulties of land travel. Beginning in the 1840s promoters capitalized on steam-driven sawmills; low-cost, readily available timber from landowners who wanted fields cleared for farming; and Americans' desire to move themselves and their goods rapidly and inexpensively. An established right-of-way could be planked to a width of eight feet for about $2,000 a mile. The road was laid quickly, and the benefits were immediate and obvious. Public and private (toll) plank roads were built wherever timber was cheap and accessible. Promoters optimistically estimated an eight-to-ten-year life span for plank roads that usually deteriorated in four or five years.

Plank roads are a footnote to American transportation history. The railroads under construction in the 1840s captured the nation's imagination, and for the remainder of the century their expansion occupied entrepreneurs and citizens alike. Capital that might have financed new plank highways and renewed established ones was siphoned off by rail promoters. Moreover, the railroads placed their own heavy demand on timber resources: Wooden sleepers (cross ties) supported first iron and then steel rails, early wood-burning engines pulled cars constructed primarily of wood, and construction crews depended on finished lumber for building terminals and shops. As railroads increased the opportunity cost of timber by extending the markets from local regions to the nation and the world, farmers began to see their trees as a product instead of a nuisance. But for nearly a century, plank roads continued to serve where primitive conditions prevailed and the cost of marketing timber remained high.[6]

Railroads were attracting transportation promoters as early as the 1820s from areas unsuited for canals, and trains were in operation by 1830, when the Baltimore and Ohio opened a thirteen-mile stretch of the line it had begun in 1828. By 1836 more than a thousand miles of rails were carrying traffic over eleven states. Railroad construction began in earnest in the 1840s, once the nation regained financial balance from the panic of 1837. The advantages of railroads, especially the speed of rolling stock and year-round usability of the tracks (canals were closed during freezing conditions), encouraged roadbed construction instead of canal digging even in areas suitable for canals.

The potential of the telegraph to break the historic connection between communications and modes of transportation inspired entrepreneurs to string wires between cities and seize the opportunity to turn a profit on the new technology. By the conclusion of the Civil War, a national telegraph system linked the entire country principally via Western Union's 44,000 miles of wire and more than 1,000 offices, American Telegraph Company's 23,000 miles of wire, and United States Telegraph Company's 16,000 miles of line. Several regional telegraph companies functioned in concert with the giants. The telegraph in Illinois and Iowa was controlled by the Illinois and Mississippi Telegraph Company; in Kentucky, Tennessee, Mississippi, Louisiana, and Texas the Southwestern Telegraph Company maintained superiority; and in Wisconsin and Minnesota lines were dominated by the Northwestern Telegraph Company. The success of the regional concerns depended on their gaining access to the national network of one of the big three. By 1866 Western Union had absorbed its two competitors to form the first national monopoly in the United States.

Competition in transportation and communications encouraged consolidation and concentration. The service provided by a single telegraph company's lines was not necessarily improved by a competitor's duplication of facilities, especially if the market was not large enough to support both: Either one firm would eventually go out of business at a loss to its investors, or the successful firm would absorb its competitor. If the equipment purchased by the surviving firm was redundant, the users of the service paid higher prices to cover the cost of useless capital carried by the firm. When Western Union acquired United States Telegraph Company in 1866, a third of the employees of the resulting company were dismissed. The excess capital, not easily eliminated, was carried as a cost covered by rates higher than would otherwise have been necessary. Waste generated by unproductive competition, as well as the lower costs of production associated with larger enterprises, forced policymakers to deal with giant businesses. At the same time that the expansion of facilities created an environment conducive to the growth and exploitation of national markets and encouraged giant business operations to accommodate those markets, the transportation and communications industries themselves were being consolidated into a few giant firms.

When the Civil War began, the United States boasted a web of lines and a rapidly emerging national telegraph system. Within months the transcontinental connection was complete, and soon after the war's end telegraph service was a continental monopoly. By the end of the decade, cables connected the United States with Europe, and the next decade brought the telephone, an accepted and dependable mechanism by the end of the nineteenth century. When the United States entered World War I, both wire-based telegraphy and telephony were established industries, and wireless telegraphy was the new darling of communications.[7]

The half-century separating the beginning of the Civil War and World War I brought changes in transportation as radical as those in communications. The idea of transmitting a voice through the air over long distances was a dream in 1860 that had by 1914 become a reality. Considering that, in 1914, people were flying through the air by virtue of machine instead of balloon, the evolution of transportation equaled that of communications. Although the airplane was the extreme change in means of transporting people and cargo, the automobile (itself an innovation in the decades between the great wars of the nineteenth and twentieth centuries) was the most pervasive addition to the transport stable. The strategic role of the gasoline-powered automobile has grown steadily since its introduction.

Airplanes and automobiles were introduced in the period between the Civil War and World War I, but their full impact would not be felt until well into the twentieth century. The railroad was the ubiquitous transportation system of the second half of the nineteenth century. Rail transportation during the Civil War had served so important a function in the Northern victory as to erase any question of its strategic place in the future of the United States. Wartime service had forced the railroads into new levels of cooperation that illuminated the potential of the rails to create a national transportation network out of the local and regional firms operating before the war. By picking up where canals left off, railroads linked together the entire landmass of the continental United States. Alfred D. Chandler Jr. indicated an even broader role for railroads in the development of business. In *The Visible Hand*, Chandler looked beyond the railroads' obvious role in creating a national market to credit them with establishing the managerial foundations for big business in the United States. Railroads were the first businesses to attain the size and complexity of giant corporations. Having no precedents to follow, they were forced to develop managerial and accounting systems to accommodate the operating needs of companies employing hundreds of managers, thousands of workers, and millions of dollars in capital. The railroads of the nineteenth century not only made giant business possible by creating an accessible mass market but laid down as well the fundamentals by which the huge business corporations of the twentieth century would operate.[8]

Before the Civil War many local and regional railroad companies worked together to expedite through-traffic, but the needs of government during the conflict accelerated the elimination of obstacles to moving freight and passengers over rails belonging to different companies. The lure of profits from through-traffic encouraged managers to cooperate. Workable linkages between lines kept trains moving in the short term; the permanent solution to multiple gauges—the 4 foot, 8½ inch standard adopted for the transcontinentals—was achieved in 1886. Sophisticated accounting systems kept pace with rolling stock moving over neighboring lines and allocated traffic among companies sharing equipment and track. The complicated procedure by which a railroad kept accounts of the disposition of its own equipment and that of other roads employing its track, paled in comparison to the difficulties of scheduling, rate setting, cost determination, tariff allocation, and maintenance. Money flowed into and out of a railroad at a number of points and through a number of people; the number of points and people expanded with the miles of line operated. There can be little argument with Chandler's thesis that the managerial revolution originated with the railroad companies' success in overcoming the hurdles encountered by the first giant business enterprises.

The internal organizational structure suitable for long-mileage railroads was worked out in its essentials on the large Eastern trunk lines—the Baltimore and Ohio, the Pennsylvania, and the Erie (before Jay Gould's takeover)—and imitated elsewhere. Railroads attained such size as to demand the attention of specialized professional management. Managers shared their operating experiences and accounting practices at regular meetings of professional associations they created to enhance the sciences of management and accounting, disciplines that transcended any one company. The American Society of Railroad Superintendents, the Roadmasters Association of America, and the American Train Dispatchers Association fostered dispersal of managerial and operating technology and encouraged cooperation among railroads.

Passenger traffic was the first priority for railroads from about 1830 until 1860. But whereas people could get themselves from one station to another, freight had to be transferred. Fast-freight lines bridged the gap between the demand for haulage and the railroads' inability to coordinate through-shipments. Transfer companies, express companies, or fast-freight lines met local transport needs with wagons, coaches, and canal barges well before the railroads appeared. Railroad construction, however, offered wider vistas to entrepreneurs who sold transit services.

Contracts with combinations of railroad companies expanded shipping beyond the confines of a single locale or railroad. The gauge differences between the tracks of the various railroads and the lack of cooperation among the early roads were overcome by the fast-freights. Instead of employing the rolling stock of the railroads, the fast-freight companies bought their own cars and contracted to have them hauled by the railroads. Freight cars equipped with adjustable trucks could operate on many gauges within a narrow range, making it unnecessary for workers to unload and reload cars to accommodate tracks of varying gauges. In the early 1870s National Dispatch had 1,000 cars equipped with adjustable trucks on the Grand Trunk and connections. If great differences in gauge demanded, a fast-freight company could offer a lucrative contract to persuade the railroad to lay a third, compensating rail. Such a rail was laid by the Great Western of Canada in 1867. Wells, Fargo & Company, the Great Western Dispatch, and the United States Express Company exemplified the independent fast-freight operations. The success of the through-freight lines encouraged railroads to initiate their own associated companies. The Pennsylvania Railroad, for example, established the Union Railroad and Transportation Company and the Empire Transportation Company.

Just as the advent of the telegraph had brought an end to the Pony Express, the advance of cooperation between the railroads removed the necessity of the express lines as organizations separate from the railroads themselves. Except for a few firms specializing in high-value freight, like Wells, Fargo or American Express, the fast-freight lines were absorbed by the railroads during the 1870s. Direct delivery of freight by the railroad companies was simplified by inter-company cooperation. The returns from the high-value products previously handled by fast-freight companies were needed by the railroads to shore up their returns on bulk cargoes that the fast-freights had been uninterested in hauling.

The first railroad companies were small operations that connected neighboring cities and seldom extended over fifty miles. The rapid advance of railroad technology in the 1840s fostered the managerial development of the 1850s and 1860s and the construction of trunk lines to connect cities in the expanding Eastern states: the New York Central, constructed from ten small locally promoted railroads extending from New York City to Albany and on to Buffalo; the Erie, built as a single-unit railroad; the Baltimore and Ohio, a system that grew with the country; and the Pennsylvania, initially designed to prevent state trade from going to New York or Baltimore and eventually the U.S. railroad with the most equipment and arguably the best management. These Eastern trunks were imitated in the West and South with roads like the Santa Fe; the Union Pacific; the Chicago and Northwestern; the Chicago, Burlington and Quincy; the Texas and Pacific; and the Richmond Terminal. There were economies of scale in railroading harnessed by clever managers who knew they could reduce costs if they carried huge numbers of passengers and great quantities of freight so that each customer paid only a small part of the otherwise tremendous fixed costs of tracks, equipment, and personnel.

But the economies of scale that made railroads profitable also made them vulnerable to competition. If railroad A offered the identical service at a lower rate than railroad B, it could take business from railroad B without substantially increasing its own total costs while reducing its cost per passenger or ton-mile of freight hauled. If the transportation demand over the route served by the two competitors was sufficient to support the facilities of two railroads at their most efficient production levels, the competition could be socially advantageous by keeping rates low and the service efficient. If, however, the route was able to support only one railroad at its most efficient production level, social loss ensued. Typically, thousands of miles of track would have been laid ahead of effective demand for services, so social loss was common. Losses included the financial collapse of one or both of the roads; deterioration in equipment as maintenance was postponed to reduce day-to-day operating costs; erosion of service; or absorption of one road by the other, which gave the surviving company an unnecessarily high capital cost and subsequently higher rates. The heaviest loss was opportunity cost: society could have employed the wasted resources for something more useful than a redundant railroad line.

By 1870 redundant and socially wasteful competition in transportation and communications invited outside interference to stabilize competitive market forces. But only government was strong enough to influence competitive combatants, and the actions of elected officials at all levels reflected the ambivalence of society at large. Competition was a national asset, and voters hesitated to support interference with markets; government was likewise hesitant to make changes that might lead to higher prices and voter dissatisfaction. Moreover, firms felt the sting of competitive vulnerability before consumers did, and managers struggled to solve market conflicts and reduce the likelihood that the public would demand political participation in market operations.

Businesses countered wasteful competition with cooperation. Railroads were already sharing rolling stock, through-traffic, and rail links and were well on the way to achieving a standard gauge. Now they must learn to share markets and rates. Cartels and pools were created to encourage member railroads to share traffic and to maintain agreed-upon tariffs. In 1870 the Rock Island Railroad, the Chicago and Northwestern, the Michigan Central, and the Chicago, Burlington and Quincy Railroad combined with smaller feeder roads to pool business in Iowa. This first formal pool foreshadowed the future of such unenforceable associations. After four years of violation by members and attacks from outside competitors, the pool collapsed. Apparently member firms expected that cheating by any single firm could greatly benefit that firm and not destroy the pool. Whereas no one cheating firm would necessarily upset the rate-holding agreement, each member tended to act with the same logic. With no means of enforcement, pools offered little aid to beleaguered railroads but generated public disapproval of actions by the member firms to guarantee, it appeared, prices higher than those permitted by competition.

Designs to curb competition between major rail lines in the West collapsed with the Iowa pool in 1874, but attempts at pooling continued among the great trunk lines of the East. Under the leadership of William Vanderbilt, the New York Central initiated a pool with the Pennsylvania, the Erie, and the Baltimore and Ohio. The pool was doomed from its inception because the Baltimore and Ohio, led by John W. Garrett, refused to join, preferring to destroy pooling agreements from the outside rather than from the inside as members did. The pool disbanded within six months, leaving behind a competitive environment as bad as that inherited, if not worse.

One regional pool did flourish, however, and its success established its director as a national proponent of cooperation among competing railroads. Albert Fink was assigned to negotiate an agreement on rates and traffic between thirty-two Southern railroad companies. The 1875 pact allowed expulsion to enforce the agreed-upon terms. The Southern Railway and Steamship Association survived, probably because the member firms were too weak financially to gamble with violations. Its success, nevertheless, encouraged other regional efforts at co-operation, efforts that failed even with Fink's leadership.

A Southwestern Railway Association established in 1876 collapsed in 1878, and the Eastern trunk lines tried another cooperative effort in 1877 but gave up within months. The failure of self-regulation forced even railroad leaders to conclude that governmental regulation was essential to prevent self-destruction by the competing lines. Railroads were unlikely, however, to obtain government aid in the form desired. A law compelling railroads to abide by cooperative contracts, the regulation espoused by railroad leaders and enunciated by Fink, was not politically viable since it would produce higher rates during a time when shippers were attacking rate setting.

Unsuccessful in preventing destructive competition or in procuring the government aid desired, railroad companies turned to system building in an effort to eliminate any need for cooperation or regulation. The traffic that railroad pools and cartel agreements had failed to guarantee was essential to the financial success of the high-fixed-cost operations that railroads represented. Aggressive railroading, then, was the apparent answer to the traffic puzzle for the large roads. Traffic could be secured if the connecting roads necessary for bringing shippers to the railroad were taken over. Unable to guarantee outlets to good markets through cooperative agreements, managers of large railroads purchased, leased, or duplicated the connecting roads. To eliminate dependence on other lines, the large carriers pursued control of all facets of their operations through ownership of essential feeder and receiver connections.

The construction of integrated railroad systems had begun as early as the 1860s, with the building of the large Eastern trunk roads. Jay Gould had attempted to take Western connections from his competitors to shore up his financially weak Erie Railroad. The defensive response of the New York Central, the Pennsylvania, and the Baltimore and Ohio railroads was to extend their control over lines needed to facilitate traffic over their own rails. The systems resulting from this expansion dwarfed previous railroad statistics. By 1874 the Pennsylvania Railroad had added over 5,000 miles of track (ten times its 1869 mileage), held assets valued at $400 million, and employed more than 1,000 managers to direct the work of over 50,000 employees within the most advanced management system developed to that time. Since guaranteeing traffic was the purpose of expanded railroad control, the systems included shipping lines and occasionally manufacturing concerns. The Baltimore and Ohio, for example, purchased coal mines, a steel rolling mill, and a chain of hotels. The depression of 1873 brought the first period of system construction to an end.

The second round of system building, an era of consolidation, was also stimulated by the activities of the speculative genius Jay Gould. Initially Gould had sought Western connections for an Eastern railroad, the Erie. Now he owned a Western railroad, the Union Pacific, a company he acquired in 1874 after its financial position had been shaken by the depression beginning the year before. Gould's eastward traffic connections were encumbered by the Iowa pool, so he simultaneously fought the cooperating lines and organized alternative links. Although Gould accumulated control of more rail mileage than any other American railroad operator, his empire was short-lived. He did not build an integrated rail network from his diverse holdings of railroad companies, whose tracks crisscrossed the continent from Boston to New Orleans to Denver, but instead took the speculative profits from buying and selling transportation properties. Gould's operations stimulated a defensive response from competitors, who expanded established rail systems and built new ones. The Vanderbilts stretched the New York Central and connectors to counter Gould's moves on every side, and their response to Gould's machinations were duplicated around the country. By 1893, according to Chandler, twenty-seven railroad systems were capitalized in excess of $100 million; these roads operated 69 percent of first-track mileage in the United States for that year. By 1906 thirty-two such systems operated 80 percent of the national first-track mileage.

The complicated financial manipulations required to put together railroad empires demanded the services of investment bankers, many of whom gained positions of power and influence over the railroads they helped construct. Sure that cooperation was the solution to destructive competition between the roads, J. P. Morgan and other financiers used their growing influence on boards of directors to fashion the workable cooperative agreements that had so long eluded the competing lines. The bankers believed they could do for the railroads what hands-on managers had been unable to accomplish. Confidence, however, did not guarantee success, and the bankers, too, failed to make cooperative agreements work. That failure, combined with a Supreme Court ruling in 1897 that effectively outlawed rate-setting associations, forced the investment bankers to seek relief from the railroads' problems in additional system building.

Government assistance was no more effective at reducing competitive problems of the railroads than the cooperative efforts had been among the roads themselves. Railroad leaders sought federal help, but Congress was under pressure from various groups to pass legislation to satisfy many different needs. Farmers, organized into granges, wanted legislative relief from discriminatory rates. Railroads tended to charge high rates over lines enjoying little or no competition to compensate for losses suffered on lines with heavy competition. Often the losers in these cases, farmers pursued relief through political action at the state and federal levels. Railroad companies operating interstate traffic preferred uniform federal regulation to state direction of their business.

Shipping interests lobbied for government aid against discriminatory rates and rebates made to favored shippers to hide rate discrimination. Firms that made extensive use of rail transportation demanded rebates and gave their business to the road willing to provide the largest repayment. The railroads saw little advantage in returning what they collected in rates, but the strong competition for traffic encouraged the practice. Merchants and shippers that opposed rebating and favored railroad regulation organized the Interstate Commerce Law Convention to press their case. Large shippers and merchants that benefited from rebates did not, of course, oppose paybacks. Smaller, less politically powerful shippers and merchants, unable to gain rebates themselves, opposed the practice that improved the competitive edge for their large rivals, but their efforts were thwarted by their own ambivalence following generally declining rates during the late nineteenth and early twentieth centuries. Rates were declining under pressure of competition among railroads—competition that threatened to destroy the railroads themselves.

The top management of American railroads were aware of the socioeconomic and sociopolitical ramifications of their position in the 1870s and 1880s but were unable to deal effectively with their endemic competitive problems, the consequences of which were generating demands for reform. Reform could have come as a government takeover of the railroads or regulation of the private companies. Regulation was the alternative least offensive to those owning or operating the companies and was viewed as a means of guaranteeing a return on railroad securities otherwise unprofitable because of competition for traffic. Regulation, however, was possible at the state as well as national level. State-level control was unattractive to companies doing interstate business because each state could be expected to enact legislation with little or no regard for national interests or the interests of the railroads. In the extreme, interstate railroading could have become impossible amid a tangle of laws requiring the railroads to operate differently in each state. Such irresponsible legislation had materialized in the early years of railroading, in the 1830s and 1840s especially, when several states established different rail gauges to prevent goods from reaching the rail lines of other states. In sum, state legislatures were not responsible for or responsive to the broader requirements of transportation in the United States at large but instead considered only the demands of the voters within their jurisdictions.

Railroad management and investment bankers saw federal regulation as their safe conduct through the perils of competitive conflict, for the federal government was responsible to all the states and had to legislate and regulate accordingly. The concentration of authority in Washington, D.C., facilitated concentration of railroad influence. The railroads were satisfied that they could influence regulators further removed than the state legislators from the scene of conflict.

Passage of the Interstate Commerce Act in 1887 established the federal precedent in railroad regulation. In less than ten years, judicial decisions had wreaked havoc with the very fiber of a regulatory commission. The railroads had been correct in estimating their ability to influence the federal commissioners: all five members on the first commission were pro-railroad. Yet the railroads gained little, for the 1887 act specifically outlawed pooling, the favored railroad approach to solving the problems of excessive, uncontrollable competition. The original act was amended frequently, but federal regulation was not a failure to be reconciled through legislation designed to shore up a faulty structure. Limited success spotted the career of the Interstate Commerce Commission in the pre–World War I era, as presidents of the United States approached the concept of federal regulation with varying philosophies. Regulation, however unsuccessful, was a harbinger of the developing relationship between big business and big government.

The problems faced by the railroads were not solved in the 1860–1914 era and indeed are extant. By the advent of World War I, however, the public focus was shifting from railroads and railroad problems. Internal combustion engines powering automobiles, trucks, and airplanes caught the fancy of a nation weary of the complex disorders associated with the iron horse, idol of half a century.[9]

The alliance between the public and private sectors of the economy that was evident in railroad development continued, if somewhat more subtly, when automobiles replaced railroads at the center of national transportation. Government participation in the spread of railroad transportation reached individuals only through aid administered directly to railroad companies. Private households benefited only insofar as the private rail firms were willing and able to absorb government aid and pass it on to their customers through service. Public funds transferred to railroads in subsidies and land grants became private property. Unless the government reclaimed public beneficence by declaring public ownership of railroad property, an option Americans did not support, public gifts to private companies left public control with the giving. American political leaders chose instead to leave private property in private hands but to guard public interests by regulating the private companies.

Well before problems with railroads became a core national issue in the United States, Europeans were laying the foundations for another transportation revolution. As Americans struggled with regional differences that led to civil war, a Belgian, Joseph Lenoir, was developing the internal combustion engine. By the first centennial of American independence, 1876, Nikolaus Otto had refined the engine, and in 1885 Gottfried Daimler, a one-time Otto employee, installed an internal combustion engine in a vehicle. The automobile was born and from it would spring a distinctively American way of life.

As many as 1,500 manufacturers eventually tried their hand at capturing what was thought in the 1890s to be a limited market for electric-, steam-, and gasoline-powered vehicles for transporting small numbers of people or small quantities of goods. Railroads provided mass transit and bulk hauling, and few pundits would have dared guess that automobiles could unseat the iron king of transit. After all, by 1890 transcontinental rail lines provided faster movement of goods and people than ever before and city railroads offered dependable local transportation. Whereas automobiles were undependable vehicles forced to function on poorly prepared surfaces, railroads owned their rights-of-way.

Automobile manufacturers were not expected to provide as much for their customers.

Local, state, and federal government became partners with auto manufacturers, much as they had earlier with rail companies. The result of public intervention in private business was again stimulation of the private sector for the benefit of private interests. One important difference was the ownership of the public donation. Public funds to the railroad companies meant privately owned and controlled equipment, rights-of-way, and roadbeds. Public subsidies to the automobile industry remained with the public in the form of improved highways on publicly owned rights-of-way. Because automobiles and trucks were at least partially household investment rather than exclusively business investment, households in the private sector were directly subsidized by public transportation funding for highways. The railroad experience could have been duplicated through public funding of private highway construction for private ownership, but that lesson had not been lost on Americans and the mistake was not repeated. Indeed, in the last years of the twentieth century, a proposed solution to the continuing railroad problem was public ownership of rights-of-way and roadbeds.

Americans had demanded roads well before they discovered the automobile, but the horseless carriage intensified their demand. State highway debt is one indicator of the extent of public involvement in the provision of highways to serve the needs of a car-buying society. An estimated $11,000 in outstanding debt from state highway construction in 1890 had ballooned to over $105 million by 1914. At least some of this money went into surfacing new and existing roads. In 1904 the 154,000 miles of surfaced roads were inadequate to serve American needs. About 10,000 miles of roads were added each year over the ten years before World War I. In those early years of road building, surfaced roads were a luxury: the number of powered vehicles using public roads expanded far more rapidly than did the miles of quality highway.

Factory sales of motor vehicles had expanded from an estimated 4,129 in 1900 to 548,139 in 1914. Automobile and truck registrations reflected the increase in vehicles sold, although not precisely, since registration is a state function and not all states required registration before 1920. In 1900 an estimated 8,000 machines were registered; by 1914 that number had grown to 1,763,018, or 220 times the 1900 figure. The wholesale value of motor vehicles sold in the United States from 1900 through 1914 is estimated at $2 billion. Americans were rolling on rubber-tired vehicles powered with gasoline engines by the beginning of World War I and demanding that city, county, state, and federal government build and pave roads, streets, and highways.[10]

The internal combustion engine was applied to powered flight in 1903, and another transportation industry was born. Public/private ownership within the aircraft industry soon resembled the American experience with railroads and automobiles. Railroads are business enterprise, whereas automobiles are owned by households and by business firms. Households willing and able to buy a motorcar were largely freed from direct dependence on railroads, trolley lines, and interurban transit companies for transportation. Cars and trains operated over roadbeds owned or subsidized by public funds, but rail rights-of-way remained private property. Air transportation demanded costly investments in airfields, terminals, and other facilities associated with flight. Public investment in air travel is more akin to investment in highways than to the subsidies given railroad companies: air facilities constructed with public money are public property.

Automobile and air travel have roots in the 1860–1914 era, though the story of their development is part of another time. The origins of these transportation innovations colored the final years before World War I and set the stage for a new world of travel. Too many automobiles were on American roads in 1914 to be ignored as a phenomenon of another time. Few aircraft were manufactured in the United States in the 1860–1914 period: only 43 planes were produced in 1913, and 49 in 1914. Just four years later, however, 14,020 air machines were manufactured in the United States, a figure neither exceeded nor equalled again before 1941. Clearly America had entered the air age by 1914.

The developments in transportation and communications in the United States between 1860 and 1914 were linked to the growth of giant enterprises— sometimes monopolies—and government participation. Government donated money and land to the railroads and eventually underwrote highway construction. Railroads in turn came under government regulation, and most highways have remained public property. In one sector of the transportation-communications nexus, government entered the business realm directly through self-declared, protected monopoly: The U.S. post office represents government participation in the predominantly private enterprise system—a form of public participation in the economic system that has been largely eschewed in the United States. The post office illustrates the limits of such government participation. There were Americans who espoused the expansion of the postal monopoly to telegraphic communications as that technology advanced, but a nationally owned and operated telegraph system did not survive the ire of private enterprise capitalists in the U.S. Congress. Continued opposition gave notice of intended federal restraint in private sector functions.

An agency for delivering correspondence (the early post office did not handle parcels), the post office limited its services to delivering mail from one place to another, using the available transportation technology. Although the national government has maintained its monopoly over the mails, the post office has advanced more in step with the private sector than in competition with it. On occasion, encouragement from the postal authority has spurred development in the private transportation sector: federal funding for post roads, contracts to haul mail on steamboats as early as 1813, and the declaration of railroads as post roads in 1838.

In the half-century following the Civil War, it was more important for the U.S. mail to unify the continental nation than it was for the postal business to make a profit. In fact, the post office was subsidized. Postage rates were kept below costs (in only six years—1865, 1882, 1883, 1911, 1913, and 1914—were revenues of the post office above expenditures), and the loss was written off as a cost of maintaining national communication. Rural Free Delivery (RFD), experimentally introduced in 1896 and made a permanent service in 1902, allowed the post office to provide Americans who lived on farms the same service offered city-dwellers. A post office serving the dense population of a city or a group of cities is potentially profitable, but if it expands into sparsely populated territory, costs of delivery rise and subsidies are necessary to maintain postal service. To the federal government, a unified nation was paramount, and Congress operated the mails at a loss, as taxpayers absorbed the costs of delivering mail to citizens who would otherwise be beyond reach at reasonable postal rates. The ultimate beneficiaries of the subsidy were the nation as a political unit; the citizens directly benefiting from subsidized mail delivery; and the business sector, able to reach all Americans at a price below the cost of service. Other postal services—such as postal money orders, special delivery mail, and registered mail—operated to the benefit of households and firms, but parcel post, in conjunction with RFD, created a mail-order business that put the entire population in reach of retailers of nearly every product, whether American-made or imported.

The post office was already a giant business operation at the beginning of the study period. In 1860 there were 28,498 post offices in the United States, a number that expanded to a peak of 76,945 units in 1901 before declining steadily thereafter. By 1914 fewer units (only 56,810) were handling more mail than had been processed in 1901. Faster transportation and the use of transit time for postal functions, along with generally improved efficiency, account for the decline in the number of facilities. In expenditures alone, the postal service qualified as a giant operation. The system paid out over $19 million in 1860 and over a quarter of a billion dollars by 1914, when nearly 20 billion pieces of mail were handled. The post office, the government monopoly mail business, was large by all measures—a giant before the age of giants.

The post office capitalized on new means of transportation to deliver mail. Railroads were used well before the Civil War, and airmail service was begun in 1917. Fast mail trains, special postal cars, electric railway post offices, and automobiles were all put to work to move the mail. The wide-ranging opinions Americans harbor about the U.S. Post Office are based on their personal experiences with the mail service and their views on government and monopoly. They watch the agency critically, and no change goes unnoticed. Postal innovations and public responses to them forecast the outcome of broader social change. If Americans would stand by while mail delivery shifted from horse-drawn conveyance to motor car, who could doubt the permanency of that vehicle on the national scene?

Although a misfit in a business history, the post office is an example of business-government cooperation during the Civil War to World War I era. Mail delivery would undoubtedly have attracted private investment, but the federal postal service met a need that private capital would have been unable to meet without subsidy—the delivery of unprofitable mail. Even so, private business has shared in the profitable portions of the postal market. The same result would have been possible with public subsidy to private enterprise, as with aid to the railroads. Although the federal affair with business enterprise in the form of mail delivery served a function and probably served it as well as the private sector could have, it also provided the limiting boundary to government entry into business. Government operation of the telegraph was rejected, as was government expansion into the telephone and wireless communications industries. Just as the railroad experience influenced public policy toward highways, the post office experience influenced public policy toward the telegraph, the telephone, and the radio.[11]

Only a series of what might be termed circumstantial miracles prevented the telephone from becoming the property of Western Union Telegraph Company, the monopoly of the wire communications industry at the inception of the modern telephone company. Invented in 1876, the telephone had within a year become the basis for a company. Western Union, determined to eliminate its potential competitor, commissioned Thomas Edison to build equipment for its own voice communications venture, the American Speaking Telephone Company. The smaller and financially weak Bell Telephone Company responded with patent infringement suits against Western Union. In 1879 Western Union settled out of court, abandoning the voice communications business to Bell Telephone. At the time of Western Union's withdrawal, Bell Telephone was under the leadership of Theodore Vail, an able administrator who would draw on his experience in federal communications monopoly to build the telephone company into a giant enterprise.[12]

Communications at the end of the period from 1860 to 1914 culminate in the telephone system. Under the leadership of former postal executive Vail (Vail had left the Bell Company in 1887 but returned in 1907), the Bell System absorbed Western Union in 1909. Joint operation of the two companies was short-lived, however; federal antitrust action threatened in 1913 forced Vail into the Kingsbury Commitment and the Bell System's sale of Western Union stock. Wireless telegraphy came under the influence of Bell in 1914, when the company bought Lee DeForest's patents on electronic amplification devices to extend the range of long distance telephone messages. On July 29, 1914, a call was successfully put through from New York to San Francisco. Bell developments in amplification devices placed that company in a strategic position for leadership in radio broadcasting in the years after World War I. Beyond the time frame here, but of related interest, is the federal takeover of the Bell System in 1918. For ten months the system operated under control of the U.S. Post Office Department, an arrangement that left little desire in the United States for permanent government ownership or operation of the national communications network.

In the 1860–1914 era, big business and big government worked together to expand communications and transportation in the United States. The first giant U.S. business organizations were railroads, the first national monopoly was the telegraph, and one of the largest monopolies was the federal post office. These became giant operations to meet the needs of a giant nation. The growth of such big businesses as the trunk-line railroads, Western Union (1,582,000 miles of wire by 1914), and the Bell Telephone Company (17,476,000 miles of wire and 142,527 employees by 1914) generated bonuses and problems. Companies large enough to exploit the efficiency found in economies of scale were also large enough to abuse their size-related advantages. The high costs of sensational speculative activities and wasteful overcapitalization fueled the public's fear of powerful businesses and stimulated voters' demands for a government role in transportation and communications. Government officials experienced in the business monopoly of the mails, however, were reluctant to expand the federal presence to railroads and the telegraph. State governments showed less restraint, despite the problems of regulating firms that did business in many states. Considerations of interstate interest finally pulled the federal government into the world of regulation, where it was welcomed by the very firms affected. At the outset of World War I government regulation of business in America was in its infancy, but it was too important to be dismissed and the future promised more of the same.

NOTES

1. Douglass C. North, *Growth and Welfare in the American Past: A New Economic History* (Englewood Cliffs, NJ: Prentice-Hall, 1966).

2. George Rogers Taylor, *The Transportation Revolution, 1815–1860*, Economic History of the United States, vol. 4 (New York: Rinehart, 1951), 137.

3. North, *Growth and Welfare*, 102; and James Saggus, "Old Bond Default Haunts Mississippi: 145-Year-Old Debt Surfaces," *Washington Post*, September 16, 1986, C1, C2.

4. Leland D. Baldwin, *The Keelboat Age on Western Waters* (Ph.D. diss., University of Michigan, 1932; Pittsburgh, PA: University of Pittsburgh Press, 1941); Erik F. Haites and James Mak, "Ohio and Mississippi River Transportation, 1810–1860," *Explorations in Economic History* 8 (Winter 1970): 153–80, and "The Decline of Steamboating on the Antebellum Western Rivers: Some New Evidence and an Alternative Hypothesis," *Explorations in Economic History* 11 (Fall 1973): 25–36; and Erik F. Haites, James Mak, and Gary M. Walton, *Western River Transportation: The Era of Early Internal Development, 1810–1860*, Johns Hopkins University Studies in Historical and Political Science, ser. 93, no. 2 (Baltimore, MD: Johns Hopkins University Press, 1975).

5. David O. Whitten, "Alternate Routes: Exceptional Road Building Materials," *Essays in Economic and Business History* 17 (1999): 229–43, and "Earth Roads Are Easy," *Essays in Economic and Business History* 18 (2000): 197–210.

6. Robert B. Starling, "The Plank Road Movement in North Carolina," *North Carolina Historical Review* 16 (1939): 1–22.

7. Robert Luther Thompson, *Wiring a Continent: The History of the Telegraph Industry in the United States, 1832–1866* (Princeton, NJ: Princeton University Press, 1947); Richard B. Du Boff, "Business Demand and the Development of the Telegraph in the United States, 1844–1860," *Business History Review* (Winter 1980): 459–79; Susan DuBrock Wendel,

"Telegraph Communications," in *Infrastructure and Services: A Historiographical and Bibliographical Guide*, vol. 3 of *Handbook of American Business History*, ed. David O. Whitten and Bessie E. Whitten (Westport, CT: Greenwood Press, 2000), 31–53; and Carole E. Scott, "Radio and Television Broadcasting," ibid., 55–101.

8. Alfred D. Chandler, Jr., "The Beginnings of 'Big Business' in American Industry," *Business History Review* 33 (Spring 1959): 1–31; *The Visible Hand: The Managerial Revolution in American Business* (Cambridge, MA: Harvard University Press, Belknap Press, 1977), *Scale and Scope: The Dynamics of Industrial Capitalism* (Cambridge, MA: Harvard University Press, Belknap Press, 1990), and *Strategy and Structure: Chapters in the History of the Industrial Enterprise* (Cambridge, MA: MIT Press, 1990).

9. Robert William Fogel, *Railroads and American Economic Growth: Essays in Econometric History* (Baltimore, MD: Johns Hopkins Press, 1964); Albert Fishlow, *American Railroads and the Transformation of the Antebellum Economy*, Harvard Economic Studies, vol. 127 (Cambridge, MA: Harvard University Press, 1965); Lloyd J. Mercer, "Railroad Transportation," in *Extractives, Manufacturing, and Services: A Historiographical and Bibliographical Guide*, vol. 2 of *Handbook of American Business History*, ed. David O. Whitten and Bessie E. Whitten (Westport, CT: Greenwood Press, 1997), 313–53; and Timothy E. Sullivan, "Water Transportation," ibid., 409–36.

10. David O. Whitten, "On the Road with King Cotton, 1926–1940," *Essays in Economic and Business History* 10 (1992): 240–56.

11. See Richard R. John, *Spreading the News: The American Postal System from Franklin to Morse* (Cambridge, MA: Harvard University Press, 1995).

12. See Chandler, *Visible Hand*, ch. 6.

PART II
Giant Commercial Enterprise

CHAPTER 3

The Commercial Response
to a Mass Market

The Civil War fostered nationalization of the American economy. Despite its divisiveness, the conflict made citizens more conscious than ever of their national ties—the South had been made painfully aware of the strength of union. After 1865 the country seemed at once larger and smaller: larger from the exposure wrought by war, smaller because of transportation innovations. Family, friends, neighbors had fought and died in places unheard of before the war, places now inscribed in the national consciousness. The war churned Americans together on an unprecedented scale, forcing a realization of commonalities and differences within a vast national habitat. The availability and rapidity of transit made Americans part of a single society: in 1865 travelers gained far-away cities with greater dispatch and ease than they could have the next town just thirty years earlier. Moreover, travel opportunities were not limited to an elite of class, status, or position; they were available to anyone with the price of a ticket.

As passenger traffic had increased on the railroads, so had freightage. Northern soldiers fighting in, and then occupying, the South were supplied by trains. When the war was over, those same trains delivered civilian as well as military goods. With railroad transit available, a seller could market products wherever the trains ran. Buyers, for their part, could purchase any items that could be shipped to them by rail. Local markets were suddenly thrown open to national competition, a competition that would intensify in the years before World War I. Within those markets yet another change developed in the years soon after the Civil War and again shortly before World War I—a change associated with transportation, intensified commercial competition, and nationalization of the American marketplace.

The growth of American cities emphasized the need for transportation within urban areas. So long as towns were small, residents could walk the distances between home and shop, home and church. Maintaining horses or mules for transportation posed few problems: Public stables in town were common, and wealthier residents could afford a stable on the grounds of their estates. Animals had long provided simple, inexpensive transport, but as cities swelled with residents and visitors from the country in the years after the Civil War, there was less room for stabling. Concentration of population not only pushed land prices up but made the maintenance of livestock within crowded areas unhealthy as well as expensive. Consequently, the proportion of the urban population that could afford to keep a horse and carriage in town declined. At the same time that people without transportation were a growing part of urban society, city boundaries were expanding so that walking was no longer feasible for getting around town.

Entrepreneurs provided conveyance in large cities well before the Civil War, but paving materials rarely afforded a smooth ride; comfortable, dependable transit awaited the laying of rails in city streets. Horse-drawn cars rolling along rails of iron or steel provided a low-cost, rapid means of public transportation within cities. Construction of street railways permitted urban expansion without loss of contact with the heart of the city. By 1870 an estimated $108 million (1929 dollars)[1] had been spent on street railways in the United States; even so, investment in street railways that year was only 1.5 percent of the value of capital in steam railroads, a complementary business. Street railways were a thriving enterprise in the years between the Civil War and World War I. As they supplied a service to satisfy a growing demand, their capital value grew annually until 1912, when $3,847 million (1929 dollars) estimated their total worth.[2] In that peak year the city railroads held not quite 20 percent as much capital as the steam-powered railroads.

Electric power was added to street railways in the 1880s, and urban transport expanded into a system of interurban railway networks. A traveler could cover hundreds of miles and visit scores of cities by boarding a series of electric-powered trolleys connecting nearby cities and towns. People living in the country found the interurbans a convenient means of transit into town and home again. Interurban companies that hauled freight expanded their local markets and gave sellers an alternative to railroads. Separate and distinct modes of travel, the steam railroad provided long-distance transportation, whereas the electric street railway served local needs. By 1890 there were 789 street railway companies in the United States. Combined, these operated 8,123 miles of track, about 15 percent of which was served by electric-powered equipment and nearly 70 percent by animal traction (the remaining equipment was operated by either steam or cable). Street railway companies employed 70,764 people in 1890 and provided transportation service to over two billion paying patrons. The demand for the service offered by the 1890 street and interurban railways is reflected in the difference between their operating revenues and operating expenses, 7.45 percent of their invested capital. (Taxes and depreciation would reduce the percentage return.)[3]

Small companies were the rule in street railways and interurban lines. Ohio alone had more than fifty different interurban transit companies with names like

Dayton and Xenia Transit Company, Lebanon and Franklin Traction Company, and Tiffin, Fostoria and Eastern Electric Railway. So well did these lines fill the demand for transit that no town with a population of at least 10,000 was excluded from that state's 2,798 miles of track in 1908.[4] Yet the life of the street railways was short: the systems peaked in the years before World War I and died quickly in the years afterward. The miles of line abandoned exceeded new construction for the first time in 1917. From that year on, miles of track abandoned ran well ahead of miles of track constructed. The three miles built in 1939 were the first since 1927. In the years 1930–33 alone, over 4,500 miles of street railway track were abandoned, leaving fewer miles in service than had existed in 1908.[5] The cable cars in San Francisco and trolleys in New Orleans that are so attractive to tourists remain today as relics, artifacts of an earlier time.

Had automobile manufacturing begun ten years earlier than it did, the street railways would probably not have developed. The motorcar made its appearance when the technology of railways was exploding. By the time automobiles were accepted in the national milieu, the street and interurban railways were fully developed but losing their market to the more flexible gasoline-powered vehicles. The decline and collapse of the street and interurban lines was tied to Americans' demand for individual determination. Waiting for a railway car did not suit the national temperament, especially in view of the alternative: an automobile that goes when and where the owner desires. The preference manifested itself in reduced earnings for the companies operating the railway lines. The 7.45 percent return (not adjusted for depreciation or taxes) of 1890 fell to 4.85 percent in 1902 and 4.59 in 1907. The adjusted returns would approximate those for the electric interurbans (not necessarily including all city networks and excluding nonelectric machines), which peaked at 3.2 percent (1911 and 1913) and fell regularly until the 1930s, when negative figures emphasized the graphic decline in demand for street and interurban railway service. The World War II years of gasoline and tire shortages and terminated automobile manufacturing for civilian markets saw the electric and interurban railways, ghosts of their pre–World War I operations, again running in the black with returns as high as 3.7 percent in 1944 and 3.5 percent in 1945. The end of hostilities and the appearance of postwar automobiles, however, brought the industry to a close.[6]

The street and interurban railways made a cameo appearance on the stage of American development. Like the cameo, their contribution was striking though truncated. The steam railroads tied the nation together, whereas the street and interurban railways turned the towns and cities of the nation into closer, more accessible units. The steam railroads offered direct transit between cities, but the street and interurban railways offered transit around town, a service so important that it was continued by underground rail networks, or subways, in major cities across the United States and abroad.

Rapid, dependable local transit was an essential link in the chain of nationalization. With post–Civil War technology people could contact one another almost instantly, and they could expect serviceable transportation both nationally and locally. For consumers, a larger marketplace meant goods from around not only town, but the nation and even the world were readily accessible. For business firms, the growth of national transportation opened sources of supply never before practical because of distance and shipping time. The creation of local transportation opened larger sales areas for local businesses. Every mile of street railway track expanded the clientele of any merchant within reach of the line. The two external economies, railroads and street railways, exposed commercial interests to economies of scale that, for entrepreneurs willing and able to capitalize on them, would eventually provide a foundation for giant business enterprise.

Grocery retailing was one of the first businesses targeted by entrepreneurs venturing to capture the profits in economies of scale promised by the exploitation of the larger markets offered by expanded communications and transportation. The small one-store operation for the sale of a limited range of food items was as much a fixture in the years around the Civil War as the supermarket was in the second half of the twentieth century. The small grocery serviced local clients who, for their part, scarcely had a choice, because distance was not easily conquered. The grocer sold neither meat nor baked goods: selling these was the province of the butcher and the baker. Multiple-store operations were not common because they were not financially attractive. Inventory was not easily secured, and there were no compelling economies of scale in stock purchasing. Furthermore, the necessary communications were lacking to manage a multiple-unit retail business. The retarding factors for multiple retail units in foodstuffs were fading by the 1860s with the advances in railroad construction and the development of dependable, inexpensive telegraph service. In the wake of these changes came innovations in grocery and dry-goods retailing.

The Great Atlantic and Pacific Tea Company, the A&P, a giant of business enterprise and an archetype of twentieth-century retailing, had its origins in the period from the Civil War to World War I. The A&P, a name adopted in 1869, was established by George F. Gilman and George H. Hartford in New York in 1859 to buy tea wholesale and sell it directly to final consumers. Gilman and Hartford absorbed the functions of various middlemen to gain a competitive price advantage, first with tea and then with other goods as they constructed a grocery business. Early expansion was slow by the standards of the era the A&P would introduce, but in the days of single-store businesses, opening 25 stores by 1865 was breathtaking. The 100-store mark was reached in 1880, and in 1913 there were 585 A&P stores. World War I saw the chain exploding to 4,200 units by 1919. Economies of scale, low markup, and rapid turnover made A&P a giant enterprise.

The market for retail grocery stores was large enough in the growing United States to permit several large-scale operations. The success of A&P and the availability of economies of scale attracted the founders of the Grand Union Company in 1872. Kroger, a name now synonymous with groceries, got under way in Cincinnati in 1882. Founded as the Great Western Tea Company by the twenty-two-year-old B. H. Kroger, the origins of the giant were modest and early growth belied the future. The chain would eventually operate over 5,000 units, but in 1891 Kroger had just 7 stores and by 1902 only 36. Other future giants in grocery retailing also came on the scene in the years between the wars: James Butler Grocery Company of Philadelphia comprised firms whose dates extended back to 1883; the H. C. Bohack Company of Brooklyn, New York, was established in 1887; and Gristede Brothers of New York was founded in 1891.

Despite an impressive response to the altered business potential created by transportation and communications advances, grocery retailing was upstaged by dry-goods merchandising. In the years between civil war and world war, three major ideas for merchandising dry goods took shape. The department store, the earliest of these modernizations, capitalized on the economies of scale of a large central facility and exploited the potential of urban and interurban transit for bringing customers within easy walking distance of shops and stores. Instead of sending peddlers out to customers or maintaining a small operation to satisfy a local clientele, the department store sought customers. A central location was one characteristic of department stores; another was their ability to spread the costs of operation over many different lines of goods. A customer's visit to one store had an impact multiplied by the varieties of merchandise presented for sale. The probability of a customer's making a purchase was pushed upward by expanding the product line carried. Maintenance of control, however, encouraged the division of the goods handled into departments of manageable size. Large size and the economies of scale accompanying it combined with the advantages of division of labor and specialization to make the department store a giant business.

Early department stores offered exceptional services (gift wrapping, exchange of or refund for returned merchandise, delivery, and comfort facilities for customers to ease the strain of shopping), a uniform price for all prospective buyers, and cash business with low markups. Low prices were built on a high sales volume that depended on an extensive range of goods, convenient location and delivery, low markup, and promotion. Advertising was one of the distinguishing features of the growing merchandising operations of the years between the Civil War and World War I, and department stores were no exception. Little was left to chance. Newspaper ads and broadsides on buildings, wagons, and the walls of trolley and interurban cars kept the public aware of a store, its location, and its special offerings. Advertising paid off by attracting customers, and the costs of promotion were spread over the wide range of items offered for sale.

Harry E. Resseguie argues that Alexander Turney Stewart opened the prototype large department store in New York as early as 1846. Not a completely developed department store, Stewart's nonetheless included many of the accepted characteristics of what would evolve from the efforts of Aristide Boucicaut at Bon Marché, R. H. Macy, and other pioneers of the department store. Stewart's store, legitimate department store or not, was a giant retail operation. Stewart began with an investment reportedly as small as $3,000 worth of Irish linens and laces that he offered for sale at 283 Broadway in 1823. By the end of the Civil War decade Stewart's business demanded over 1,000 employees. Stewart carried on both a wholesale and a retail dry-goods business with a degree of success illustrated by the $50 million in total sales registered in 1865. As a retail merchant, Stewart is distinguished by being the first to retail as much as $10 million in dry goods in one year. In both 1872 and 1873 he surpassed that mark and retailed $12 million worth of merchandise. Stewart's name was removed from his giant business establishment shortly after his death in 1876.[7]

Giant department stores became part of the growing urban sector of the United States in the years between the Civil War and World War I. Some of the giants had roots extending back into the time of small establishments; others were begun fresh in response to the attractive, if vacillating, business conditions of the era. The Lord & Taylor establishment opened in New York in 1825. Samuel Lord undertook the enterprise on a loan of $1,000 from his wife's uncle, John Taylor, and during the second year of operation, Mrs. Lord's family provided a partner in the person of George Washington Taylor. Arnold Constable & Company, also of New York, shared the opening date of 1825 with Lord & Taylor. Both enterprises attained giant size after the Civil War. Another New York department store, Hearn Brothers, located at 425 Broadway, was established in 1842—well before the war—but reorganized in 1860 as James A. Hearn & Son and relocated to 775 Broadway.

Although New York was the center of department store growth, other cities partook in the development, though on a smaller scale. The John Shillito Company of Cincinnati was founded in 1830. Two others, Jordan Marsh in Boston and F. R. Lazarus in Columbus, Ohio, opened in 1851—Marsh with an investment of only $5,000, Lazarus with an even smaller sum of $3,000. That $3,000 beginning launched a store that, by 1914, was making sales in excess of a million dollars a year. By 1855 Klein & Mandel was prospering in Chicago (after 1877, Mandel Brothers Department Store). A year earlier Samuel Carson and John Pirie had started a small dry-goods business in La Salle, Illinois, a business destined to become Chicago's Carson, Pirie, Scott & Company, another retailing giant of the years between the wars.

Two of America's prominent retail giants were founded before the Civil War. Both Macy's of New York and Marshall Field of Chicago got under way in the late 1850s. The origin of Marshall Field & Company can be traced to 1856, when young Field became a traveling salesman with the embryo of his future concern, Cooley, Wadsworth & Company on Lake Street in Chicago. Later Field was taken into the firm as a partner, and in 1864 his name went on the store then known as Farwell, Field & Company. Early in 1865, however, Field and Levi Z. Leiter, chief accountant and junior partner, formed a new company with Potter Palmer, a major competitor. By 1881 Field, Palmer & Leiter had given way to Marshall Field & Company. The vastness of Field's business success is suggested by the $120 million value of his estate at his death in 1906.

Rowland Hussey Macy opened his famous store at 204–206 Sixth Avenue, New York, on October 28, 1858. Unlike Marshall Field's smooth career, Macy's retail success followed years of disappointment. When he contracted for the

$1,600-a-year rental on his first New York store, Macy drew on fortitude and the experience gained from several failed enterprises: Macy's business acumen was more suited to the huge market of New York than it was to the smaller markets he had plied in the towns of his early mistrials. He expended nearly twice his rental obligation for advertising in the first year and reaped a harvest of about $85,000 in sales. Success begot success, and Macy enjoyed million-dollar-a-year sales by the early 1870s. At his death in 1877, an estate valued at more than $300,000 stood as testimony to his retailing achievements.

Like Marshall Field & Company, Macy's continued beyond the death of its founder, but R. H. Macy's heirs sold their shares in the store. Several attempts to change the famous name fell short before the Straus family gained complete control of the establishment in 1896. They steered Macy's to $10 million-a-year sales shortly after taking the helm, an achievement that augured well for the future of the store. Isidor and Nathan Straus, the heirs to Rowland Macy's creation, developed their business acumen working with their father Lazarus Straus, a glass and china merchant. Lazarus put his sons in contact with Macy and other retailers by means of his profit-sharing concessions to run glass and china departments in those stores. From such beginnings the Straus family became the owner of retail giants.[8]

Philadelphia in 1861 was the setting for John Wanamaker's renowned Oak Hall. Wanamaker, the owner of the largest U.S. men's clothing store by 1869, experimented with branches in Pittsburgh, New York, Washington, D.C., and other cities before abandoning interstate commerce in favor of concentrating in Philadelphia, where he introduced a second store on Chestnut Street. Wanamaker employed over eight hundred people in the two stores. During 1875–76 he rebuilt an abandoned railroad freight depot into what was nearly a department store and named it the Grand Depot. The Depot was not an immediate sensation with customers, but as Wanamaker continued restructuring the buildings, shoppers were attracted. By 1886 the giant retail outlet provided employment for 5,000 people and displayed many of the characteristics of a department store.

Macy, Field, and Wanamaker stand out as creators of giant department stores, but they do not stand alone. In Macy's New York, dry-goods retailing was rapidly taking the form of department store merchandising. Benjamin Altman established B. Altman & Company in 1865. At Altman's death in 1913, $20 million of his $50 million estate represented ownership in his giant store. Across the river in Brooklyn, Wechsler & Abraham opened in 1865 and was a $2.5-million-a-year business by 1884. The Straus family of Macy connection bought out Joseph Wechsler's share of the business in 1893. Together with Abraham Abraham, they developed the famous Abraham & Straus business. When Abraham died in 1911, the store was a giant, employing 2,700 people and turning $13 million in sales annually. During the 1860s Stern Brothers opened in New York (1867), Rich's in Atlanta (1867), and Strawbridge and Clothier in Philadelphia (1868).

Bloomingdale Brothers opened in New York in 1872, keeping the lead in department stores in America's principal city, but other growing metropolitan areas supported department stores as well. E. J. Lehmann opened for business in 1875, planting the seed for the Fair, a Chicago landmark. Within ten years of its 1881 startup, the J. L. Hudson Company of Detroit had built a $2-million-a-year business. The J. W. Robinson Company ("Boston Dry Goods Store") was established in Los Angeles in 1883, and Arthur Letts' dry-goods store on Broadway and Fourth Street, precursor of Bullock's, Incorporated, opened in the same city ten years later. San Francisco had the Emporium by 1897, and Wanamaker's Philadelphia was the location for Lit Brothers in 1891. Not to be left without distinction, Dallas, Texas, was the site of the first Neiman-Marcus Store. Established with $30,000 in 1907, Neiman-Marcus had by 1914 moved to a new building at Main and Ervay. In the first year at the new location the store almost doubled its sales volume, making a profit of $40,000 on sales of $700,000 of its exclusive merchandise.

While department stores were opening in America's growing urban districts, a second dry-goods retailing innovation was emerging in recognition of the vast rural and small-town market. Department stores served shoppers able to reach these establishments, and theirs was a growing clientele, but millions of Americans still lived beyond convenient reach of urban areas during the period from 1860 to 1914. These people bought from peddlers and from general stores in the vicinity or from city stores when their needs could not be met near home. For the most part, rural dwellers simply did without many items considered necessities by those able to secure them easily. Two giants were created in response to rural and small-town demand for the wide variety of goods readily available to city people through the growing, evolving department store.

The mail-order origins of Montgomery Ward and Company and Sears, Roebuck and Company are all but lost to generations of consumers accustomed to these stores across the modern landscape. Twentieth-century shopping malls often housed retail facilities of one, or both, of the firms. But neither company operated retail stores between 1860 and 1914 and instead concentrated on catalogue sales. Eventually, in the 1920s, they began to run mail-order business and on-site sales simultaneously. Montgomery Ward and Sears, Roebuck stores represent a hybrid of the major dry-goods retailing innovations of the Civil War–World War I era. They were at once department stores, mail-order stores, and variety stores, all operating within the framework of a chain. In the late twentieth century, the two firms attempted to incorporate another retail innovation, discounting. Yet early in the twenty-first century, Sears struggled to survive, while Wards entered bankruptcy, as did K-Mart, one of the discount giants that had fomented conflict at Sears and insolvency at Wards.

Aaron Montgomery Ward opened his Chicago mail-order business in 1872 with $2,000, a post office box number, and the help of his wife. From a twelve-by-fourteen-foot room, Montgomery and Elizabeth sent locals of the National Grange their price lists of goods for sale through the mail. Response was slow during the early years—people were suspicious of strangers offering sales by mail—and 1873 was a year of financial panic. Ward managed his mail-order operations at night and worked for salary in a supply house during the day. As business picked up, capital was added to the original meager stock through the purchase of a partnership by George R. Thorne, Elizabeth Ward's brother-in-law. Thorne brought in $500. (The partnership was later changed to a corporation in 1889 and capitalized at $500,000.) The handbills carrying the earliest price lists were supplanted in 1874 by a catalogue, a three-by-five-inch booklet of eight pages. Just two years later, the company was grossing $300,000 and mailing out 150-page catalogues. In 1880, only eight years into operation, Montgomery Ward enjoyed sales of $2 million. (Because of deflation, a period of falling prices, the increase represented growing sales of merchandise, not just increasing money totals.) Total sales in 1906 were $18 million and by 1920 were over $100 million. Ward died in 1913, but he had lived to see his company grow from a one-room mail-order business into a retail giant. He created his giant around a sound merchandising idea, an idea that also gave rise to the competition—Sears, Roebuck.[9]

Sears, Roebuck and Company's origins are as humble as those of Wards'. Richard W. Sears discovered firsthand that mail-order sales could be profitable as a young railway station agent in Minnesota. Assigned to deal with a consignment of watches refused by the addressee, Sears, with the approval of the shipper, sold them to friends by mail. Sears was so impressed at how fast the timepieces moved at a low markup that in 1886 he started a mail-order business in Minneapolis. He later moved the center of his operations to Chicago and added a partner, Alvah C. Roebuck. In 1893 the name Sears, Roebuck and Company was adopted for the young firm that generated $338,000 in sales that year. Two years later Sears sold out to Julius Rosenwald. When Rosenwald began running Sears, Wards had sales five times larger than his. Sales at Sears reached $11 million in 1900, $61 million in 1910, and over $245 million in 1920—almost two-and-a-half times the Wards total for 1920. Sears, like Wards, had grown from a small cottage business to a giant enterprise in the years between the Civil War and World War I. Changes in American society and the economy during that period combined with transformations wrought by World War I and the 1920s to encourage Wards and Sears to broaden their sales to incorporate the advantages of department stores and variety stores into their mail-order business.

The variety store was as much a part of retailing in the United States between 1860 and 1914 as the department store and the mail-order house. Although variety stores, or five-and-ten-cent stores, conjure up names like Woolworth, Kress, Kresge (Kresge was the origin of K-Mart, the discount giant of the late twentieth century), Murphy, and Grant, only Woolworth had constructed an obvious giant by 1914.

Frank W. Woolworth, like so many of the creators of giants in his day, started with little. The notion that a retail business could be built around a large variety of inexpensive items—items to be sold for five or ten cents—and $800 capital ($300 of which was a merchandise loan from his previous employers) were Woolworth's foundation stones for his first store, which he opened in Utica, New York, in 1879. The venture failed, and Woolworth moved to Lancaster, Pennsylvania, the same year and tried again. The second store was successful enough to carry Woolworth through the failure of stores three and four. Store five, the second success, was opened in Scranton, Pennsylvania, late in 1880. Philadelphia was the target for store six—another failure, but one that emphasized the importance of the location studies that had preceded the Scranton opening. Having learned that variety-store profits were dependent on high turnover, Woolworth began selecting properties that promised heavy buyer traffic, a criterion that proved as important as the cost and availability of the real estate. In 1886 Woolworth had seven stores and a total sales volume of $100,000; in 1895, twenty-five stores and $1 million in total sales; and by 1900, fifty-nine stores and sales of $5 million.

Woolworth helped family and friends who followed him into variety-store retailing, and these related firms grew along with his own. To take advantage of economies of scale in buying, distributing, and selling, Woolworth proposed a consolidation of six chains. When the merger was finalized in 1911, the F. W. Woolworth Company was operating 596 stores with total sales of over $52 million; by 1914, the 737 Woolworth stores were yielding almost $70 million in sales. Three more years found the giant operating 1,000 stores with total sales of over $98 million. By World War I the variety store (or five-and-ten-cent store), the mail-order house, and the department store were the established hallmarks of twentieth-century American merchandising.[10]

The retail giants that emerged between the Civil War and World War I did not all fit neatly into the categories of chain, variety, or department store, however. Variations, while not the rule, were not unusual. Gimbel Brothers, a name immediately recognizable as a famous New York department store, was more exactly a chain department store that grew strong enough to compete in the New York market. Adam Gimbel landed in New Orleans in 1835, a Bavarian seeking his fortune in the New World. He entered retailing as a peddler, an occupation that permitted a review of the American landscape as well as a living. Vincennes, Indiana, was the part of that landscape where Gimbel settled and opened a store in 1842. Content to do business in Vincennes, Gimbel left expansion to his heirs. Forty-five years after he opened his store, Adam's sons, the Gimbel brothers, established an additional one in Milwaukee (1887). Success there was followed by a Philadelphia opening in 1894, and New York, the haven of department stores, was attacked head-on by the Gimbels in 1910. Not content to buy and build for a trial run, the brothers paid $9 million for a lot on Herald Square (the original arrangement was for rental of the site for $655,000 a year): Gimbel Brothers was prepared to compete with giants as a giant, and it succeeded.

J. C. Penney made variations on the principal retail innovations of the 1860–1914 era. Although Penney's first store, opened in 1902, did only $28,898 in sales that year, by 1914 he had 71 stores doing sales of more than $3.5 million. Three years later, 177 stores were producing almost $15 million in sales. Neither department stores nor variety stores, Penney's retail units were instead outlets for clothing and dry goods, the diversity of which depended on the size of the unit and the nature of the market area. Penney took ideas from the three basic innovations—the department store, the variety store, and the mail-order house—and constructed a chain that was a giant only a dozen years after its founding.[11]

In the early years of the twenty-first century Wal-Mart, the late Sam Walton's creation, is the retail leader in a global market; K-Mart, its closest contender, has declared bankruptcy. Wal-Mart SuperCenters that sell everything from groceries and housewares to garden supplies and household maintenance equipment dwarf the revolutionary retail outlets of the 1860–1914 era and indeed have helped drive out of business many of the remaining department, mail-order, and variety stores that survived into the late twentieth century. Woolworth, Montgomery Ward, and Grant are gone, and Sears has restructured several times as it skirts bankruptcy. Walton seized the retailing lead not by developing a novel approach to consumer sales, but by pushing the ideas of the first giant retailers along a declining long-run average cost curve that offers lower costs as quantity sold increases. The Wal-Mart chain operates out of immense distribution centers. The logistics of supply for an enormous chain of superstores could not have been managed before computers added to the battery of technologies available to entrepreneurs capable of harnessing them.

Walton's creation was not so much innovation as extrapolation of the retailing ideas put into practice in the post–Civil War years. Railroads and the telegraph made large-scale retailing more profitable than peddling and small-unit sales in general stores and specialty shops. Motorcars, trucks, and the telephone permitted yet larger retail units and lower per-unit costs. In the current era air freight and computers have increased the speed of business and pushed per-unit costs even lower as volume increases. The 1860–1914 advances in consumer sales were the first installment in an ever-changing retail environment that continues to bring households a broader selection of goods at lower prices. What changes lie ahead are a matter of conjecture; that changes will come is certain.

NOTES

1. U.S. Bureau of the Census, *Historical Statistics of the United States: Colonial Times to 1957* (Washington, DC: U.S. Government Printing Office, 1960), ser. V212, 590.

2. Ibid.

3. U.S. Bureau of the Census, *Census of Electric Industries: 1917 Electric Railways* (Washington, DC: U.S. Government Printing Office, 1920), 12–13.

4. George W. Hilton and John F. Due, *The Electric Interurban Railways in America* (Stanford, CA: Stanford University Press, 1960), 254–55 and passim.

5. Ibid., 186–87.

6. Ibid.

7. Harry E. Resseguie, "Alexander Turney Stewart and the Development of the Department Store, 1823–1876," *Business History Review* 39 (Autumn 1965): 301–22; and John William Ferry, *A History of the Department Store* (New York: Macmillan, 1960), 41–45.

8. Robert Sobel, *The Entrepreneurs: Explorations within the American Business Tradition* (New York: Weybright & Talley, 1974), 89.

9. Cecil C. Hoge, Sr., *The First Hundred Years Are the Toughest: What We Can Learn from the Century of Competition between Sears and Wards* (Berkeley, CA: Ten Speed Press, 1988); and Frank B. Latham, *1872–1972: A Century of Serving Consumers; The Story of Montgomery Ward*, 2d ed. (Chicago: Montgomery Ward, 1972).

10. Charles F. Phillips, "A History of the F. W. Woolworth Company," *Harvard Business Review* 14 (January 1935): 225–36.

11. Godfrey M. Lebhar, *Chain Stores in America, 1859–1950* (New York: Chain Store Publishing Corporation, 1952), 11–14.

CHAPTER 4

The United Fruit Company

The United Fruit Company, a giant firm that imported bananas into the United States, was founded and developed in the era between the Civil War and World War I. The perishable fruit was grown or purchased by United in the tropics, shipped to U.S. ports, and transported by rail to inland markets at a profit, despite numerous natural and technological obstacles. Pitted against a hostile, unfamiliar environment, the North American business struggled to subdue the vagaries of tropical climates and the ravages of endemic diseases. Severe storms and hurricanes frequently destroyed banana crops and occasionally company ships. Tropical politics were as hostile as tropical weather. With little or no warning, governments friendly to the company became, or were replaced by, contentious administrations. The tropical countries supplying bananas, and eventually other products as well, were technologically backward at the time American businesses began looking their way for profitable products: If a railroad were needed to move a crop, the company had to construct it. To turn a profit on bananas, United Fruit treated tropical diseases of people and plants, appeased politicians, and financed infrastructure. United Fruit's profits depended on strong leadership, sound decisions, good fortune, and its practice of putting the earnings of stockholders before the best interests of the Latin peoples in the targeted countries.[1]

Giant enterprise in bananas began in 1885, when twelve New Englanders familiar with the nascent banana trade founded the Boston Fruit Company, an informal partnership launched with a total paid-in capital of $15,000 and an agreement to pay no dividends to stockholders for five years. Despite competition with banana companies in the other major port cities (the inland distribution system was yet to come) of New Orleans, New York, and Philadelphia, Boston Fruit turned its $15,000 into $200,000 in two years. In 1890, at the end of the five years of reinvestment, Boston Fruit was valued at $531,000 and incorporated at that value in Massachusetts.

During the 1890s, Boston Fruit bought into companies that sold bananas in rival port cities. In a period when banana importing firms were initiated and terminated with regularity and little fanfare, Boston Fruit survived and expanded, creating, for example, the Fruit Dispatch Company in New Orleans to facilitate the movement of bananas from boats to trains bound for inland markets. Bananas had been shipped inland before Fruit Dispatch was created, but the condition of the fruit on arrival at final points of sale was more a function of chance and chicanery than good business operations. The bananas Fruit Dispatch sent to inland dealers were guaranteed marketable.

Eight years after the Boston Fruit Company was incorporated (1898) its estimated value had increased by six to eight times its original capitalization of $531,000. The following year Boston Fruit contributed $5,105,000 toward the $20 million capitalization of United Fruit, incorporated in New Jersey. To complete the capitalization, United Fruit stock was exchanged for holdings in other companies in the banana business. Within two months United Fruit, a working association of twelve banana firms, controlled properties in Baltimore, Boston, New York, Philadelphia, and New Orleans, and in Costa Rica, Cuba, Colombia, the Dominican Republic, Jamaica, Nicaragua, and Panama.[2]

The United Fruit Company continued the vertical integration begun by the Boston Fruit Company. The firm acquired extensive acreage for the production of bananas, sugar, and other tropical products and built railroads to connect company lands and private supply sources with shipside loading facilities, infrastructure that frequently had also been developed by United Fruit. The company purchased its own merchant vessels, painted them white to make them distinctive—the famous Great White Fleet[3]—and attracted media attention by offering luxury berths to well-heeled travelers interested in visiting exotic ports at a leisurely pace. Where infrastructure was lacking, United Fruit constructed housing for employees and built and operated hospitals. If products required processing (like grinding sugar cane, then manufacturing sugar from the molasses and refining the raw sugar for consumption), United Fruit carried on whichever of the functions were profitable. Conglomerate expansion was not ignored, either. United Fruit used its fleet to build the tropical tourist trade. A Caribbean vacation aboard a United Fruit Company vessel became a coveted treat of the early twentieth century. The absorption of competing enterprises frequently added to the company both horizontally and vertically.

Although United Fruit continued to grow beyond the study period, eventually becoming a multinational corporation, it had attained giant size within fifteen years of its founding. In 1900 the company's assets were just under $17 million, a figure that would more than double by 1908, when company assets exceeded $35 million. By 1913 United Fruit assets had more than doubled again, to over $82 million.[4] The United Fruit Company expanded to capitalize on the demand for tropical products. Never a monopoly in the U.S. market, United Fruit was nonetheless the largest single firm importing tropical goods in the years before World War I and a giant enterprise in the years before giants were commonplace.[5]

NOTES

1. Stacy May and Galo Plaza, *The United Fruit Company in Latin America, Case* Study, NPA Series on United States Business Performance Abroad, no. 7 (Washington, DC: National Planning Association, 1958), 2.

2. Charles Morrow Wilson, *Empire in Green and Gold: The Story of the American Banana Trade* (New York: H. Holt, 1947), 109.

3. John H. Melville, *The Great White Fleet* (New York: Vantage Press, 1976).

4. Frederick Upham Adams, *Conquest of the Tropics: The Story of the Creative Enterprises Conducted by the United Fruit Company*, Romance of Big Business, vol. 1 (Garden City, NY: Doubleday, Page, 1914), 332.

5. For more information about United Fruit, see the United Fruit Historical Society website at www.UnitedFruit.org. This site has pages for bibliography, biographies of people associated with United Fruit, a chronology of company history, and information on the Great White Fleet.

CHAPTER 5

The Singer Sewing Machine Company

The founders of United Fruit Company, like the entrepreneurs who established department stores and mail-order businesses, created a new enterprise in response to America's expanding commercial opportunities. Singer Sewing Machine Company, a manufacturer that circumvented wholesalers and retailers to sell directly to its customers, is another wrinkle in the unfolding fabric of American market capitalism.

Isaac Merritt Singer (1811–75) invented and patented a variety of improvements on the sewing machine. Though he did not invent the sewing machine, Singer's work, beginning in 1850, made possible the manufacture of a dependable, durable model considerably more useful than the temperamental devices first marketed.[1] Yet beyond the mechanical advances he created, Singer contributed little to the company bearing his name: the business of the Singer Company was conceived and directed by Edward Clark, an attorney and partner.[2]

Singer Company's commercial operations launched the modern household appliance market. The sewing machine was the first major machine for household use that could not be manufactured at home. Moreover, its purchase price seriously limited demand at a time (early nineteenth century) when most households had little access to money. If sewing machines were to be manufactured at the lowest possible cost and sold at a market-stimulating price, a mass market was essential so that the cost of machine tools designed for the exclusive production of the interchangeable parts could be spread over many machines. And mass production demanded mass consumption.

To sell its sewing machine, the Singer company would have to create a mass market. The obstacles to mass sales were price and the specialized customer services buyers would need if they were to make maximum use of a complicated technical device. Potential buyers would want to see the sewing machine at work, so sellers would need to maintain not only a sales force trained in operating Singer's sewing machine but, since buyers would be taught to use the machine, teaching facilities and personnel as well. Once a machine had been purchased, Singer replacement parts and personnel trained in repair would guarantee its continued functioning. And if credit sales were introduced to offset the high purchase price of a sewing machine, collections and recordkeeping could be rationalized.

Early sewing machine manufacturers used territorial rights and commission agents to supplement direct sales in the distribution of their products. Territorial rights to specified geographic areas were sold for a cash payment: The manufacturer surrendered retail control over those tracts, and the owner of the purchased rights enjoyed a monopoly on the sale of the machine in that territory. Commission agents were usually established sellers—retail, wholesale, or both—who agreed to buy the machine from the manufacturer at a 25 to 40 percent discount. The agents' return came from reselling the product. The manufacturer's influence over such agents depended on the attractiveness of the product to consumers. If the market were good, the agents would strive to meet the manufacturer's specifications rather than lose the commission to sell the product, but if the market were indifferent, the manufacturer could do little to force agents to comply with their directives. Direct sales permitted control of retail conditions but at the producer's expense for creating and maintaining the essential showroom, demonstration facilities, instructional space, spare parts, and service space, as well as a staff to demonstrate and repair sewing machines and instruct buyers in their use.

In the early stages of its development, the Singer Company employed all three methods of distribution. Isaac Singer and Edward Clark had decided from the beginning to manufacture their product themselves; in contrast, Elias Howe, the recognized inventor of the sewing machine, always licensed others to manufacture and sell his model. The earliest sewing machines were hand-produced in machine shops. Each part was custom-made to fit the other individually shaped components. While working as a machinist, Singer had seen his first sewing machine, one brought in for repair. As he worked on this early model, Singer realized he could improve it and did.

Clark, contacted by Singer for legal advice, recognized the market value of Singer's improvements to the sewing machine and became the business force behind the Singer Company. Together Singer and Clark established a company office as a center of operations for machine production and marketing—the first Singer Sewing Machine Center. The founders did not have enough capital to expand retail facilities when their first priority was building a production organization. In 1851 and 1852 Singer and Clark sold territorial agreements in the hope of facilitating sales, but the arrangements were not financially remunerative. They also could not control marketing in the assigned territories: The territorial rights were exploited according to the whims of the holders, and by 1856 Clark had begun buying back the agreements.[3]

In the early 1850s Clark experimented with retail alternatives. Territorial rights were sold, and commission agents were contracted to add the Singer machine to their line of wares. Although Clark would have preferred contracts that precluded the Singer model being retailed side-by-side with competing models, the sewing machine was too new and the company too small for him to negotiate the contracts he wanted. Recognizing that commission agents would neither guarantee customer services nor differentiate the Singer machine from other models, Clark began to create the company's direct-sales organization by establishing branch offices as early as 1852. (It is a measure of Clark's entrepreneurial talent that at a stage in the company's development when all energies and funds would normally have been flowing into production, he considered marketing as important as production.) The cost of direct sales was even higher than that of commission sales. Commission agents usually received a 25 percent discount, whereas the branch offices cost the company about 28 percent of sales. The Singer Company was operating 14 branch offices by 1859; the number was up to 200 by 1877 and 4,552 in 1905.

Although Elias Howe is credited with inventing the sewing machine, he is more contributor than inventor to a working model shaped by himself, Isaac Singer, and six others. Each of the models offered for public sale included parts patented by someone other than the manufacturer. Moreover, because many innovators made improvements in the early models, sewing machine manufacturers were numerous in the first several decades after Howe's invention. Every maker hawked his own machine's advantages over the others', but when an obvious improvement appeared on any one machine, each maker quickly incorporated it into his model. Patent laws did not deter infringement but did keep manufacturers in court. Howe, for example, received his patent in 1846, but eight more years passed before a court order forced sewing machine manufacturing companies to pay him royalties. Howe sold licenses to manufacture and sell sewing machines under his patent rights. Once the manufacturers had settled with Howe, they set upon each other for patent infringement. The expense and inconvenience of court actions encouraged producers to create the first patent pool in the United States (1856). Members of the pool shared the patents they all needed to build a functional sewing machine.

During the years of the patent pool (1856–77), sewing machine prices settled at roughly $65. Member firms wrestled for market share. Since prices were almost identical from machine to machine and every manufacturer had access to the same technology, the only route to market dominance was radical cost reduction that could translate into drastic price cuts. Sewing machines were hand-constructed in machine shops by skilled machinists. The alternative, which was not obvious in the middle of the nineteenth century, was mass production with machine tools designed to produce each part of the sewing machine to specifications that would allow assembly of the final product from stockpiles of the requisite components. Using part-specific machine tools meant manufacturers would have to spread a huge fixed-cost investment over so large a number of output units that the unit cost would fall well below that of the handmade product. But attaining low costs per unit was only half of the equation for success: the huge volume of output had to find a market.

Selling was closely related to manufacturing: large-scale manufacturing was the key to reduced costs but was feasible only when large-scale selling was possible. In the year the patent pool began, Singer Company tried increasing sales by offering a hire-purchase plan that let buyers rent machines and apply the rental payments to the purchase price. The adoption of these installment sales complicated company bookkeeping but paid off in expanded sales. In the second half of 1854, Singer produced only 331 machines, but in ten years' time, output had risen so much that in the third quarter of 1864 the firm turned out 7,368 units. In 1873 Singer opened a factory at Elizabethport, New Jersey, that could produce 1,000 machines a day, and three years later, in 1876, the firm manufactured and sold 262,316 sewing machines. Singer Company took the lead in the sewing machine race and pulled far ahead of its nearest competitor, Wheeler and Wilson, who sold only 42 percent as many units in 1876 as Singer. The following year, at the end of the patent pool, Singer reduced its unit price to $30 cash or $40 on installments. The reduction expanded the company's sales and essentially destroyed all competitors except Wheeler and Wilson. The economies of large-scale manufacturing attained by Singer Company permitted production for as little as $12 a unit, 40 percent of the $30 price.

The I. M. Singer Company of New York that Edward Clark joined as a partner in 1852 was restructured as a corporation in 1863. In 1873 the company was reincorporated under New Jersey's more liberal corporate laws as the Singer Manufacturing Corporation. A limited liability charter freed the company of partnership restraints—especially the burden of Singer himself, a partner more interested in spending the firm's profits than in directing its operations—and facilitated the efforts of active officers to expand the business. Isaac Singer and Edward Clark, directors of the corporation, each agreed not to assume the presidency during the other's lifetime. Clark became president after Singer's death.

Economies of scale in production, the successful construction of a mass sales organization, a superior product, and the freedom of the corporate form of business enterprise combined to help the Singer Manufacturing Corporation exploit foreign markets. Although company experiences differed in detail from country to country, foreign business, like its domestic counterpart, was successful. The first of the factories Clark built abroad to support international sales opened in Kilbowie, Scotland, in 1885. It had a capacity to produce 10,000 sewing machines a week and employed 5,000 workers. The Kilbowie facility provided products for European markets, which were divided into national sales companies for: Germany in 1895, Russia in 1897, the Scandinavian countries in 1901–02, and Great Britain in 1905. By 1900 Singer employed 60,000 sales people around the world. The extensive international business was organized under a world sales subsidiary in 1904 as Singer Sewing Machine Company. Two other subsidiaries were established before World War I: one in 1904 for employee insurance, the other in 1913 for corporate investments.

In 1890 Singer, a giant enterprise, manufactured an estimated 75 percent of the sewing machines sold worldwide—800,000 machines in 121 styles produced in six factories employing 12,000 men and women. The company had amassed a surplus of $14.5 million, reserves of $12.8 million, and accounts receivable of $20 million. In 1900 the directors declared a 200 percent stock dividend to increase corporate capitalization to $20 million. Growth continued apace into the twentieth century: by 1905 Singer employed 61,444 sales personnel working out of 4,552 branch offices and 30,000 production employees manufacturing 200 styles of sewing machines in eight factories, for a total of 1,250,000 units.

World War I demonstrated the versatility of firms geared to a mass consumer market. Although Singer plants in the United States had little time to adapt production lines before the conflict ended, the Clydebank plant in Scotland illustrated the company facilities' potential for manufacturing armaments. In just the final quarter of 1915 Clydebank produced 3,000 six-inch artillery rounds (half of the amount all of Scotland was expected to turn out in a week). Working under more than 5,000 government contracts, the plant's predominantly female labor force of nearly 14,000 had by 1918 manufactured more than 300 million artillery rounds along with shell and fuse components, parts for airframes and aircraft engines, tank components, small arms parts, and hundreds of thousands of horseshoes.[4]

The population of the United States more than tripled from 31 million in 1860 to nearly 100 million in 1914, but because Americans were spread out over a vast continent, the increase was insufficient to generate a mass-market nation. The great land policy controversy of the pre–Civil War years had produced the argument that a rapid opening of land to citizens would dilute the market and deal a serious blow to U.S. commercial interests. But though the conservatives opposed to opening the frontier to fast settlement were right about the scattering of consumers over the continent, they were wrong about the loss of markets. The telegraph and the telephone allowed communication between people in all parts of the country. The steam railroads offered, at a moderate cost, the means for those seeking to transport themselves and their possessions to far-flung places. The street and urban railways and then the automobile moved people and goods about within cities and adjacent areas. The combination of a population growing through natural increase and extensive immigration and the developing transportation and communications technologies created a mass market that attracted entrepreneurs who appreciated the profits promised by economies of large scale in production and distribution.

The domestic commercial developments between 1860 and 1914, giant department stores, mail-order houses, and variety stores, created and extended within a framework of a chain of stores—retail merchandising on a grand scale— were obvious features of the times. A change less visible to citizens benefiting from the transformation of the market infrastructure was expansion of the international sector. Globalism had been a critical part of the American experience from the time Europeans immigrated to the New World, but the years after the Civil War brought changes in the international sector that dovetailed with the mass marketing developments in the domestic market. The United Fruit Company drew on the heritage of the seventeenth-century East India companies when it constructed a multinational corporation that loomed as large as the challenge of the market it served. Singer Sewing Machine Company, another early multinational, also built on the legacy of international business enterprise, contributing to the evolution of the global marketplace that burst into bloom during the final decades of the twentieth century. These large-scale businesses in the commercial sector set the pace for the years beyond World War I, when giants would be the rule rather than the exception in American business.

NOTES

1. For a biography of Singer, see Ruth Brandon, *A Capitalist Romance: Singer and the Sewing Machine* (Philadelphia, PA: Lippincott, 1977).

2. Robert Bruce Davies, *Peacefully Working to Conquer the World: Singer Sewing Machines in Foreign Markets, 1854–1920*, American Business Abroad (New York: Arno Press, 1976); Don Bissell, *The First Conglomerate: 145 Years of the Singer Sewing Machine Company* (Brunswick, ME: Audenreed Press, 1999); and Charles M. Eastley, *The Singer Saga* (Braunton, Devon: Merlin Books, 1983).

3. Andrew B. Jack, "The Channels of Distribution for an Innovation: The Sewing Machine Industry in America, 1860–1865," *Explorations in Entrepreneurial History* 9 (February, 1957): 113–41.

4. Davies, *Peacefully Working to Conquer the World*, 170.

PART III

Giant Firms to Exploit Natural Resources: Extractive Industries

CHAPTER 6

Giant Farms

Although the rise of giant commercial enterprise in the United States over the years between the Civil War and World War I reflected America's genius at selling on a grand scale, big business was not limited to commerce. American industrial production in those years was led by firms capable of harnessing the advantages of large-scale operation. Small business remained, but leadership was seized by the large firms.

The most basic extractive industry is agriculture. Large-scale farming is not unusual in human history: Big farms helped feed ancient cultures, and the medieval manor, a large farming operation, had roots in the Roman *latifundium*. Abortive attempts to establish feudalism in the Western hemisphere introduced large farms in what would become the United States. Colonial and antebellum farming in the United States was punctuated with large-scale agriculture, especially in the plantation South; nevertheless, until about 1820 big agricultural units were rare.[1] Large sea-island cotton plantations and rice plantations along the coasts of South Carolina and Georgia were exceptions.

Americans took advantage of the Erie Canal to access the rich lands of western New York and central Pennsylvania, where they built large farms. By 1820 cotton cultivation was entrenched in the older Southern states and moving west. Yields in the new cotton states, dotted with large plantations, surpassed production in their Atlantic coast predecessors by the mid-1830s. Large-scale farming was an established part of the American scene, North and South, by 1860.

At the onset of the Civil War large-scale agricultural units were common in cotton planting in the Southwest, rice production in South Carolina and Georgia, and sugar growing and manufacturing in Louisiana. The Census of 1860 reported 5,348 farms of 1,000 acres or more in the United States (excluding territories). Nearly 70 percent of these were located in the Southern states of Alabama (696),

Georgia (902), Louisiana (371), North Carolina (311), South Carolina (482), Tennessee (158), Texas (87), and Virginia (641). Employing slave labor, these large, sometimes giant, operations were managed along lines more resembling a business than a family farm. Gangs of slaves planted, cultivated, and harvested a staple crop under the supervision of an overseer or the owner. For some crops, sugar and rice in particular, the slaves were additionally directed in the manufacture of the crop. Slave labor was recognized as capital and worked accordingly. Slaves were only profitable in agricultural pursuits that occupied their time completely. Grain farming, for example, was more profitably undertaken with free labor that bore its own cost of unemployment during slack periods. In his *Journey in the Back Country, 1853–1854*, Frederick Law Olmsted published a firsthand account of large-scale cotton planting with slave labor that accurately illustrates employment of the labor force over the entire year.[2]

The task system favored in Southern rice and sugar production was rarely employed in cotton farming. The large cotton plantations of the antebellum years were instead worked with gangs of slaves. Production methods of the slave-labor era died with slavery: Freed men and women refused "slave work" even for a wage, and landowners rarely had sufficient cash to offer wages. Sharecropping, a system established to accommodate the workers' desire to be their own bosses, the landowners' desire to hold title to the soil, and the lack of financial resources in either group, replaced the ubiquitous large cotton plantations of the antebellum years. The cotton plantation survived to the extent that large holdings remained in the hands of a few landowners, but the farming itself was fragmented into many small units controlled with credit advances on the cotton yet to be grown. The extent to which large plantations were centrally controlled by landowners manipulating the croppers and tenants has yet to be determined. The large antebellum cotton farms disappeared in the years between 1865 and 1914. Giant twenty-first century cotton farms are rarely rooted in land holdings of the slave-labor era.

Heavy investments in land improvements and processing machinery gave many sugar and rice plantations more in common with large commercial and manufacturing enterprises than with cotton farms. Along the tidal rivers of coastal South Carolina and Georgia, slaves cleared, drained, diked, and ditched swamps into level fields for rice cultivation. Opening and closing sluice gates flooded fields with fresh water backed up by a rising tide or drained the fields into rivers receding with a falling tide. Plantations equipped with processing machinery powered by tides or steam to prepare rice for market were factory-farms, impressive examples of working capital. In 1850 Solon Robinson visited the estate of William A. Carson in South Carolina, where he reported seeing a farm with 650 acres in rice, 90 in sweet potatoes, 180 in corn, 26 in oats, and additional acreage in "gardens, yards, lots and roads, of which last he [Carson] can show a pattern worthy of imitation." Robinson appraised Carson's holdings at $130,000 for 3,300 acres of land, "a very large tidewater hulling mill, steam threshing mill, steam saw mill, a noble mansion, a very good lot of Negro houses, overseer's house, barns, stables, store houses, shops, &c., enough to make up a town in California worth a million."[3]

Robinson also visited the rice plantation of William Aiken, an estate comprising 3,300 acres, 1,500 of which had been improved for rice planting and 500 reserved for other uses. Aiken employed 700 slaves, worth an estimated $210,000, on land valued at $170,000. Rice was big business in antebellum South Carolina and Georgia.

The Civil War brought an end to large hand-operated rice plantations and shifted America's center of rice production to Louisiana, Arkansas, and Texas. South Carolina and Georgia rice fields, neglected during the war years, suffered the destructive wrath of severe hurricanes in addition to direct war-related damage. Recovery was slow with a free labor force, whereas slave-driven field maintenance had been carried out at marginal cost as a by-product of an industry that produced slaves and rice for market. Rice planters needed more than they received from rice sales to make their capital returns comparable with alternative investments of similar risk.

The Aiken plantation earned $15,000 on an estimated $380,000 investment in 1850. There is no reason to expect much of an increase in rice sales in the 1850s, but slave values rose, as did the number of slaves through natural increase. As slave capital value increased, planters had to reduce capital and increase income through slave sales. The alternative was to allow income to run substantially behind the opportunity cost of investment (the return the investment could bring if transferred from current use to the best alternative available). Investments in slaves were sufficiently liquid (easily changed to cash) for planters to adjust their holdings as necessary in a changing market. The Aiken estate earned less than a 4 percent return at Robinson's conservative estimates. Slave prices rose rapidly in the 1850s, and as they rose—and Aiken's slave force increased—the plantation generated a smaller and smaller return. Rice planters responded to such conditions by selling off surplus slaves.[4]

Emancipation abolished slavery and eliminated slaves as a plantation by-product. The surplus labor associated with the production of slaves had been available for maintaining the rice fields in the antebellum industry. The legacy of the war was a free labor force and a rice industry that had to be productive enough to pay its own way, including the costs of land maintenance. Without the superfluity of labor it had enjoyed in the antebellum years, the Carolina-Georgia rice industry did not return to its antebellum vigor, as table 6.1 indicates. At the end of the Civil War the industry was at low ebb, producing less than 2.5 million pounds of rice in 1865.[5] Economies of scale disappeared as owners divided plantations of thousands of acres into farms of 150 to 250 acres.[6] Rice as a giant business enterprise expired on the east coast.

Between 1860 and 1880 rice culture expanded along the Mississippi River but contracted on the Carolina-Georgia coast to small farm units and a few remaining plantations. Small amounts of rice had long been grown on the rich, wet soil of southern Louisiana, but competition from sugar cane had limited its scope. The

TABLE 6.1 Rice Production in South Carolina and Georgia, 1839–1919
(millions of pounds of rough rice)

1839	1849	1859	1869	1879	1889	1899	1909	1919
118	322	278	88	125	73	95	31	8

Source: Derived from Census of Agriculture (Washington, DC: U.S. Government Printing Office). When production figures differ in older and newer census publications, the newer data are used here.

disruptions of the Civil War encouraged many sugar planters to divide their lands into smaller units for the cultivation of rice. The availability of water combined with rich soil to produce a competitive rice region, but the farm units remained small, even smaller than those on the east coast.

The 1880s, however, brought a return to large-scale rice growing in the United States. Jabez B. Watkins, an enterprising land promoter who had had some success in Kansas, undertook to develop southwestern Louisiana, an area recently opened by a new Southern Pacific Railroad line. Watkins organized English investment funds into seven corporations he operated as the Watkins Syndicate, headquartered in London but managed by the freewheeling Watkins from the United States. The funds provided by the syndicate were used to purchase 1.5 million acres in southwestern Louisiana. The tract comprised thinly settled prairie and about two-thirds swampland considered to be of little or no value. Reclaiming the swamp on a grand scale was Watkins's original plan, but before it came to fruition, the project was diverted to activities on the prairie lands held by the syndicate.

Watkins had recruited the president of Iowa State College, Seaman A. Knapp, into the development enterprise early in its operations. While Watkins handled finance and reclamation, Knapp devoted his time to attracting settlers onto the syndicate's lands. After resigning his position with the college, Knapp worked to determine crops and livestock best suited for the area and displayed his successes to prospective immigrants through model farm exhibits. Knapp's efforts to attract potential buyers and lessees for syndicate property—the ultimate goal of a land development company—were reinforced by Watkins's expenditures for advertising throughout the Midwestern United States. Watkins established a weekly newspaper, the American, to spread the word and provided inspection trips into the Louisiana tract for members of the press. He installed exhibits at fairs and dispatched a special advertising railroad car on a tour of the Northwest. On mainline roads he paid railroad station agents to encourage land seekers to go South.

Settlers in the syndicate region initially grew rice like the native Louisianans had, using pockets of water held from rains to flood fields prepared for seed. But the prairie soil, unlike the mud of Carolina and Georgia or the Mississippi River delta, proved firm enough to support the agricultural machinery employed for grain farming in the Midwest. The machinery revolutionized rice culture, permitting large farms that could be worked by a few mechanics and laborers instead of the small farms worked by many hands that had characterized the established industry. Experiments in prairie rice farming gave way to permanent farms relying on deep wells and steam-powered pumps for irrigation. Even the seed rice was chosen with scientific calculation. Around the turn of the twentieth century, Knapp made an Asian tour in search of a rice variety capable of withstanding hulling with minimum breakage (the broken grains sell at a discount). The new industry, based on machinery, returned rice culture to its large-scale antebellum character.[7]

Rice production reflected the vigor of the new enterprise. The 136.8 million pounds harvested in 1890 had risen to 586 million pounds by 1904. The cultivated area expanded westward, reaching Texas in 1895 and pushing northward into the Grand Prairie region of Arkansas in 1902. Mechanized techniques were introduced in the San Joaquin Valley of California in 1908. A giant land development syndicate succeeded in restoring life to a dying industry and, in the process, provided the means by which many large rice farms exploited the country's rich resources.

Like rice farming, sugar cane planting was associated with large units. Growing and manufacturing sugar cane on a grand scale dates from the beginnings of the commercial cane industry in the United States. Although many commercial producers operated on a small scale, the industry, located almost entirely in Louisiana, was regarded as the province of large grower-manufacturers.[8] In 1861 Louisiana boasted 1,291 sugarhouses, of which 80 percent were steam-powered. (A sugarhouse was a factory, usually located on the plantation proper, where sugar cane was put through a mill to extract the juice, and the juice was processed into raw sugar. The raw sugar was not the familiar refined product but a light brown crystal that contained molasses. Refining was usually carried out in a separate factory—a sugar refinery.) As much as $100,000 was invested in some of these facilities. Most represented at least $50,000, and few fell below an investment of $20,000. The total estimated value of the 1861 Louisiana sugar industry was $200 million, or an average value per farm of nearly $155,000. If the estimated value of slaves is subtracted to leave a figure for land, machinery, stock, etc., the average remains a large $73,500.[9] Those parishes producing a million or more hogsheads of sugar in 1860 held an estimated investment of $10.85 per improved acre of land, whereas investment per improved acre in Virginia was $0.82, in Alabama $1.16, in Ohio $1.38, and in Pennsylvania $2.14.[10]

The years immediately following the Civil War were difficult for Louisiana sugar farmers. Fields that required drainage and protection from river flooding suffered clogged ditches and deteriorated levees. Few planters found their manufacturing equipment untouched by some facet of the war. Sugarhouses that had escaped direct war-related damage held machinery wasted from years of misuse or no use. Maintenance and repair were hindered by shortages of adequate spare parts. Rolling stock and livestock had been confiscated for the war effort. Labor was uncertain, for the freedmen were reluctant to return to the heavy labor of the sugar farm.[11] The condition of southern Louisiana after the war made a return to sugar planting and manufacturing tenuous, as sugar farmers tried the less demanding cotton production as an alternative to cane. The sugar cane industry did rebound, but only after major adjustments to new circumstances.[12]

Although some antebellum sugar plantations resumed operation after the war in the mode long established in Louisiana, the general lines of the industry changed. The solution to the labor problem combined with an alternative to on-site manufacturing to separate the cultivation and processing functions of sugar production. The tenant system shifted the responsibility for the crop at least partially to workers. Wage workers were often unreliable, but tenants—owners of a contracted percentage of the crop—could be counted on to protect their interests. Some planters attempted to increase their control over tenants by paying them only a portion of their earnings during the season. The final payment, which would include the forced savings of previous months, was not made until the crop was taken care of for the year. Unpopular with tenants, the system gave planters almost as complete control of land and labor as in the antebellum era.

Whereas the planting unit was decentralized into many small farms once the economies of scale associated with large slave forces were gone, manufacturing facilities were centralized to ease the difficulties of gathering capital to rebuild sugarhouses. The 1,291 sugarhouses of 1861 had been reduced to 240 by 1910. The economies associated with sugar manufacturing were spread over a large number of planting units in the post–Civil War years, in contrast to the attempts to dilute high fixed costs with a single large planting unit in the antebellum years. Smaller planting units were not an end to the sugar plantation but were a change in its form from a single centrally controlled operation to a combination of many smaller and somewhat independent units.[13]

The large farm-factory unit no longer characterized the cane sugar industry in the 1865–1914 period, but giant size had not disappeared from the sugar industry so much as it had shifted position. Several enterprises, operating on a very large scale, endeavored to introduce commercial sugar cane culture and manufacturing into the Everglades of Florida. Millions of dollars were expended, but the results were disappointing. The Florida sugar investment did not come to fruition in the period between the Civil War and World War I.[14] The successful giants of the sugar industry during this period were to be found not in cane culture but in refining.

Production on the giant farms of the 1860–1914 period was not restricted to Southern staples but included corn in Iowa, Illinois, and Indiana from 1850 to 1870 and wheat in the valley of the Red River of the North (Dakotas) from 1870 to 1890. The big corn farms and wheat bonanza farms anticipated agribusiness operations of the twentieth century but were not their contiguous predecessors.

Several factors combined to encourage large farms in the Illinois region in 1850. Forested land in the East had been cultivable only after years of clearing, but soil on the treeless prairies lay ready for turning. A liberal national land policy favored large units: good land could be had for as little as (and sometimes less than) $1.25 an acre.[15] And by making their land grant subsidies available on similarly generous terms, the Illinois Central and other roads fostered extensive farm units. The cattle industry exerted its own brand of influence. Small-scale cattle ranching frequently led to larger scale operations as ranchers took advantage of unclaimed land for grazing. A small farm abutting open range could support great herds. As the open land was claimed, the ranchers, wealthier from their use of free land, bought vast areas to protect their businesses.

Technological advances in farm machinery in the 1850s and 1860s expanded the acres that could be worked per man-hour, permitting many of the farms to produce corn despite their large size. Inventions and improvements included the reaper, corn planters, plows for prairie soil, the corn cutter and stacker, power sheller, disc harrow, cultivator, and mechanical ditchers. Farms of over 1,000 acres, a size all but unknown beyond the cotton South, appeared on the prairies, and by 1870 Illinois had 302 such farms, Indiana 76, and Iowa 38 (whereas Mississippi had 233, Georgia 419, and Virginia 317).[16]

One example of the giant corn farms was Broadlands. In the mid-1850s Michael Sullivant assembled 80,000 acres of government land and Illinois Central Railroad holdings. From a block of 23,000 acres, he created Broadlands. Sullivant pastured livestock on the farm and planted 1,800 acres of corn, 300 of winter wheat, and 40 of oats. In one year the farm produced a surplus (beyond the fodder needed for the livestock) of 22,000 bushels of corn for market. Sullivant sold Broadlands in 1866 to avoid financial embarrassment. The new owner, John T. Alexander, continued to operate the farm much as Sullivant had, while the founder began operations anew on another block of 40,000 acres.

On his new farm Sullivant had 18,000 acres in corn by 1871 and 5,000 acres in other crops. The machinery required to run his giant farm illustrates the scale of the operation: 150 steel plows, 75 breaking plows, 142 cultivators, 45 corn planters, 25 gang-harrows, and a ditching plow needing 68 oxen and 8 men to operate. A force of 350 mules, 50 horses, and 100 oxen powered the machinery.

Sullivant and Alexander anticipated the giant agribusinesses of the next century. Although they employed machinery extensively to operate the farms, their dependence on animals for a power source limited the extent of their mechanization. The modern capability of rapid movement on the ground (cars, trucks, motorcycles, etc.) and in the air (airplanes, helicopters), as well as immediate communications between units with convenient radio or cellular equipment, allows the coordination of huge numbers of men and machines over extensive distances. The rapid transit (railroads) and high-speed communications (telegraph) of the 1860s and 1870s lacked the flexibility for coordinating a giant centrally operated farm. Most of the giants in the corn belt in the post–Civil War era were divided into many small units to simplify coordination. Isaac and Jesse Funk, for example, used tenants to run their 30,000 acres in Illinois. William Scully, who owned 200,000 acres over four states (Kansas, Nebraska, Missouri, and Illinois), divided portions of his land into 160-acre farms for tenant use. Jacob Strawn was yet another operator of a large farm (20,000 acres) who employed tenants in addition to hired hands to tend his cattle and cultivate thousands of acres of corn.

Farms of 1,000 acres and more were exceptions in the 1850–70 corn belt, and farms of 20,000 acres and more were exceptions among these giants. Most of the large farms held around a thousand acres, a small portion of which was actively cultivated. But even these giants were dismantled after 1870. Increasing land values encouraged ranchers to push west and south for cheaper rangelands. The economies of large scale that would later accrue to corn planters were not evident in the 1850–70 period, so large farms for growing corn were not profitable enough to guarantee their continued existence. As late as 1899 the most productive corn planters maintained, on average, between 175 and 260 acres (31.4 bushels per acre).[17] Ranchers moved on and farmers reverted to smaller, more productive farm sizes. The giant farms of the corn belt first appeared in the years between the Civil War and World War I, then disappeared until a later time.

The giant corn farms of the 1850–70 period received little public attention, probably because they were established and dismantled during the decades dominated by sectional conflict. The primary purpose of many of these, ranching, may have further reduced the visibility of the attendant farming operations. The bonanza wheat farming, however, attracted extensive press coverage. *Atlantic Monthly* for January 1880 offered its readers the following description of the "Bonanza Farms of the West":

> The valley of the Red River of the North, in the northern part of Dakota and the southern portion of Manitoba, is about three hundred and fifty miles in length, north and south, and sixty miles wide, east and west, of unsurpassed fertility and beauty, the timber being confined to the immediate margins of the streams. The surface is nearly level, with hardly sufficient dip to afford to all parts a thorough drainage; but much the larger part is well drained by the smaller water-courses that empty into the Red River, giving large bodies of rich vegetable and alluvial loam, well adapted to the growth of wheat, rye, barley, oats, and the vegetables grown in the Northern States. It is too far north for corn. The wetter portions of the valley afford abundant grass, which is used for feeding and cut for hay. It is claimed that the capabilities of this valley are equal to the present wheat production of the whole United States.[18]

Wheat farming in the valley of the Red River of the North was undertaken on a small scale by pioneer farmers in the early 1870s.[19] The bonanza operations were set in motion by confirmation of the high flour quality of the wheat grown there, the completion of the Northern Pacific Railroad line from Duluth to Fargo, and a downturn in the financial sector.[20]

With the failure of Jay Cooke in 1873, the price of Northern Pacific Railroad bonds fell to a low of 40 cents. Expectations for a recovery being weak, bondholders invoked their privilege of exchanging bonds for land held by the company. Over the next two years the railroad dispensed almost half a million acres of land. Most of the acreage went to one small group of bondholders.[21] The Northern Pacific reorganization of 1876 provided bondholders with stock in the company in time for another market collapse. The new stock fell to a low of 10 cents. Again security holders turned to railroad land in an effort to recoup their losses. From 1873 to 1878 the land department of the Northern Pacific (headed by James B. Power) dispersed ownership of over 1.7 million acres. Over a third of the total went to forty individuals, who each secured an average of 14,685 acres, most of which was Red River Valley land.[22]

During those years (1873–78), when ownership of large parcels of Red River land was accumulating in the hands of a few Eastern financiers, enterprising farmers were investigating the profitability of wheat farming in the valley. In 1873 one forty-acre tract produced 1,600 bushels, showing the attractive possibilities of the valley for that grain.[23] James Power brought together the necessary ingredients for attempting wheat cultivation on a bonanza scale. He encouraged recipients of railroad lands to cultivate their holdings, rewarding promises to do so with choice tracts close to the railroad line. The encouragement elicited interest from George W. Cass, president of the Northern Pacific Railroad, and Benjamin P. Cheney, a member of the board of directors of that railroad. Beyond assigning the two men choice sections along the railroad right-of-way, Power secured ownership of the alternate sections for them. By doing so he created huge contiguous tracts for efficient farming on a grand scale.[24]

James Power contributed to the bonanza wheat project when he persuaded his friend Oliver Dalrymple, an experienced wheat farmer, to undertake management of the Cass-Cheney lands. Dalrymple directed the breaking of 1,280 acres during the summer of 1875. From that planting, he harvested 32,000 bushels of choice wheat in 1876. Dalrymple parlayed his ten years of farming the Cass-Cheney tract into lucrative returns for himself and the absentee owners. Power, in turn, capitalized on Dalrymple's success, using an account of his operations as the basis of an advertising campaign to further promote the Red River Valley holdings of the Northern Pacific Railroad.

By 1880 there were 82 farms of over 1,000 acres in the Red River Valley. Some of these were owned by individuals—Cass-Cheney, the Lockhart and Keystone farms in Minnesota, and the Dwight, Fairview, Keystone, Cleveland, Donning, and Antelope farms in Dakota—and some (the 30,000 acres of the Sharon Land Company, for instance) were held by corporations. By 1890 there were 323 farms of over 1,000 acres in the valley.[25]

The giant farms, like the 38,000 acres belonging to the Grandlin brothers, were subdivided into managerial units of about 2,000 acres. Economies of scale associated with equipment, however, were spread over the aggregate operation.[26] The Grandlins owned 300 horses, 100 plows, 50 seeders, 75 binders, 10 separators, and 10 steam engines, and employed 300 men to operate the equipment.[27]

On the general calendar followed by the bonanza farms, plowing began in September (in July on new ground) and was completed in about three months. When the plowing was finished, the bulk of the labor force was released, leaving a skeleton crew for maintenance work until the March seeding and harrowing began. Full operations awaited August and the beginning of the harvest. Crews directed by foremen used haresters, binders, and thresher-separators to bring in the crop. Most of the grain was immediately shipped to market, ending one crop-year and signaling the plowing phase of another. On the bonanza farms wheat and hay for the livestock were the only crops: food stuffs were purchased as needed over the year.[28]

Although bonanza wheat farms distinguished the Red River Valley, large-scale farming was not the most important feature of agriculture in the area: The majority of farms in the valley were smaller than 500 acres, and wheat was not cultivated on most of them. Bonanza farming proved short-lived, for only large investors could afford to put immense sums into a single crop, and even they were forced to diversify after 1890.[29] Drought in the valley reduced the size of crops, financial difficulties destroyed many bonanza owners operating on borrowed capital, and declining wheat prices combined with rising land values to make profits elusive.[30] Large farms were broken up, and wheat gave way to diversified agriculture.[31] Yet the lure of bonanza farming has maintained for it a solid place in American history, especially the history of American giants.

The promotion of the Red River Valley by the railroads that held contiguous land grants is an early example of the use of communications media to broadcast information. Americans and foreigners alike read of the bonanza experience in newspapers, magazines, and books. The image of America as the land of plenty was reinforced by stories of endless stretches of golden grain. Press coverage of the bonanza wheat farms pales, however, against the global spread of stories about a contemporary American business known for its giant operations. Beef cattle production in the late nineteenth century and early twentieth century remains, without a doubt, the most renowned experience of American extractive industry.

Giant operations in Western cattle followed the pattern of bonanza farms in corn and wheat. Rising in response to favorable economic, social, and political conditions, the large ranches prospered for several decades and then declined in response to changes in their environment. Change was the essence of their existence: environmental factors forced alterations in ranching, alterations that in turn further changed environmental factors. By the end of World War I, the world of giant ranches lived in books and on film, casting an image larger than the real-life experience.

American farmers raised livestock for sale in nearby towns and cities. Cattle drives from farm to market were not uncommon, even in the colonial period. As towns flourished and nonfarm population increased, the livestock business grew to meet the demand for meat. Bonanza ranching was a response to the growth of markets and the disappearance of nearby grazing land. Spreading municipal boundaries drove up prices for surrounding acres. Pastureland earned small returns per acre, so ranchers were forced away from their expanding markets. Railroads offered transportation from inexpensive pastureland farther from populated areas, and livestock could be shipped long distances by rail yet arrive at market in edible condition. As urban markets grew large enough to absorb huge amounts of meat, thousands of cattle were profitably sold by ranchers far from the cities to middlemen who directed transportation and sale to packers and abattoirs. The large and growing demand in American cities for meat, expanding railroads, and vast open pastureland in the public domain combined to produce the fabled giant ranches of the post–Civil War era.[32]

Cattle ranchers were not distinguished by their ownership of vast acreage because public domain, used without charge and shared with others, was not associated with a particular person or ranch. So long as the range provided feed for the cattle, ranchers expanded herds at the cost of cattle and the hands to manage them, increasing profits with every animal since no charges were levied for feed. John W. Iliff of Weld County, Colorado, held an estimated million dollars' worth of cattle in 1877 on a land investment valued as low as $10,185. George W. Littlefield's LFD Ranch near Roswell, New Mexico, was based on $1,600 paid for land (in the early 1880s) that gave access to thousands of square miles of public range.[33]

Just as population pressure made profitable ranching on the plains a possibility, it changed the terms under which profits could be extracted by pushing farmers onto the public domain to compete with ranchers for the land. By the time of the landmark winter of 1886–87, when blizzards destroyed cattle and fortunes, the cattle kingdom was already making the changes often traced to the heavy losses from cold weather. Farmers had begun competing for the plains land even before the Civil War, and that competition grew in the postwar period.

Bonanza ranchers exploited public land until competition from farmers willing to buy the acres or gain title to them through the Homestead Act forced the cattlemen to sell their small holdings and move farther west, where farmers had not encroached. George Littlefield used public lands extensively and moved when spurred by population pressure. In the 1880s population pressure on the plains might be little more than a handful of farm families. Littlefield sold his herd and the "range rights" of his Texas Panhandle ranch to a Scottish syndicate in 1881 for $253,000. Range rights represented claims to the use of land based on prior use, not ownership. In 1888 Littlefield and his partners controlled 1.5 million acres, the Four Lakes Ranch in New Mexico, from their ownership of 15,000 acres (one hundred acres of public land for each acre owned in fee simple). Littlefield held this ranch until 1910. His buyer went bankrupt competing with the farmers Littlefield had escaped by selling out. Littlefield did eventually buy a ranch in Texas in 1901, paying $2 an acre for 235,858 acres, but only after decades of extracting profits from ranching on land belonging to the public.[34]

Homesteaders forced bonanza ranchers to shift away from their reliance on free land for feeding cattle. No one or two small farmers could drive a rancher from the range, but numbers and the law were on the farmers' side as the American population moved westward, attracted to the free land. Unused to the arid rangeland, inexperienced homesteaders staked claims on acres poorly suited for farming, at once depriving ranchers of the pasture and ruining themselves financially. Ranchers met the coming of the nesters in a variety of ways. Some few attempted to repel the onslaught with violence and intimidation, thus giving future writers a theme for untold numbers of books and movies.[35] The violence reflected frustration and ignorance on the part of the perpetrators, who often mistook a social problem for a personal one. Homesteaders as individuals might have been intimidated, but as a group they were not likely to avoid indefinitely that public domain controlled by ranchers.

The purchase of carefully selected acreage proved a more effective, if less exciting, method for discouraging small farmers from settling on or near a rancher's claim. John Hittson was able to control all the water in his part of Colorado through ownership of as little as 320 acres. Another Colorado rancher, J. P. Farmer, controlled the West Bijou River through ownership of 640 acres.[36] Conflict was not always prevented by outright ownership of strategic acres: ranchers fenced public land as well as titled land, providing no clue to the difference and defending both with fervor.

Aggressive farmers cut fences to gain access to water, grass, and timber, sparking confrontations with ranchers, who viewed such action as an invitation to battle. Corporate land claims received less respect generally than private ones, and foreign-owned corporations commanded the least respect of all. The west-ward development of institutional law enforcement eventually ended the practice of fencing the public domain and offered protection to private property rights. Although the law forbade fencing public land, ranchers took down fences less because of the law and more to protect their herds. During blizzards cattle sur-vived by moving with the storm. Fences stopped the herds, and mounds of dead cattle accumulated at fence lines.

Ranchers had yet another way of dealing with the competition for rangelands. Some purchased the public domain lands they needed to support their cattle operations. Such land acquisitions allowed the rancher to continue fattening his cattle indefinitely with the support of the legal structure against encroachments by homesteaders. Richard King founded just such a ranch in 1852, one that still operates on holdings exceeding a million acres. If ranching failed to pay off, the owner of large blocks of land could recoup the real-estate investment by sell-ing off small parcels to farmers or large blocks to others in the cattle industry; the Prairie Cattle Company, Western Ranches, Inc., and the Matador Ranch are three examples of this strategy. The Matador Ranch operated profitably through the final decades of the nineteenth century and the first half of the twentieth. When sold in 1950, the ranch brought over thirty times the original cost, that after annual earnings of about 15 percent since the 1920s. Those investors who stayed with the Prairie Cattle Company and Western Ranches also prospered from rising land prices. In most cases, however, investors would have found yet higher returns than those forthcoming from rising land values had they invested elsewhere than the cattle industry.[37]

By the disastrous winter of 1886–87, the bonanza cattle business was in de-cline. Investors were aware of the high opportunity cost of leaving large sums tied up in land. Homesteaders were squeezing ranchers unable to purchase their rangelands onto smaller and smaller tracts to compete with other ranchers for overgrazed areas. The need to cultivate food for the cattle forced ranchers into farming. The competition for markets drove out producers of blooded stock: highbred cattle could not be turned loose to fend for themselves but required careful attention. All these pressures nudged ranchers away from their extensive techniques (huge herds, thousands of acres, minimum of care) to intensive farming-ranching (smaller herds, less land, careful husbandry).

Bonanza beef ranching was dead by the opening of World War I, after two decades of decline. The dependence on free public land to fatten scrub cattle turned out to fend for themselves until market time was no longer rational or profitable. The cattle business, like bonanza corn and wheat farming, responded to a changing environment that no longer favored giant operations with economies of scale but instead encouraged smaller, more intense operations. Not all the giant ranches disappeared, however; some, like the renowned King Ranch, are still in business, employing vast landholdings to efficiently produce much more than grass-fattened cattle. The King and the other surviving giant ranches are not carryovers of the bonanza era but enterprises evolved to adapt to modern conditions in the beef cattle industry (and the other industries in which they compete). The imagination nonetheless attaches them to the romantic times when bonanza ranches were more prevalent than anachronistic.

NOTES

1. Morton Rothstein, "The Big Farm: Abundance and Scale in American Agriculture," *Agricultural History* 49 (October 1975): 592.

2. Frederick Law Olmsted, *A Journey in the Back Country, 1853–1854* (New York: Mason Brothers, 1860), 46–54; and Gavin Wright, *The Political Economy of the Cotton South: Households, Markets, and Wealth in the Nineteenth Century* (New York: Norton, 1978).

3. Herbert Anthony Kellar, ed., *Solon Robinson: Pioneer and Agriculturalist*, (Indianapolis: Indiana Historical Bureau, 1936), 350–54.

4. Dale Evans Swan, *The Structure and Profitability of the Antebellum Rice Industry, 1859* (Ann Arbor, MI: University Microfilms, 1972), ch. 3; and David O. Whitten, *Antebellum Sugar and Rice Plantations, Louisiana and South Carolina: A Profitability Study* (Ann Arbor, MI: University Microfilms, 1970), ch. 5.

5. Edward K. Phillips, "The Gulf Coast Rice Industry," *Agricultural History* 25 (April 1951): 91–96.

6. Arthur H. Cole, "The American Rice-Growing Industry: A Study of Comparative Advantage," *Quarterly Journal of Economics* 41 (August 1927): 595–643.

7. Ibid., 607; and David O. Whitten, "American Rice Cultivation, 1680–1980: A Tercentenary Critique," *Southern Studies* 21 (Spring 1982): 5–26.

8. David O. Whitten, "Tariff and Profit in the Antebellum Louisiana Sugar Industry," *Business History Review* 44 (Summer 1970): 226–33.

9. Walter Prichard, "The Effects of the Civil War on the Louisiana Sugar Industry," *Journal of Southern History* 5 (August 1939): 315–32.

10. Whitten, "Antebellum Sugar and Rice Plantations," 24.

11. J. Carlyle Sitterson, "The Transition from Slave to Free Economy on the William J. Minor Plantations," *Agricultural History* 17 (October 1943): 216–24, and "The McCollams:

A Planter Family of the Old and New South," *Journal of Southern History* 6 (Summer 1940): 346–67.

12. B. I. Wiley, "Salient Changes in Southern Agriculture Since the Civil War," *Agricultural History* 13 (April 1939): 65–96; and Roger Wallace Shugg, "Survival of the Plantation System in Louisiana," *Journal of Southern History* 3 (Summer 1937): 311–25.

13. Shugg, "Survival of the Plantation System," 311–25.

14. J. Carlyle Sitterson, *Sugar Country: The Cane Sugar Industry in the South, 1753–1950* (Lexington: University of Kentucky Press, 1953), 361–78.

15. Paul Wallace Gates, "Large Scale Farming in Illinois, 1850–1870," *Agricultural History* 6 (January 1932): 14–25.

16. *Ninth Census of the United States, 1870: The Statistics of the Wealth and Industry of the United States*, vol. 3, table 6, 340. California had 713 farms of over 1,000 acres in 1870, but these were for the most part made up of holdings much larger than the employed land area.

17. *Twelfth Census of the United States, Agriculture*, part 2, 26 (1902).

18. [P. Bigelow], "Bonanza Farms of the West," *Atlantic Monthly* 45 (January 1880): 37. Also see C. C. Coffin, "Dakota Wheat Fields," *Harper's New Monthly Magazine* 60 (March 1880): 529–35.

19. Harold E. Briggs, "Early Bonanza Farming in the Red River Valley of the North," *Agricultural History* 6 (January 1932): 26–37.

20. Stanley N. Murray, "Railroads and the Agricultural Development of the Red River Valley of the North, 1870–1890," *Agricultural History* 31 (October 1957): 57–66.

21. Ibid., 60.

22. Ibid.

23. Ibid., 61.

24. Ibid. Railroad land grants comprised alternate sections along the right-of-way. The railroad could buy the sections not in the grant at public auction.

25. Briggs, "Early Bonanza Farming," 29–30.

26. Ibid., 32–33.

27. Ibid., 30.

28. Ibid., 32.

29. Morton Rothstein, "A British Investment in Bonanza Farming, 1879–1910," *Agricultural History* 33 (April 1959): 72–78.

30. Briggs, "Early Bonanza Farming," 35–37.

31. Murray, "Railroads and the Agricultural Development of the Red River," 57–66.

32. Maurice Frink, W. Turrentine Jackson, and Agnes Wright Spring, *When Grass Was King: Contributions to the Western Range Cattle Industry Study* (Boulder: University of Colorado Press, 1956), 5–58.

33. Lewis E. Atherton, *The Cattle Kings* (Bloomington: Indiana University Press, 1961), 172; and Agnes Wright Spring, "A 'Genius for Handling Cattle': John W. Iliff," in Frink *et al.*, *When Grass Was King*, 335–450.

34. Atherton, *Cattle Kings*, 173.

35. For example, see George A. Wallis, *Cattle Kings of the Staked Plains* (Dallas, TX: American Guild Press, 1957).

36. Atherton, *Cattle Kings*, 173.

37. Ibid., 176–77; and Harmon Ross Mothershead, *The Swan Land and Cattle Company, Ltd.* (Norman: University of Oklahoma Press, 1971).

CHAPTER 7

The American Sugar Refining Company

The sugar refineries and confectionaries that appeared in Boston, New York, Philadelphia, and other towns and cities in America as early as 1730 offered consumers white sugar and a range of brown sugars. Refiners processed sugar for resale. Confectionaries sold reprocessed sugar too, but they also made and sold sweetmeats—candied fruit, sugar-covered nuts, sugarplums, bonbons, and balls or sticks of candy. Before reprocessors opened their doors, sugar buyers were offered raw sugar that had been made on cane plantations then imported and sold in bulk, usually in a general store.

In cane-growing regions sugar makers squeezed the juice from cut sugar cane and then clarified and boiled it until crystals appeared. These molasses-laden crystals were suspended in a dark brown sediment, which was ladled into drain boxes and set over catch basins for months to allow the molasses to drain off, leaving behind light brown plantation, or raw, sugar. The best manufacturing equipment produced the lightest raw sugar. Crude processing in open kettles turned out a sugar dark brown with molasses. The lighter sugars were in greater demand because they did not taste strongly of molasses.[1]

After purchasing raw sugar in bulk, usually from Caribbean sources, refiners and confectioners melted and remanufactured it for resale. Until the 1850s refining was little more than a repetition of the manufacturing routine, with the aim of removing more molasses from the crystals. The melted liquid was poured into molds and allowed to sit until most of the molasses in it had settled to the bottom. The process was repeated until the desired products were obtained. The final product was a loaf or cone of sugar with nearly molasses-free white sugar at the top and molasses-heavy dark brown crystals at the bottom.[2]

The whiter the sugar, the higher the price. Because molasses-laden light brown and dark brown sugar sold at a discount, domestic and commercial cooks and bakers used it in cakes, cookies, and other dishes. Technological advances in the 1850s made possible the near complete removal of molasses from the crystals, allowing confectioners to produce a uniform refined sugar. But brown sugars had become an established ingredient in many recipes, and refiners found it remunerative to add molasses back into the crystals and market the resulting light and dark brown sugars. The molasses-laden sugars discounted in the pre-refining period became premium-priced products in the age of advanced refining.

Loaf sugar was as good as the confectioner who made it. Buyers were attracted by special qualities inherent in the output of a particular refinery (product differentiation), but sugar refined with equipment available after 1850 (efficient filters, steam pans, and especially the centrifuge) was of uniformly high quality and varied imperceptibly from refinery to refinery. This homogeneous product found ready markets in the expanding post–Civil War United States, where rail networks offered every refiner a potential national market. These features of sugar refining combined with fairly easy entry into the industry to create what has been called the golden age of competition in the sugar industry.[3]

A competitive market, as economists define it, comprises many firms (so many that no one firm, acting alone, has any influence over market price) producing a homogeneous product in the absence of obstacles to entry into the industry. Buyers recognize the product as homogeneous and see little or no reason to purchase from one seller rather than another. The sugar refining industry took on these characteristics in the years following the Civil War. Profits attracted new firms into sugar refining, but market stability was compromised when industry capacity outstripped market demand. Competing firms were forced to reduce their prices to sell enough refined sugar to cover at least the out-of-pocket, or variable, costs of production. Some firms operated at a loss rather than close down. So long as the losses of operation were smaller than the losses of closing down, the refiners continued to produce, hoping for the return of profits. At that time, the capital cost of refineries was so high that even a loss-level of production was preferable to closing down. The scrap value of the machinery was low enough to discourage producers from going out of business permanently. As more refineries opened, more were forced to produce at a level that could not earn a return as high as that made on comparable alternative investments. Unable to liquidate their refinery investment, these refiners continued to produce sugar and sell it for what they could get, accepting returns below the market opportunity cost of the capital.

By the 1870s falling sugar prices were squeezing refiners who could not keep their costs moving downward with the prices; nevertheless, industry profits were not so low as to discourage expansion. Advancing processing technology allowed the newest plants to refine the best sugar at the lowest unit cost. But higher capital costs (fixed costs) meant that newer firms must seize large market shares to realize their lower average cost (unit cost). In other words, firms with the newest plants and equipment enjoyed lower unit costs than older competitors, but to get the lower costs the newer firms had to seize large market shares. To capture more of the market, cover their costs of production, and make a profit, operators of the newest plants reduced their prices below what the older ones could charge.

Refiners with anything but the latest equipment had high sunk costs, fixed costs that cannot be recovered. Once new refining machinery was available, the market for the old disappeared, but many refiners continued producing and selling sugar at the falling prices set by those with the newest machines so long as some of their sunk costs could be recovered. When prices fell so far that the lagging firms were financially better off to stop production, the plants were closed unless, of course, the owners scrapped the old machinery and invested in new, which rotated the re-equipped firms to the top of the industry. The improvements in profit positions attained through plant expansion and modernization lasted only until the industry caught up, when the same old squeeze came back into effect.

Refiners were locked into a losing proposition. New plants and technology could lower costs, but the scramble for market shares sufficient to spread high capital costs over enough sales to provide a profit pushed prices ever lower. Even a surge in demand large enough to cover the available supply from producing firms was not enough to ease the problem, for the industry included plants that operated only at certain price levels. These were plants that lost less by closing down than by operating at normal market prices. When prices rose enough to make operating losses less than the losses associated with closing, the plants started back up. Some firms chose to operate on the margin rather than close down and scrap the machinery, so a rise in price for whatever reason brought an increase in output and a return to lower prices.

Each cycle of expansion and catch-up left the industry with fewer, but larger, refineries. New York had as many as thirty-three refineries in 1872 and 1873. This number was down to twelve by 1887, and several of the twelve were marginal plants. Philadelphia, a refining city competitive with New York, had twenty refineries in 1870 but only twelve by 1887. About nine of that number were marginal. Boston, the other East Coast rival, had seven refineries in 1868, 1869, and 1873. Five remained in 1887, but only one was competitive. St. Louis had one competitive refinery, and New Orleans supported two by 1887. In that same year there were only two competitive refineries in California.[4]

As the number of competing firms declined and their average capital cost soared, the practicality of collusion among them increased. On several occasions many firms were brought together under an agreement to limit output and thereby increase the market price. Producers of sugar were no more able, however, to maintain output agreements than producers of other products had been or would be. For any one producer to cheat meant higher returns for that firm. The chance of being caught was small, the consequences nil. When several producers reacted with the improved returns and negligible consequences in mind, the agreement collapsed. A more manageable arrangement was necessary, so in 1887 John Searles, an associate of the Havemeyer sugar interests, began crafting an innovative alternative.

Searles persuaded competing refining companies to consolidate their operations into a single business unit, a monopoly that could be manipulated to provide maximum returns to them all. Details could be worked out once enough refiners agreed to the arrangement. The entire scheme would collapse if too many producers remained outside the controlling unit. In late 1887 the Sugar Refineries' Company was established. Had Searles chosen to incorporate as a holding company, by law a corporation, the refiners would have been required to divulge many of their activities. Instead, to ensure secrecy, he organized a trust, an arrangement whereby the participating firms continued operation under the authority of a board of trustees. The trustees held ownership in the participating firms, ownership taken in exchange for trust certificates. Member firms received their financial remuneration from payments made on the certificates by the trustees. Furthermore, a developing market in trust certificates provided the holders a means of liquidating, cashing in on capital gains, and avoiding capital losses.

By October of 1887 seventeen of the then twenty-one competitive sugar refineries in the United States were under the control of the sugar trust: Havemeyer & Elder, DeCastro & Donner, F. O. Mathiessen & Wiechers, Havemeyer Sugar Refining Company, Brooklyn Sugar Refining Company, Dick and Meyer, Moller & Sierck, Oxnard Brothers, North River Sugar Refining Company, Standard Sugar Refining Company, Boston Sugar Refining Company, Continental Sugar Refining Company, Bay State Sugar Refining Company, Planters Sugar Refining Company, Louisiana Sugar Refining Company, St. Louis Sugar Refining Company, and Forest City Sugar Refining Company. With a near monopoly over sugar refining east of the Mississippi River, the trust undertook to limit supply to maintain a profitable market price for refined sugar. At the same time Searles and his employers, the Havemeyers, prepared to add the region west of the Mississippi to the trust empire.

The West was already under the dominant hand of another giant: Claus Spreckels. Spreckels had gained his command over West Coast sugar refining through a combination of technological advantages—several of which he had personally invented—and control over a substantial portion of the sugar cane grown in Hawaii. When faced with the prospect of membership in the sugar trust, Spreckels declined to join, choosing instead to enjoy the fruits of the monopoly he had carved out of the West Coast sugar industry. The trust, for its part, chose to fight, not wanting an outside competitor influencing its pricing policies.

The battle of giants began on Spreckels's home ground, with the trust buying the American Sugar Refinery, a California company. Like so many wars that take a heavy toll, this one was expected to be short. The trust, after all, was in a position to operate the California refinery at a loss until Spreckels surrendered, a loss to be more than covered by the monopoly profits from the East. And indeed there were profits: the trust paid about 10 percent dividends annually from its founding until it was succeeded by the American Sugar Refining Company (the holding company) in 1891. The 10 percent was paid on all certificates, even on those representing unproductive (closed down) refining capacity, as well as on certificates representing no capacity at all, which had been given out solely to encourage refiners to join the trust. Nevertheless, Spreckels was not sufficiently impressed with the strength of his assailant to surrender without a fight. In 1890 he brought the battle to the trust by opening his own $3 million refinery in Philadelphia. His action doubled the refining capacity of the independent refineries on the East Coast.

Before Spreckels advanced their capacity, the East Coast independents had enjoyed a lucrative position vis-à-vis the trust. Their combined capacity was small enough that the trust could afford to ignore them, and the trust limited its own output to maintain prices at a profitable level. The independents shaded that price ever so slightly and sold all they could produce at a price well above that prevailing before the formation of the trust. The increased capacity represented by the new Spreckels refinery made a continuation of that policy on the part of the trust too expensive in terms of sales lost to the independents. Instead of maintaining high prices, the trust now forced them down to pressure the independents to either close or join the trust. Its size and the advanced technology it employed allowed the trust to operate profitably at lower prices than most competitors could. The trust also had a cash reserve to shore it up over periods of loss operation.

The losses to both Spreckels and the trust—lower prices to consumers—were enough to stimulate negotiation and eventually an agreement between the parties that would ultimately award control of Spreckels's Philadelphia refinery to the trust. Before the agreement was actually fabricated, the trust, operating in secret, had used the low-price period of their battle with Spreckels to lure the other independents into their organization. Once the agreement was settled, a true refining monopoly ruled supreme—or so it would seem.

By the date of the agreement with Spreckels, the trust had changed form. Legal pressure at state (New York) and federal levels forced Henry Havemeyer, the chief executive officer in the trust, and the other trustees to seek a different form of business organization. Although the monopoly position of the trust was the target of legal attacks, the secrecy in which it operated was the soft spot the courts were hitting. The trust was composed of corporations; every member firm was incorporated as a prerequisite to entry. The courts questioned the legality of a combination of supposedly open business units operating under the cloak of secrecy afforded by a trust agreement. Moreover, at the national level the passage of the Sherman Antitrust Act (1890) made combinations of businesses for restraint of interstate trade illegal. The Sugar Refineries' Company chose to defend against these attacks from a sturdier organizational position by reorganizing as the American Sugar Refining Company, a holding company chartered under the laws of New Jersey. From this new position, the newly founded company fended off legal attacks and competitive forces. Success was limited in both areas.

On the market side, the development of the beet sugar industry in the western United States in the late 1880s threatened the American Sugar Refining

Company's monopoly of refined sugar. Beet processing plants were established in the Utah-Idaho region (Utah-Idaho Sugar Company, six plants in 1907; Amalgamated Sugar Company, two plants in 1907; and the Lewiston Sugar Company), Colorado (Great Western Sugar Company, eight plants in 1907; American Beet Sugar Company, three plants in 1907; Holly Sugar Company, two plants in 1907; National Sugar Manufacturing Company; United States Sugar and Land Company), Michigan (Michigan Sugar Company, six plants in 1907; Continental Sugar Company, two plants in 1907; Holland Sugar Company; Owosso Sugar Company, two plants in 1907; West Bay Sugar Company; German-American Sugar Company; Mount Clemens Sugar Company; St. Louis Sugar Company; West Michigan Sugar Company), and California (Spreckels Sugar Company; American Beet Sugar Company, two plants in 1907; Alameda Sugar Company; Union Sugar Company; Los Alamitos Sugar Company; Sacramento Valley Sugar Company; Pacific Sugar Company). Although concentrated to a lesser extent, beet sugar processing plants were opened in other states, including New York, Washington, Oregon, Nebraska, Wisconsin, Illinois, and Iowa.[5]

Henry Havemeyer employed his personal resources in concert with those of the American Sugar Refining Company to secure and maintain a degree of control over the emerging beet sugar industry. The new beet companies were characteristically capital hungry. Havemeyer and the American were rich capital lodes. So one by one the beet companies entered the controlled market orbit of the American in return for the capital necessary to attain efficient size. Some of the funds originated with Havemeyer and some with the American, but the result was the same: control by the sugar monopoly. By 1907 this arrangement had netted the sugar monopoly control over 69 percent of the beet sugar slicing capacity in the United States.[6]

While the American Sugar Refining Company engaged competition from beet sugar in the West, it battled more conventional problems closer to the East Coast heart of its sugar refining empire. The prices on refined sugar were high enough to attract new firms into the industry. To protect its monopoly or near monopoly position, the American tried to make entry into sugar refining unattractive by taking advantage of its competitive edge in transportation. The American Sugar Refining Company shipped a large enough volume of sugar to demand and receive from the railroads preferential treatment that included rebates (returns to the company of portions of its own and even competitors' paid freight bills) and free storage. These advantages, combined with the American's size, its distribution links, and its hold on sugar manufacturing know-how, discouraged some— but not all—potential competitors.

Havemeyer and the American Sugar Refining Company failed to eliminate all competition. How competitors were dealt with depended on their ties with Havemeyer and the other owners of the American Sugar Refining Company. The National Sugar Refining Company (incorporated as a holding company under the laws of New Jersey in 1900), for example, was made up of three independent refineries (New York Sugar Refining Company, Mollenhauer Sugar Refining

Company, and the National Sugar Refining Company) doing business peacefully alongside the American simply by following the American's production and pricing policies. National was not attacked by Havemeyer because its owners were tied in with the American's owners in diverse ways. The pressures of a price war between the American and Arbuckle and Company, a firm Havemeyer had tried to destroy, forced the three independents to seek refuge in combination. Havemeyer personally oversaw and directed the development of this rival sugar refining company. The Arbuckle war, for its part, was fought to a standstill: the two sides eventually learned to live together for mutual financial benefit.

The American Sugar Refining Company's quest for monopoly control made it a target for promoters. Adolph Segel, a professional promoter, found profit in building plants for the production of goods normally controlled by a monopoly or near monopoly. Once completed, the plant could be sold for a profit to a company eager to keep out competition. Segel had succeeded in selling a match plant and a soap-rendering factory before building a sugar refinery. In 1894 he organized the United States Sugar Refining Company and erected a refinery at Camden, New Jersey. As Segel anticipated, the American bought out the new firm in 1895. Segel promoted similar enterprises in steel, shipbuilding, and asphalt before trying sugar again in 1901. This time he organized the Pennsylvania Sugar Refining Company and built a larger refinery across the river from his first one. Caught up in his own web of dealings, Segel was overextended financially and the second venture did not go as smoothly as the first, but the result was the same: the new refinery was drawn into the orbit of the American Sugar Refining Company. But the American could not maintain its monopoly position indefinitely against such attacks. The Justice Department of the United States encouraged recognition of that fact.

Theodore Roosevelt breathed new life into antitrust action at the national level. Although President Roosevelt refused to condemn corporate existence on the basis of size alone, he was aware of the misuse of large size to manipulate interstate trade. One step toward reducing misuse of size was the Elkins Act (1903) and its stiff criminal penalties for railroad rebating. A second step was the establishment of a competent Justice Department to enforce federal legislation against restraint of trade. With William H. Moody in the office of Attorney General and Henry L. Stimson as United States Attorney for the Southern District of New York, the department began investigating suspected violators. The American Sugar Refining Company was a prime suspect.

The Justice Department had gained access to records of the American that left little doubt that rebating was a regular part of the company's activities. Rather than make one spectacular case against the American, Stimson determined that many smaller cases would keep the company in the public eye and bring pressure to bear on its managing officers. Such pressure, it was supposed, would encourage the company to cease and desist illegal activities that might continue if fines alone were levied. Stimson's success in court led the American Sugar Refining Company to plead guilty to all charges for the sake of escaping the bad publicity of multiple prosecutions. In late 1906 the company paid $150,000 in fines and so ended one trauma in time for the unfolding of another.

In 1907 federal agents uncovered massive customs frauds by the American Sugar Refining Company. The American was cheating on the weighing-in of imported sugars and thereby paying illegally low tariffs on these sugars. The publicity associated with the company's fraud and rebating combined with a court decision that revitalized the Sherman Antitrust Act to bring the American face to face with a federal suit to dissolve the company (1909). That suit dragged on until 1922, by which time the American Sugar Refining Company had substantially reduced its holdings in competitive enterprises. World War I and federal price controls dominated the intervening years. The American was asked, for the good of the nation (through price stabilization), to price like a monopoly—just as it had for its own profit—all the while under threat of court-ordered dissolution for such behavior. When the courts finally handed down a decision in 1922, the value of large size in gaining economies of scale was better appreciated as an advantage to business and customer alike. The American Sugar Refining Company was permitted to continue as a giant corporation in competition with giant rivals who recognized the lameness of price cutting in what was now an oligopolistic market.

NOTES

1. Manuel Moreno Fraginals, *The Sugarmill: The Socioeconomic Complex of Sugar in Cuba, 1760–1860* (New York: Monthly Review Press, 1976), 33–41.

2. J. Carlyle Sitterson, *Sugar Country: The Cane Sugar Industry in the South, 1753–1950* (Lexington: University of Kentucky Press, 1953), 133–56.

3. Alfred S. Eichner, *The Emergence of Oligopoly: Sugar Refining as a Case Study* (Baltimore, MD: Johns Hopkins Press, 1969); and David O. Whitten, *Andrew Durnford: A Black Sugar Planter in the Antebellum South* (New Brunswick, NJ: Transaction Publishers, 1995).

4. Eichner, *Emergence of Oligopoly*, ch. 4 and apps. A, B, and C.

5. Ibid., app. F.

6. Ibid., 349.

CHAPTER 8

The American Tobacco Company

Sugar was not the only farm product to attract giant business enterprise. Tobacco underwent a similar takeover by managerial moguls. Sugar planting had long been associated with large farms and giant enterprise, but tobacco had been grown and processed on plantations and small family farms since the beginning of the industry in early colonial America. Cultivating the tobacco plant included seedbed planting, selective transplanting, and calculated pinching-back during the growing season. Once harvested, the leaf was cured in an exacting, time-consuming process. The intensiveness of tobacco culture inhibited economies of large scale and encouraged small operations. In the years before the American Civil War, the tobacco-growing states were Virginia, Maryland, North Carolina, and Missouri.[1]

The Civil War brought changes in tobacco culture. The end of slavery encouraged the breakup of plantations into small farms, and production spread into Kentucky, Tennessee, South Carolina, and southern Ohio. Tobacco farmers abandoned the land-sacrificing techniques of the antebellum years in favor of land conservation and higher yields per acre. Between 1880 and 1905, yields were increased by almost 10 percent in Kentucky, 29 percent in North Carolina, 9 percent in Tennessee, and 19 percent in Virginia. On the business side, the creation of a trust concentrated control of nearly 80 percent of the 1906 Southern tobacco crop. Giant business in tobacco took root in its manufacture.[2]

Tobacco products are sniffed (snuff), chewed (plug), and smoked (cigars, pipes, cigarettes). With the exception of cigarettes, tobacco markets were well developed in the United States and the industrialized world and in those regions influenced by that world. Cigarettes were popular with tobacco users who had easy recourse to fire, but most smokers found it difficult to light their cigarettes. The free paper matchbook, an advertising gimmick introduced by traveling salesmen toward the end of the nineteenth century, made fire readily available and increased the popularity of cigarette smoking.[3] Before cigarettes became the income-generating darling of the tobacco industry, plug tobacco—simple and inexpensive to make and to use—led tobacco sales. Plug was made with a variety of ingredients to hold it together and offered special taste sensations. Small firms with carefully guarded recipes made and sold their private brands in local markets. Granulated tobacco for pipe smoking, powdered tobacco for sniffing, and leaf tobacco for cigars were produced and sold similarly.

In addition to their garden crops, small farmers in tobacco country usually grew leaf as a source of cash and a trade good. One such farmer was Washington Duke. On returning to his North Carolina farm from a Union prisoner-of-war camp, he found a part of his store of tobacco unscathed by the war. Duke granulated the leaf, packed it in muslin bags, and sold it around his part of the country under the name *Pro Bono Publico*. From this humble postwar beginning, Washington Duke built a company around the sale of tobacco products. But it was Washington's son James Buchanan Duke, known from childhood as "Buck Duke," who would use the family business as a foundation for building the country's dominant tobacco firm, the American Tobacco Company—the tobacco trust.

By 1880 the twenty-four-year-old Buck Duke was running Duke Sons and Company. Postwar adjustments in the tobacco industry had created a market with few competitive gaps. Plug manufacture was dominated by firms in Winston, North Carolina, and granulated pipe tobacco by the popular Bull Durham brand; cigar production was centered not in the South but in Ohio, New England, and the Caribbean, where cigar leaf was grown. Young and aggressive, Buck was neither content to head an also-ran tobacco business, nor foolish enough to expect to wrest much of the market from established masters. His best chance for success lay in cigarettes, for that market was not dominated by any single company but rather offered opportunities to anyone with a little capital and a lot of ambition. Buck Duke had a little capital at his disposal and limitless ambition, so in 1881 he led his firm into cigarette production and sales.

The cigarette was an attractive product for tobacco manufacturers. From an estimated 1.8 million cigarettes sold in 1869, the market had expanded to nearly 278 times that number by 1880, when 500 million were marketed.[4] Most of the market increase was for cigarettes made with domestic tobacco grown in the Southern states. Although the growing market for cigarettes appealed to many tobacco companies, there were clouds on the horizon that discouraged would-be entrants: cigarettes were easy targets for taxation. A 0.1 cent per-unit tax ($1.00 per 1,000) had been established in 1864 to help finance the war. In 1867 the tax was raised to 0.5 cents a cigarette ($5.00 per 1,000), reduced in 1868 to 0.15 cents a unit ($1.50 per 1,000), and then increased again in 1874 to 0.175 cents ($1.75 per 1,000), where it stood when Buck Duke entered the business. Uncertainty regarding the tax discouraged manufacturers from entering the cigarette business. A return to a $5 tax, or higher, would in all likelihood reveal the power to tax as the power to destroy the cigarette industry.

Buck Duke bet the future of his company on the bright side of the tax question. In 1881 he hired a cigarette rolling team from New York to relocate to Durham, North Carolina, to hand-roll his two major brands: Duke of Durham and Pinhead. Duke discovered an inert retail market for cigarettes, despite the statistics on the growth of demand. Retailers were reluctant to stock his brands, so Duke hired Edward Featherstone Small to lead a sales campaign. The addition of Small to Duke's cadre was a fortunate stroke, for the man anticipated modern advertising techniques. Small decided to differentiate Duke's products from the competition's by seeking ordinary publicity in unordinary ways. Employing an attractive woman to represent the company to sellers assured the retailers' attention and coverage in the press. Giveaways for carton purchases and bulk orders from jobbers proved popular, and, persuaded by Small, prominent people endorsed the products he was promoting. Small's novel methods worked, and Duke's cigarettes became big sellers.

On the political front, Duke joined other cigarette manufacturers in lobbying to reduce the tax on cigarettes. Success came in the form of an 1883 tax cut on cigarettes from $1.75 to 50 cents per thousand. The timing was excellent for Duke. His cigarettes were well known in the distribution network, so when Duke cut his prices in half in response to the tax reduction, the reaction on the market was immediate, and his sales increased at the expense of firms that did not follow the cut. To gain and to hold a larger market share, however, Duke had to instill customer loyalty and gain a production advantage over his competitors. The loyalty was pursued with advertising budgets, and the production advantage was found in a machine to roll cigarettes.

When Buck Duke entered the business, cigarettes were hand-rolled. A supervisor and a team of ten rollers, the standard production unit, could manufacture about 20,000 cigarettes a day. No technical economies were associated with a larger scale of output. To increase output, another supervisor and team would have to be employed to provide the most product for the expenditure. Since a firm turning out 20,000 cigarettes a day could expect substantially the same costs per unit as one producing 200,000 a day, small firms predominated in the cigarette industry. Because large size brought no financial advantages in cigarette rolling, Duke was free to enter the competition when he did; yet those features of the industry that prevented others from keeping Duke out of the industry kept Duke from gaining control once he was in.

Although producers had some misgivings about the marketability of a machine-rolled cigarette, they were on the lookout for a workable machine. Buck Duke made another of his well-timed decisions when he contracted for two rolling machines patented by James Bonsack of Virginia. Because Bonsack had yet to market any machines, Duke extracted rebates and other special concessions to guarantee his ability to roll cigarettes more cheaply than his competitors could.[5]

Machinists perfected the Bonsacks in 1884; Duke sealed his advantageous contract with the inventor the following year. Duke estimated that he could produce cigarettes for a total cost of $1.85 a thousand if (1) the tax remained at 50 cents, (2) tobacco could be bought at 25 cents a pound, and (3) he could roll and sell 250,000 units a day, a staggering amount for the time. If the product could be sold wholesale for $4, the profit possibilities were tremendous.[6]

Duke controlled about 10 percent of a one-billion-a-year cigarette market in 1885. He wanted the entire market, so he moved to take over his major competitors: Allen and Ginter of Richmond, Virginia; Kinney Tobacco of New York; Goodwin and Company of New York; and William S. Kimball and Company of Rochester. Duke carried the battle to New York, where he installed Bonsacks in a loft, spent large sums for advertising, and began cutting into the Northeastern market. By 1889 Duke and the other four major cigarette producers were selling almost 2.2 billion cigarettes. Duke was selling over 39 percent of that total—over 60 percent more than Allen and Ginter (number 2) and nearly five times the sales of Goodwin and Company (number 5).

The competing firms could not match Duke's low costs, for he held an unmatched contract with Bonsack. The pressure of Duke's lower costs and expensive advertising campaigns forced his competitors to accept his terms: the reorganization of the cigarette industry into a trust with Duke at the head. The trust, capitalized at $25 million, was formally established in January of 1890 as the American Tobacco Company.

Duke controlled the cigarette industry through his trust, but he wanted more. Cigarettes represented a small part of the total tobacco market. The trend of annual cigarette sales was upward, but the growth was neither even nor regular. The ups and downs reflected the newness of the market and social reformers' attacks on the use of tobacco.[7] Duke was not content to rationalize the industry he had monopolized and cash in on the product that had brought him to power. His empire was a gathering of competing firms operating under single ownership but not single management. Duke left it that way while he undertook to monopolize the entire U.S. tobacco industry, and beyond that goal stood the world. The profits from cigarettes would provide the war chest for this grand crusade to build an even larger empire.

To conquer the other tobacco markets, Duke employed the techniques that had won him the cigarette industry. The first target was plug (chewing) tobacco. In 1893 American Tobacco increased its capitalization by $10 million. The additional stock was used to buy control of a key plug manufacturer: the National Tobacco Works of Louisville, Kentucky. That firm's already well-known brand, Battle Ax, was used to show other producers what Duke had in mind—the absorption of the entire plug industry by American Tobacco Company. Duke suggested merger to the major plug competitors (P. Lorillard, Liggett and Myers, Drummond, and Brown) in 1893 but was rebuffed.

Profits from cigarettes gave Duke the latitude to make drastic price cuts in plug tobacco, starting in 1894. American Tobacco frequently sold below the cost of manufacture with the intent of driving the competition to the wall. Liggett and Myers and the Drummond Tobacco Company attempted Duke's own tactics by entering cigarette manufacturing in 1896. They were unable to match Duke on his own field, however, as he enjoyed well-established brands and an advantageous contract with Bonsack.

Duke seemingly won the plug war in 1898 with the creation of a new holding company, Continental Tobacco of New Jersey. Continental was capitalized at $97.5 million, only about $3 million of which was sold for cash. The remainder of the stock, divided between common and 7 percent noncumulative, was used to buy existing plug firms. American Tobacco Company, for example, sold its plug companies to Continental for $1.1 million in cash and $30.4 million in stock (half common, half preferred).[8] Duke and his staff ruled both Continental and American.

The plug war was not won without Duke's engaging an adversary willing and able to employ Duke's own tactics. The encounter proved a valuable experience for Duke and left him with some powerful allies. A group of Wall Street speculators, including Thomas F. Ryan, Anthony N. Brady, Thomas Dolan, and William H. Butler (a director of American Tobacco Company) formed Union Tobacco Company of America in 1898. Union was offered to survivors of Duke raids as a vehicle of protection against Duke's monolith. An important independent cigarette producer, National Cigarette and Tobacco Company of New York, gave up its stock in exchange for shares in Union. At that point, Butler left American and took charge as president of Union Tobacco. Having acquired a cigarette company, the speculators went on to attract into their operations a smoking tobacco firm, Blackwell's Durham Tobacco Company of Durham, North Carolina.

The Union Tobacco Company scheme was recognized for what it was by other speculators interested in profiting on tobacco. Oliver H. Payne, a millionaire through his Standard Oil associations, in concert with other millionaires, had been accumulating American Tobacco stock for some time. They joined the Union Tobacco forces and used their wealth and influence to gain for that company an option to buy Liggett and Myers, the country's largest producer of plug tobacco.

Duke faced the challenge of a viable producer of cigarettes and plug and smoking tobacco in Union Tobacco and a loss of control because of a takeover engineered by Payne. The outcome was more a victory for both than a loss or conquest for either one. Duke played his trump card—his own services. He assured Payne that he would resign and establish a competitive tobacco company unless he were permitted control of American and Continental Tobacco companies. To allow Duke to leave would have defeated a major purpose of Payne's forces in seizing American, Continental, and Union: the creation of a stable monopoly in tobacco.

Payne gave Duke his way in return for heavy monetary remuneration and a number of positions on the various boards of directors for himself and colleagues. Union Tobacco was absorbed by American for $12.5 million in American stock (American gained Union stock plus $3 million cash). Continental received Liggett and Myers plus $5 million in cash in exchange for $35 million in Continental's common and preferred stock. The speculators also gained from the 100 percent stock dividend declared on the $21 million in American stock outstanding when the readjustments began.[9] Ryan and his speculative associates netted $20 million on the deal.[10]

In the same year that Duke placated Payne, Ryan, and their allies, 1899, he acquired R. J. Reynolds Tobacco Company for Continental. Before that takeover, Continental controlled 60 percent of the national output of plug tobacco. Seizing Reynolds was the beginning of a series of expansions that would give Continental almost 85 percent of national plug output in 1910.[11]

Once cigarettes and plug tobacco were securely in Duke's control, he made fast work of the snuff business. Several of the firms acquired for American and Continental had brought snuff markets with them. American bought additional independents and held a third of the market by 1899. As though anticipating Duke's drive for consolidation, the Atlantic Snuff Company had been organized in 1898 to bring several small firms under single control. Together, Atlantic's firms accounted for about half of the snuff market, but Duke employed his proven tactics to force Atlantic into his sphere of influence. After a brief price war, Duke established American Snuff Company of New Jersey. The new holding company, capitalized at $23 million, took over Atlantic Tobacco, added it to what Continental had held in snuff, and then combined it all with some other independents it took over. The new firm held about 80 percent of the national market for snuff, a proportion that would grow through continued expansion and acquisition to over 96 percent by 1910.

In 1901 Duke attacked the cigar market in the United States and the tobacco industry worldwide. He enjoyed little success in the first endeavor and limited success in the second. The cigar industry was as decentralized as the cigarette industry had been before Bonsack. Duke's inability to alter that basic feature of the cigar market underlines the role of mass-production techniques, economies of large scale, and heavy fixed-capital investment in the concentration of American industry and the rise of oligopolies in the American market. In 1901 Duke formed American Cigar Company with a $10 million capitalization. The cigar holdings of American Tobacco and Continental Tobacco were secured with $7 million of American Cigar stock.[12] American Cigar then began buying established firms and using them like Duke had done earlier to gain control of cigarettes, plug, and snuff, but that strategy did not work in the cigar industry. Duke's other commitments may have kept him from launching the full-scale attack necessary to conquer the cigar business, or he may simply have been restrained by the persistent decentralization of the industry. As late as 1910 the trust held only about 14 percent of the cigar market.

Duke invaded England in 1901, buying Ogden's, Ltd., an important U.K. tobacco firm, and using it to wedge his way into British tobacco markets behind heavy advertising and gifts to jobbers. The British tobacco interests retaliated by combining thirteen major firms as the Imperial Tobacco Company, Ltd., and threatening to use it to push into the U.S. market. A truce was signed. American Tobacco turned Ogden's over to Imperial in return for stock. Additionally,

American agreed to refrain from selling in Great Britain and Imperial from selling in the United States. With the intention of seizing tobacco markets outside the United States and the United Kingdom, American and Imperial combined to organize the British-American Tobacco Company. American Tobacco retained ownership of two-thirds of British-American Tobacco.

Duke created British-American Tobacco to delineate his international empire. On the domestic front Duke controlled American Tobacco and Continental Tobacco, through which he dominated markets in cigarettes, plug, smoking tobacco (holdings were acquired as parts of firms seized for other reasons), and snuff. Although his empire was primarily in tobacco, as Duke acquired horizontal holdings he also expanded vertically, securing operating companies in licorice, tin foil, cotton bags for tobacco, wooden crates, machinery, and retail outlets (United Cigar Stores with 392 units).[13] That far-reaching empire inspired business historian Robert Sobel to entitle Duke a conglomerateur.[14]

By the first years of the twentieth century, Duke's empire was much like other giant businesses of the time. Representatives of the trust's many financial backers were wielding more influence over tactical and strategic decisions governing Duke's now diverse holdings, and company owners and operators were increasingly concerned about antitrust laws. In 1901 the Consolidated Tobacco Company was established to concentrate ownership of American and Continental in the hands of those best able to exploit the profitable future of monopoly operations in tobacco. Stock in Consolidated sold for cash—$30 million initially, then later $40 million. Bonds from Consolidated were offered in exchange for stock in American and Continental. The terms were lucrative enough to attract most of the stock to the new company. The reorganization so concentrated the tobacco industry that the holdings of just sixteen directors of the firm combined with those of the financial house of Moore and Schley accounted for 94 percent of the capital of Consolidated, which in turn held 98 percent of Continental and 90 percent of American by late 1901.

Shortly after the creation of Consolidated Tobacco, a windfall enriched its owners. Tobacco taxes had been increased to $1.50 a thousand on cigarettes in 1898 (and other tobacco products were also taxed at higher rates), and prices were raised to cover the taxes. In 1902 the taxes were reduced substantially, but because competition had been drastically reduced Consolidated was able to maintain the tax-driven higher prices and reap greater profits. Consolidated was a step toward a tobacco monopoly securely in the hands of a ruling elite. In 1904 Consolidated, Continental, and American were reorganized into the American Tobacco Company, a firm engineered to fend off antitrust attacks.

Like American Sugar Refining Company, American Tobacco Company was a target for antitrust action. Initially, sugar refineries did not differentiate their products to create brand loyalties as tobacco producers did; selling a homogeneous product like sugar under different brand names began later in the century. A new sugar refiner could find buyers because American Sugar did not control its wholesalers. In contrast, American Tobacco spent millions on advertising to create consumer loyalty. A new cigarette brand had to attract smokers away from existing brands if it was to succeed. Maverick cigarette, snuff, or plug makers were not welcomed by wholesalers, most of whom were remunerated in one way or another by the tobacco trust to carry only trust-approved brands, and retailers risked the ire of the trust and the wholesalers if they bought wares directly from manufacturers. Wholesalers who ran afoul of American Tobacco would be cut off from the best-selling brands. If a particular brand of cigarette became a problem for the trust, wholesalers were given increased margins to carry brands from American instead of the brand targeted for destruction. American Tobacco's bellicose reputation discouraged some potential competitors from head-on marketing.

After American Tobacco took control of tobacco consumer markets, it moved to guarantee its supply of tobacco. Duke's empire was so large a part of the tobacco industry that farmers either sold to American or did not sell at all. Competitive bidding at tobacco auction deteriorated to American's bid or no sale. By 1906 American had stopped bidding in open auction and offered only personal deals to farmers. These deals paid prices considerably below what farmers expected—demanded—for their leaf. Frustrated farmers turned to violence.

The American Tobacco Company was a monopsony buyer of tobacco leaf (the one buyer in that market). The natural option open to sellers was the creation of a monopoly selling apparatus. If farmers could form pools and sell only from the pools, they could use their collective power in negotiating with the monopsony buyer. Pooling, however, was as elusive a solution for farmers as it had been for railroads, sugar refiners, meat packers, steel makers, and oil drillers seeking to harness its obvious power. A farmer outside the pool—or one in it willing to cheat—could undersell, ever so slightly, the pool members and thereby capture a disproportionate market share. The tobacco pools used violence and fear to force cooperation from both sides of the leaf market. Non-pooling farmers were visited by "night riders," masked horsemen who burned crops, barns, and houses, and beat and even murdered farmers.

The holdings of American Tobacco and Imperial Tobacco Companies were attacked by the enforcers operating beyond the law. In November and December of 1906 an Imperial plant and two American warehouses in Princeton, Kentucky, were burned by armed riders who used their weapons to turn back firefighters. The riders' activities continued unabated through 1907, culminating in a large-scale attack on Hopkinsville, Kentucky. Lawmen and firemen were held at gunpoint while two factories were burned.[15] Violent opposition to his bullying tactics drove Buck Duke to call for law and order, a call that brought the underlying causes of unrest to the attention of federal officials. President Theodore Roosevelt himself was aware of the operations of the American Tobacco Company. Much to Duke's chagrin, the president was more concerned with American Tobacco's monopsonistic behavior that had occasioned the farmers' unusual and extreme actions than he was with the violence itself.

The tobacco trust was no stranger to litigation: Several states had attempted to thwart its monopoly power, but regulation of the company's interstate business demanded federal authority. That authority was brought to bear in 1908 by a government suit under the Sherman Antitrust Act to break up the monopoly or at least prevent it from dealing in interstate commerce. The court ruled against the trust. Barring Imperial Tobacco, British-American Tobacco, and United Cigar Stores, the trust was enjoined from interstate commerce until competitive conditions were restored. Both sides appealed.

The U.S. Supreme Court handed down its decision in 1911. Imperial Tobacco Company, British-American Tobacco Company, and United Cigar Stores were not to be exempt. Eight months were allowed to dissolve the monopoly. Under the direction of the attorney general, Duke and his associates prepared a plan, and the court accepted the plan later that year, providing three years in which to reconstitute the monopoly as an oligopoly. The new firms destined to dominate the tobacco industry were American Tobacco Company, Liggett and Myers Tobacco Company, R. J. Reynolds Tobacco Company, and P. Lorillard Company.

Two further changes reinforced the new direction of the tobacco industry in the years before World War I. The first was the combination of many of the independent companies. Smaller independents had resisted the tobacco trust more successfully than they would the powerful new oligopolies: the breakup of the monopoly had permitted more competition but at a level so hostile as to discourage all but large firms. The stage was set for the next half-century.

The second major change in tobacco before World War I related to output of that product through which the industry had been monopolized in the first place, the cigarette. The court-approved division of the spoils of Duke's empire allotted no cigarette brands to Reynolds, butReynolds had never been a cigarette producer. In 1913 Reynolds introduced the Camel cigarette and concentrated its promotional efforts on that brand. While other firms continued the practice of promoting several brands, Camel went from less than 1 percent of the national market in 1913 to 35 percent in 1914. The explosive success of Camel forced the other oligopolies to copy the approach of heavy advertising and concentration on a single brand. The Camel revolution brought forth Chesterfield from Liggett and Myers, Lucky Strike from American Tobacco, and eventually Old Gold from Lorillard.

By the beginning of World War I, U.S. tobacco markets were dominated by giant oligopolies with roots in the monopoly Buck Duke created from the competitive industry he had inherited from his father. From civil war to world war, tobacco, like many other industries, evolved from competition to monopoly to oligopoly. Giant firms, like the economies of scale that spawned them, were characteristic of American industry from the 1860s to the 1920s.

NOTES

1. Paul Wallace Gates, *The Farmer's Age: Agriculture, 1815–1860*, Economic History of the United States, vol. 3 (New York: Holt, Rinehart & Winston, 1960; New York: Harper

Torchbooks, 1968), 99–115; and Carol J. Miller, "Tobacco Manufacturing," in *Manufacturing: A Historiographical and Bibliographical Guide*, vol. 1 of *Handbook of American Business History*, ed, David O. Whitten and Bessie E. Whitten, (Westport, CT: Greenwood Press, 1990), 65–86.

2. Meyer Jacobstein, "The Conditions of Tobacco Culture in the South," in *Economic History, 1865–1909*, vol. 6 of *The South in the Building of the Nation*, ed. James Curtis Ballagh (Richmond, VA: Southern Historical Publication Society, 1909), 66–72.

3. Robert Sobel, "The Match," ch. 4 in *They Satisfy: The Cigarette in American Life* (New York: Doubleday, Anchor Press, 1978), 64–71.

4. Robert Sobel, *The Entrepreneurs: Explorations within the American Business Tradition* (New York: Weybright & Talley, 1974), 166.

5. Maurice Corina, *Trust in Tobacco: The Anglo-American Struggle for Power* (New York: St. Martin's Press, 1975), 24.

6. Ibid., 27.

7. Sobel, *They Satisfy*, 49–56.

8. Richard B. Tennant, *The American Cigarette Industry: A Study in Economic Analysis and Public Policy* (Hamden, CT: Archon Books, 1971), 29.

9. Ibid., 30.

10. Corina, *Trust in Tobacco*, 60.

11. Sobel, *Entrepreneurs*, 178–79; Corina, *Trust in Tobacco*, 61; and Tennant, *American Cigarette Industry*, 31.

12. Sobel, *Entrepreneurs*, 179.

13. Tennant, *American Cigarette Industry*, 33.

14. Sobel, *Entrepreneurs*, 176.

15. Corina, *Trust in Tobacco*, 117.

CHAPTER 9

The Forest Products Industry

Trees were among the first crops harvested by Europeans who moved to the New World. Colonists cut timber to repair old ships and build new ones; construct houses, barns, and other outbuildings; make furniture, wagons, and fences; and supply fuel for warmth, cooking, curing, and light. Most of the forests were cut and burned to clear farmland and the ashes used to make lye for home manufacture of soaps, candles, and tanning preparations. Early American culture was built on wood.

Until about 1860, the forest products industry comprised many small-scale producers. Farm families provided their own timber products in the years before mills appeared along waterways convenient to a supply of logs and a market for lumber. The mills, local operations, cut timber from public land or on acres purchased inexpensively. After trees had been cut, mill owners could sell the partially cleared land for more than they had paid for it. As towns and cities developed, the market for lumber attracted investment in sawmills. For access to water power and cheap transportation, these mills were constructed along waterways. (Even later, during the antebellum years when powerful steam-driven sawing equipment replaced the slower, simpler water-driven saws, mill owners continued to locate along waterways to reap the benefits of moving bulky logs into the plant easily and inexpensively and then shipping the unwieldy timber products to market.) Forests were cleared within log-rolling and dragging distance of the water. The felled trees were trimmed of branches and pushed into the water: lumberjacks maneuvered the dangerous cargo to mills downstream, where it was cut then either loaded onto boats for shipment to market or formed into rafts and floated to market.

A premier advantage of railroads was their capacity for hauling people and goods through areas lacking water transportation, so construction engineers often used the emerging railroads to bring in the timber for building railbeds, bridges, and shops. During construction, mills were erected along the right-of-way. Trains delivered logs to the mills, then hauled the timber products to the point of construction. Once the local work was finished, these mills were dismantled and relocated to construction sites farther down the line or sold, for they were unlikely to be cost-competitive with waterside operations for other forest products markets.

In the years before the Civil War, technology and market size made the forest products industry a competitive business in which large numbers of small enterprises produced and sold products without distinguishing characteristics; hence, a buyer would have no reason beyond price to prefer the products of one mill over those of another. The costs of establishing a sawmill were so low that the hint of a profitable market attracted competitive investors bent on harvesting the local forests and profits. Trees were free for the taking or obtained at modest prices and available in such quantities that Americans of that era and for decades thereafter thought the supply inexhaustible. When competing mills did not meet market demand and lumber prices were driven up, new mills were attracted into the competition.

If, however, the mill owners saturated their markets, falling lumber prices would force them to abandon their machinery—which they did readily when more productive mills made it obsolete—or relocate closer to fresher, more competitive markets. But markets were not the only driving force behind mill relocation. A mill might be moved every few years as nearby timber was cut to a distance from the water source that made further logging too expensive for that mill to compete with mills that had access to trees that could be dropped and rolled into water immediately at hand. Mill owners routinely evaluated market potential and log availability. By relocating at irregular intervals, mill owners tempered market shifts and helped keep supply and demand in workable relation to one another.

Although integral to the forest products industry, the naval stores industry was subject to pressures distinct from those shaping the market for forest products in general. In the age of sail, tar was a caulking material essential for sealing the gaps between a ship's planks. Pitch was plastered over the tar for tighter, more flexible sealing, and turpentine was used to thin out tar and pitch to make it more elastic and to reinvigorate tar and pitch in place. Tar, pitch, and turpentine, along with trees suitable for ship's masts and spars, were naval stores.(The organic compounds would later be supplemented and then largely supplanted by mineral derivatives just as iron and steel would eliminate the need for wooden masts and spars for commercial and military vessels.) If trees meeting the specifications for masts and spars could be located near a water source, they were harvested there first; but their high value and short supply encouraged producers to haul their finds great distances to reach a water route to market. Tar, pitch, and turpentine could also be produced at some distance from cheap transportation if necessary (although producers carefully sought out waterside locations to keep their costs low), since processing not only increased value but decreased weight.

The decade of the 1860s, a watershed in sawmill technology, reshaped the forest products industry. Technologically advanced mills equipped with steam-driven multiple gang saws and conveyer systems manufactured vast quantities of lumber, laths, and shingles in less time and at costs well below those of mills using earlier generation machinery. Advanced mills cost more to equip than mills using older, simpler saws, but owners could spread their high costs over a huge output. Of course, the output had to find a market, because mass production is built on mass consumption. The more productive mills—those that cut the most products in the shortest time—were dependent on a ready supply of logs to keep the machinery going. If the log supply faltered and the mill closed, expensive machinery that could have been turning out goods for market sat idle. A mill with a capacity of 10 million or more board feet of lumber a year would exhaust immediately available timber stands in less time than it took to pay the costs of building and equipping the plant.

Heavy investments in mills were accompanied by efforts to guarantee a log supply. Large operations required timber rights or outright purchase of timbered land as free land passed from the American scene to be replaced by private and government land holdings. With the need for logs and the cost of land rising, it was no longer feasible to cut only timber near a water route, and distant timber stands were bought and cut to maintain a steady supply of logs to giant mills. Steam winches called donkeys replaced mules and oxen for dragging logs from the cut to the transit point. Where water transit was lacking, entrepreneurs bought steam locomotives and laid rails to carry logs directly to the mill or to the nearest waterway.

Lumbering with the advanced techniques developed in the years after 1860 was an industry apart from early American logging, for which there had been almost no fixed costs—costs producers have to pay whether or not their facilities are running. Loggers in the pre-1860 era hired crews of men and draft animals to cut and haul trees that had cost little or nothing. If the market for lumber fell, a logger had only to dismiss the crew and sell his livestock, if indeed he had not leased the animals with the crew. When the market revived, operations began anew. The only essential investment was money to pay the crew until payment arrived from the mill purchasing the logs.

Once free and inexpensive timber rights were exhausted in an area, loggers moved on to newer logging regions or increased their fixed costs by purchasing cutting rights where they could and buying timberland where they could not. To spread the fixed costs over as much timber as possible, loggers maximized harvests, increasing fixed costs still further with investments in steam donkeys, locomotives, and rail lines to extend access to trees beyond those close to a water route. When loggers expanded their fixed cost with investments in capital equipment, they created additional pressure to expand operations even more and spread the cost as thinly as possible. The logger had to plan ahead, buying more land or timber rights (more fixed costs) to keep expensive capital equipment in use. If the market fell, the logger could not pay the mortgage on loans for equipment and might well be pressed into bankruptcy. The loss was no less if the logger owned fixed capital outright, but it was an internal loss as the opportunity cost of idle equipment and uncut trees accumulated.

Logging and milling were separate businesses in the early period of the American lumber industry, and mill owners could usually depend on independent logging crews to bring them as much timber as they needed to keep the sawmills working. As lumbering became a higher fixed-cost business, loggers grew increasingly dependent on mill owners and the market to keep business afloat. Mill owners had the same problems as their log suppliers. When their capital costs (fixed costs) rose, mill owners were forced to spread the costs. The mill that worked twelve hours a day would eventually be driven out of business by one cutting twenty-four hours a day. Had technology been fixed, the twenty-four-hour-a-day plant would have simply worn out about twice as fast as the twelve-hour-a-day plant. But in a world of advancing mill machinery, the full-time plant would be refitting with more productive equipment while the half-day mill was still paying for what it had. Survival for loggers and mill owners meant producing the greatest possible output in the shortest possible time to spread the high fixed costs as thinly and as rapidly as possible.

The pressure of rising fixed costs concentrated forest products manufacturing into a diminishing number of firms, even as growing capital costs limited the number of industry participants. New entrants as well as established firms recognized the advantages of scale economies attendant on large size, whether that size was attained through growth of the individual firm or through cooperation between firms. Mergers and growth, encouraged by economies of the industry and its advancing technology, accounted for the rise of giant companies turning out forest products. Mill owners soon recognized both their dependence on a steady flow of logs and the obstacles to expansion facing the loggers who had historically provided the supply. To guarantee their log supply, mill owners expanded vertically into logging by underwriting existing loggers or by purchasing land (or timber rights) and establishing their own logging operations. By 1915 the cost of building a sawmill in Mississippi with a life expectancy of fifteen years was $500,000[1] plus $2,500,000 to $3,000,000 worth of timber to keep the mill working.

The market did not always cooperate to alleviate the growing pressures on lumber producers. The millions of dollars tied up in timber rights, logging equipment, and mills were frequently idled by a slow market or a market saturated by the lumber products of mill owners striving to cover costs and make a profit through high-volume output. Mill owners expanded their financial influence into logging to guarantee sufficient supply to keep their expensive mills running and, to improve their sales outlets, moved into wholesale and retail sales. The opportunity costs of closing down a sawmill were high, and just as logs had to keep moving to the mill, lumber had to move away from it. As producers became slaves of their high fixed costs, they could no longer allow local markets to dictate their sales levels—they were forced instead to actively seek sales outlets for their high output. Initially, producers were able to stimulate local sales with multiple outlets for the buyers' convenience and prices below costs of production; but larger markets offered more opportunities to sell, so producers used the expanding transportation technology in rails to exploit national and international markets.

Between the Civil War and World War I, the changes outlined above re-structured the forest products industry from small-scale production by many independent operators to large-scale production concentrated in large inter-related firms owning millions of acres of land and millions of dollars in equipment. Change in the structure of the industry was accompanied by change in location: lumbering moved westward ahead of the population. By the advent of the Civil War, small-scale lumbering was an established local industry in most populous areas of the United States. New England, the Old South, and the Atlantic coast had lumber industries that dated from the colonial period.

The economic expansion associated with the Civil War swept the lumber industry into the national market that war production created. The Great Lakes states were positioned to respond best to the changing conditions of the market and advancing technology. While small-scale lumber companies continued to operate in their historical preserves, large-scale lumbering rose to dominate the Lake states industry and the national market. By the end of the Civil War the Lake states dominated national lumber production. Output peaked about 1890 and then began a long decline, although the region maintained its lead until about 1910, when production in the Pacific Northwest and the South surpassed pro-duction in the Lake states. The figures in table 9.1 illustrate shifts in the lumber industry and the comparative importance of each region during the period from the Civil War to World War I.

Knapp, Stout and Company of Menomonie, Wisconsin, was a forest products firm in the Lake states that grew into a giant in the years after the Civil War.[2] The company was begun in 1846 by John H. Knapp and William Wilson. Doing most of their own work, the owners ran a mill with a 15,000 board feet daily capacity. Fifty years later the company maintained an average employment of 2,000 people and cut 750,000 board feet daily in its several mills.

The company grew both horizontally and vertically within lumbering and expanded into areas beyond forest products. Knapp, Stout started with mills to cut timber and fashion laths and shingles. As the company expanded, it bought land to guarantee timber, set up logging camps to cut and load timber, established farms to grow food to feed the employees, built dams for water control and power generation, and constructed railroads to haul logs from forests to mills and from mills to markets. The company's wholesale and retail businesses were outlets for its lumber products, as well as for the output of its grist mill, pork-packing plant, foundry, machine shop, and wagon and cooperage shop. Knapp, Stout even expanded into land development, an outgrowth of its huge investments in land.

Started as a partnership, Knapp, Stout was incorporated in 1878 with a capital of $2 million. Only four years later the capital was doubled. The firm's output

TABLE 9.1 Lumber Production: United States and Regions, 1869–1920
(millions of board feet)

Year	U.S. Total	Old Industry[a]		Great Lakes[b]		South[c]		Pacific[d]	
		Amount	%	Amount	%	Amount	%	Amount	%
1869	12,756	4,922	38.6	6,290	49.3	923	7.2	621	4.9
1879	18,125	5,416	29.9	10,107	55.8	1,755	9.7	847	4.7
1889	27,039	6,603	24.4	14,100	52.1	3,875	14.3	2,461	9.1
1899	35,078	8,422	24.0	14,761	42.1	8,404	24.0	3,489	9.9
1904	34,127	7,480	21.9	10,826	31.7	10,499	30.8	5,323	15.6
1905	30,503	6,293	20.6	9,163	30.0	8,238	27.0	6,808	22.3
1906	37,551	8,043	21.4	10,192	27.1	10,996	29.3	8,321	22.2
1907	40,256	9,341	23.2	10,565	26.2	12,341	30.6	8,008	19.9
1908	33,224	7,518	22.6	8,476	25.5	10,711	32.2	6,520	19.6
1909	44,510	10,374	23.3	11,101	24.9	14,796	33.2	8,239	18.5
1910	40,018	8,138	20.3	9,782	24.4	13,249	33.1	8,850	22.1
1911	37,003	7,377	19.9	9,012	24.4	12,222	33.0	8,391	22.7
1912	39,158	8,293	21.2	8,811	22.5	13,538	34.6	8,516	21.7
1913	38,387	7,080	18.4	7,819	20.4	14,329	37.3	9,158	23.8
1914	37,346	7,970	21.3	7,552	20.2	13,384	35.8	8,441	22.6
1915	37,012	8,165	22.1	7,115	19.2	13,590	36.7	8,142	22.0
1916	39,807	7,407	18.6	7,386	18.6	15,325	38.5	9,689	24.3
1917	35,831	5,753	16.1	6,208	17.3	13,900	38.8	9,971	27.8
1918	31,890	5,014	15.7	5,733	18.0	11,135	34.9	10,009	31.4
1919	34,552	5,958	17.2	5,730	16.6	12,704	36.8	10,160	29.4
1920	35,000	5,529	15.8	5,458	15.6	11,914	34.0	12,099	34.6

[a]Connecticut, Delaware, Maine, Maryland, Massachusetts, New Hampshire, New Jersey, New York, North Carolina, Pennsylvania, Rhode Island, South Carolina, Vermont, Virginia.
[b]Illinois, Indiana, Iowa, Kansas, Kentucky, Michigan, Minnesota, Missouri, Nebraska, Ohio, Tennessee, West Virginia, Wisconsin.
[c]Alabama, Arkansas, Florida, Georgia, Louisiana, Mississippi, Oklahoma, Texas.
[d]Arizona, California, Colorado, Idaho, Montana, Nevada, New Mexico, Oregon, South Dakota, Utah, Washington, Wyoming.

Source: Historical Statistics of the United States: Colonial Times to 1957, ser. L 36–44, p. 313.

climbed from 50 million board feet of lumber in 1871 to 100 million in 1879 and 150 million in 1882 as the company became the largest lumber business in the United States.[3]

The giant lumber companies of the Lake states had parallels in the South and West. The L. N. Dantzler Lumber Company dates from 1873, when Lorenzo Nolley Dantzler established his own business after the dissolution of a partnership in his father-in-law's lumber company. Ten years later Dantzler, with the financial backing of Henry Buddig (a New Orleans lumber merchant), constructed a large double circular mill at the mouth of the Pascagoula River in Mississippi. Dantzler guaranteed a flow of logs to his mill by underwriting loggers and buying timberlands. He also bought land well ahead of his needs, so when his competitors were closing operations for want of timber, Dantzler was well supplied. Early into the twentieth century the firm was producing 90 million board feet a year, making it one of the giants in American lumbering.[4]

Under the direction of the founder's three sons, Dantzler enterprises continued to grow well into the twentieth century. The company expanded its southern operations by acquiring mills, timberland, tramroads, and other capital associated with the forest products industry. To distribute its huge output, Dantzler exploited foreign markets, especially in South America. Company ships carried cargoes of timber products to Cuba, Mexico, and Caribbean islands. Products bound for Europe and South America were marketed through the Standard Export Company. In 1907 the Dantzlers exported over 145 million board feet, a company record that was broken in the peak year of 1913, when 149 million board feet were shipped. The value of the Dantzler enterprises that year is estimated at about $5.5 million. As southern native timber was exhausted in the years after World War I, some companies shifted their operations to the Northwest; but the Dantzlers retired from manufacturing in the 1930s and turned to tree farming on their cutover land.

Another giant in the southern lumber industry was one of those that moved south when northern white pine was exhausted. The Eastman-Gardiner Lumber Company established a 60-million-board-feet capacity mill at Laurel, Mississippi, at the turn of the twentieth century. To supply their mill, the Gardiners bought 180,000 acres of timberland. By 1904 the company employed as many as 1,000 people to cut and haul timber and operate the mill.[5]

The United States Lumber Company was a giant forest products firm with interests in Pennsylvania, New Mexico, and Mississippi. In Mississippi alone the company owned the Mississippi Central Railroad (Hattiesburg to Natchez) and lumber mills producing as much as 200 million board feet a year. To market its huge output, the firm ran a wholesale lumber business. The giant company's estimated value in 1905 was $26 million.[6]

The Edward Hines Lumber Company began at the wholesale and retail levels, and integrated backward into sawmilling and logging to guarantee a steady supply of lumber for its Chicago market. Hines moved from Lake states lumbering to the South as the supply of white pine dwindled. He purchased 250,000 acres of Mississippi yellow pine to supply his markets until that source expired as well. Hines shadowed the industry by moving his lumbering from the Lake states to the South, then from the South to the Pacific Coast.

Much of the Pacific Coast lumber industry had roots in the westward shift of the Lake states lumber giants, but some large-scale forest products firms were indigenous to the West Coast. One of these, the Puget Mill Company (later Pope & Talbot, Inc.), was begun in 1852 by Andrew Jackson Pope and William C. Talbot and associates. Within ten years their firm was operating two mills and shipping 19 million board feet a year in the company-owned fleet of ten vessels. In 1875, when Lake states lumber dominated the American market, Pope and Talbot were operating four mills with a combined daily capacity of 335,000 board feet.[7]

Pope and Talbot combined successful management practices with foreign sales of their products to maintain a leading position in West Coast lumbering through the end of the nineteenth century. Instead of relying solely on their own abilities, the two founders employed their complementary managerial skills in concert with those of hired supervisors to provide a complete management team. Foreign markets gave Pope and Talbot an alternative to the fluctuating domestic market—most competitors lacked a readily available fleet of ships. Pope actively sought new markets, dispatching loaded vessels to uncertain ports in search of agents to carry Pope & Talbot products. Pope and Talbot recognized that a firm needed a broad marketing base to maintain the economies of large scale. Through aggressive marketing, the company expanded its Southern California sales and eventually established a strong position in the lumber trade with Hawaii.

The Port Blakely Mill Company was a giant forest products firm dating from the 1860s. Captain William Renton and Daniel S. Howard established their mill on Puget Sound in 1864, and its initial capacity of 50,000 board feet a day had expanded to 200,000 by 1881. Renton and Howard acquired their own ships to distribute the growing output of the enterprise. The company enjoyed sufficient capital backing to prevent collapse during short-term reverses, a sound management that used the available capital profitably, and a well-developed foreign market to stabilize sales. Adept at acquiring and exploiting timber stands distant from waterways, the company constructed logging railroads before other firms considered such backward integration. When domestic markets were slow, the Port Blakely Mill Company, like the Puget Mill Company, kept its mills and ships busy servicing foreign customers.[8]

Another giant lumbering operation, one following the same pattern of growth as the Puget Mill Company and the Port Blakely Mill Company, was the Tacoma Mill Company established by Charles Hanson on Commencement Bay. The 40,000-board-feet-capacity mill began operation in 1869; by 1883 capacity was 225,000 board feet. Like his giant competitors, Hanson shipped lumber to markets along the Pacific Coast when profitable and exploited foreign markets (Central America and Australia) to guarantee sale of the large output necessary to keep his investments remunerative.

Puget Sound had no monopoly on giant forest products operations based on the West Coast. Humboldt Bay, the center of the redwood lumbering area, was home to several giant firms that exploited the redwood forests. Several problems associated with the redwood lumber industry—the high costs of moving timber to the mill and consumer preference for fir and pine, for example—kept redwood lumbering in the shadow of the Douglas fir industry. Giant enterprises, nevertheless, did emerge. The apparent leader in the redwood business was the California Redwood Company. By 1884 this firm employed a labor force of around 1,000 to operate three mills and two logging camps, as well as a machine shop to service its extended operations.

The redwood producers, like their Douglas fir competitors, served the West Coast markets and, when possible, established foreign outlets to stabilize their sales. The U.S. market east of the Sierra Nevada was less accessible to Western lumbering firms than were most foreign ports. Until the close of the nineteenth century, when railroad connections to the lumbering areas of the West were completed, Western timber producers bore the expense of shipment from the forests to rail facilities, then rail transport across the country or water transit around South America. Once in the eastern United States, Western products had to compete with products from the East Coast states and the South, as well as from the Lake states. The turn of the twentieth century, however, brought a change in the competitive position of the West Coast vis à vis the principal U.S. market.

Although West Coast lumbermen gained access to transcontinental rail facilities in 1883, the exploitation of their forest products for sale in the central and eastern United States was delayed until the turn of the century. The decade of the 1880s was nonetheless a prosperous one for the industry, as the demand for ties and structural materials for bridgework on the transcontinental railroads and the requisite linking lines helped large lumbering firms maintain profitable output levels and opened markets to marginal firms. Foreign markets in South America, Hawaii, Australia, and China and local markets on the West Coast boomed in the 1880s. The heavy demand for forest products combined with the declining availability of easily accessible timber stands to spur Sierra Nevada lumbermen to invest in railroads into the forests to bring out the timber. These rail investments further contributed to the prosperity of the industry. Freight rates for lumber hauled to the transmontane United States were too high to permit the West Coast interests to compete successfully with the still dominant Lake states lumber industry, but alternative market opportunities were sufficient to support boom times.

Although the U.S. economic prosperity of the 1880s dissolved into the depression of the 1890s, the West Coast lumber industry continued its transformation from a regional to a national to an international industry dominated by giant firms. The depressed economy encouraged the transformation by forcing marginal firms out of the industry and by encouraging railroads to reduce rates to attract lumber shipments east. The hard times coincided with declining timber stands in the South and the Lake states; Southern and Lake states timber barons were looking for new forests to conquer with flush bank accounts that reflected their earlier lumber successes. By the end of the decade, when the Spanish American War was spurring the economy into renewed prosperity, Lake states lumber capital held a substantial and growing place on the West Coast. Rail rates low enough to make mass shipments profitable and huge expanses of Douglas fir and redwoods at attractive prices had enticed the capital westward despite the economic downturn. Even international shipping shifted to the advantage of the large, well-financed lumber firms.

By the 1890s the economics of ocean shipping had tipped in favor of large steamships constructed of iron and steel. Not only was it cheaper to haul timber products in steamships (not to be confused with steam-powered sailing vessels and steam-powered schooners, both of which continued in service well into the twentieth century), but the size of the shipments necessary to fill these giant ocean-going vessels outstripped the capacities of small firms and frequently strained the capacities of the large ones. The technological advantage of large ships, then, encouraged giant firms and discouraged smaller ones.

Giant firms were the product of the economies of lumbering. Conditions on the West Coast were essentially the same as they were in the other U.S. lumbering areas: survival required growth. Firms that did not grow technologically were priced out of the market by firms that had grown. To spread the costs of technology thinly enough to allow a profit at the competitive prices available, firms had to increase output capacity. But if the number of firms surviving through expansion generated a production capacity greater than the market demand for the product at the lowest cost-covering price, adjustments were necessary. Cooperation among surviving firms to align output with demand to permit a profit for everyone was a potential alternative to the long wait for someone to drop out. Pooling arrangements and cooperative associations were tried on the West Coast as they had been tried in all the other lumbering areas, but the results were unsatisfactory. Whenever lumbermen were successful in pushing prices into the profitable range by limiting output, cheating on the limitation agreements became attractive, and new firms were attracted into the competition. Although giant firms grew out of the competitive conditions in lumbering—just as they did in other industries at the same time—lumbering did not give rise to a trust with the degree of control found in other areas, the sugar industry, for example. The industry did, however, produce a giant figure who was frequently regarded as the ultimate lumber baron: Frederick Weyerhaeuser is still a name synonymous with forest products.

Weyerhaeuser emigrated from Germany to the United States in his teen years. He was working as a stacker for a lumber yard in Rock Island, Illinois, when the panic of 1858 resulted in the financial failure of his employers. Instead of costing Weyerhaeuser his job, the collapse propelled him into management—creditors of the yard put him in charge of the operation. The following year Weyerhaeuser and his brother-in-law F. C. A. Denkmann bought the Coal Valley yard and the Rock Island Sawmill that supplied it. Denkmann managed the operations and Weyerhaeuser worked in the field, ably negotiating with landowners, lumber gangs, customers, and competitors.

The Weyerhaeuser and Denkmann business prospered in the surging markets of the Civil War era and the postwar period. Their firm was one of many exploiting the growing Midwest and the ample Lake states timber resources. Weyerhaeuser was never the ironfisted powermonger found in steel, sugar, tobacco, and other industries. The freedom to enter lumber production discouraged a dominating force in forest products when many other industries were being turned into monopolies. Weyerhaeuser's strength was not that of a Buck Duke wresting control of the competition but, rather, that of a man bringing competitors together for common profit.

In 1868 Weyerhaeuser began buying logs in the Chippewa River area of Wisconsin and floating them down the Mississippi to the two mills then owned and operated by himself and Denkmann. The Chippewa Valley was the location of vast timber resources, estimated in 1840 to comprise nearly 20 percent of the white pine in the Lake states. As Weyerhaeuser became more active in the pursuit of lumber profits in the Chippewa area, he was pulled into a raging battle between local and out-of-state interests. His success in resolving the conflict proved his approach to business dealings and made him extremely wealthy.[9]

The Chippewa war was waged by Eau Claire lumber interests allied with steamboat operators against out-of-state mill owners who purchased Chippewa timber to float downriver to their mills. The local lumbermen used the Chippewa to float in their logs and the Mississippi to float their timber products to market. As out-of-state lumber interests grew, so did the inconveniences to Eau Claire lumbermen. Jams of out-of-state-bound logs slowed down timber entering the local mills and lumber headed South. The steamboats did not navigate the Chippewa above Eau Claire, so they had little concern for the inflow of timber to that point. But the growing number of logs (about 12 million board feet of logs in 1867) endangered shipping from Eau Claire to the Mississippi and southward.

The Eau Claire interests consequently moved to stop the growth of out-of-state log shipments. In 1866 they purchased land along Beef Slough, the only feasible place from which to dispatch logs from the Chippewa to points down the Mississippi. They also gained, from the Wisconsin legislature, the exclusive right to develop the slough for handling lumber. Their plan was to obstruct other lumberers' construction of processing equipment.

The following year the Mississippi River mill owners incorporated the Beef Slough Manufacturing, Booming, Log Driving and Transportation Company. They immediately began construction of a jam and sorting facility at Beef Slough, in clear violation of the franchise of their local competitors. The battle was waged in the Wisconsin legislature, in the courts, and on the slough itself.

In 1870 the war appeared won by the Eau Claire combatants. The Beef Slough Company had won a hollow victory by gaining legislative authority to operate sorting facilities in the slough, for by that time the company was bankrupt. Weyerhaeuser joined the battle at this point, encouraging other Mississippi River lumbermen to join him in leasing the facilities of the Beef Slough Company. Later that same year the firms participating in the lease formed the Mississippi River Logging Company (an Iowa corporation capitalized at $1 million), and the following year the new organization took over the lease of the Beef Slough works. Eventually the Mississippi River Logging Company purchased the Beef Slough Company.

The 1870s found the new Weyerhaeuser company fighting and prospering. The Eau Claire combination did not give up what had, for a short time, appeared to be their victory. They worked to obstruct the flow of logs through Beef Slough with legal, as well as physical, force. The Weyerhaeuser group fought back using the same weapons. By 1879 the Mississippi River Logging Company had succeeded in constructing log-handling works sufficient to guarantee millions of board feet of logs to its owners annually. During Weyerhaeuser's presidency (1872), the company had begun acquiring timberlands. The thousands of acres of timber it purchased provided the company with a valuable capital asset, secured its access to timber resources, and gave rise to the myth that Weyerhaeuser monopolized the upper Mississippi lumber industry. As the Weyerhaeuser company's power grew, the opposing Chippewa lumbermen came to recognize that the Mississippi River Logging Company was not to be stopped. They sued for peace and found the Weyerhaeuser group willing to negotiate. By the end of 1880 the Chippewa group was, through the establishment of several new companies, a component of the Weyerhaeuser interests.

By the turn of the twentieth century the Weyerhaeuser group was exhausting its Lake states timber and looking west for new territory. The syndicate had closed shop in the Midwest by 1910 to pursue the resources in the American Northwest. On January 3, 1900, the Weyerhaeuser group announced its purchase of 1,406 square miles of timberland from the Northern Pacific Railroad. The $5.4 million deal involved Weyerhaeuser and Denkmann ($1.8 million) and fifteen associates. The strength of Weyerhaeuser's leadership was his ability to combine potential competitors in a complex of interrelated companies such that they all profited from the arrangement. The West Coast corporation was christened the Weyerhaeuser Timber Company, and Frederick Weyerhaeuser was president until his death in 1914.

The lumber industry was threatened by the antitrust spirit of the Progressive Era. The absence of a monopoly trust and the growing recognition that size alone does not make a business good or evil, combined with the large firms' policy of avoiding headlines, protected Weyerhaeuser and other giants from court-ordered division. The industry did encounter government intervention, however, in the form of the conservation movement. Gifford Pinchot is largely credited with the establishment of a government-business-conservation system in the American forests. Pinchot, trained in forestry in France, became Chief of the Division of Forestry, Department of Agriculture, in 1898. His goal was less the regulation and control of the lumber producers and more the introduction of conservation techniques on public lands. If the business sector could see the profitability of forest management programs, he reasoned, the timber barons would not have to be forced to copy them. Although lessons in conservation were learned slowly, time was on Pinchot's side. As the supply of available timber declined, lumbermen had no choice save that of the farmer: someonewho must consider the requirements of tomorrow's crop, unable simply to seek out one provided by nature.

Pinchot's approach to future needs permitted the cutting of selected trees in federal forest preserves. Lumbermen who bought the federal timber gained firsthand exposure to fire-control techniques, timber selection, replanting, and general forest management principles. Pinchot practiced his planned-future ideas in the area of forestry training: If lumbermen were to emulate the federal timber practices, they would need trained foresters. Pinchot was in the vanguard of conservationists responsible for the introduction of forestry training schools at American universities—Yale and Cornell, for example.

The year 1900 saw the introduction of a forestry school at Yale, the beginning of the Society of American Foresters, and the creation of the Weyerhaeuser Timber Company. On the surface, the three were independent events, but long-run analysis would suggest their interdependence. Weyerhaeuser was a timber-land owner of too many millions of acres to ignore the implications of the forestry conservation movement. By the end of the study period (World War I), the Weyerhaeuser Company was well on the way to the modern tree farming company it is today. In the forest products industry, as in so many other American industries of the period between the Civil War and World War I, giant firms rose to preeminence. The role of government was a cooperative one. Giant firms were the product of American economic conditions, not of avarice and greed. Rather than attempt to redirect the product of those conditions, government guided the giant businesses along a path determined as most suitable to the long-run needs of the firms and the nation.

NOTES

1. Nollie Hickman, *Mississippi Harvest: Lumbering in the Longleaf Pine Belt, 1840–1915* (University, MS: University of Mississippi, 1962), 160.

2. Robert F. Fries, *Empire in Pine: The Story of Lumbering in Wisconsin, 1830–1900* (Madison: State Historical Society of Wisconsin, 1951), 124–28.

3. Ibid., 125.

4. Hickman, *Mississippi Harvest*, 168–75.

5. Ibid., 179–80.

6. Ibid., 181–82.

7. Thomas R. Cox, *Mills and Markets: A History of the Pacific Coast Lumber Industry to 1900*, Emil and Kathleen Sick Lecture-Book Series in Western History and Biography (Seattle: University of Washington Press, 1974), 116–21.

8. Ibid., 121–23.

9. Robert F. Fries, "The Mississippi River Logging Company and the Struggle for the Free Navigation of Logs, 1865–1900," *Mississippi Valley Historical Review* 35 (June 1948–March 1949): 429–48.

CHAPTER 10

Mining

Like lumbering, mining has roots deep in the American experience. Europeans were attracted to the New World by the lure of mineral wealth barely touched by Native Americans. Spanish explorers seized stores of precious metals from their American hosts, located the mines, and then founded mining colonies around the extraction of ores. Although the Dutch, French, and English searched for gold and silver in their American land claims, they had more success stealing from the Spanish. Mining in the area of the future United States was largely limited to diggings for iron ore, peat, and bituminous coal. Mineral extraction on a large scale was delayed until the late 1820s and the exploitation of rich beds of anthracite coal in Pennsylvania.

Before 1820 Americans burned bituminous coal mined in Virginia and Nova Scotia and shipped into the metropolitan areas of the northeastern United States.[1] American coal supplemented wood and charcoal on the hearths of homes and businesses convenient to water transportation. English coal was imported, often as ballast, for sale in that same market.[2] Residents of Pittsburgh burned bituminous coal mined locally, but the mountains separating western Pennsylvania from the seaboard obstructed the sale of western soft coal in the principal American market. The abundant American anthracite deposits that would later fuel rapid industrial development in the northeastern and north central states and yield the first American mining giants remained inaccessible and unappreciated.

Alfred D. Chandler Jr., dean of American business historians, credits the exploitation of anthracite with sparking U.S. industrialization. Anthracite deposits were concentrated in rugged mountainous areas, far from the waterways needed to carry the fuel to even the nearest markets. Additionally, anthracite was not easily recognized as a fossil fuel and was taken for nothing more than black stones. European settlement in North America was more than three centuries old before the energy potential of anthracite enticed entrepreneurs to invest in canals and railroads to haul the hard coal to markets.[3]

In 1749 the Proprietary Government of Pennsylvania bought land from the Indians of the Six Nations and became the unknowing owner of the greatest concentration of anthracite coal on the globe. The tract, 125 miles by 35 miles, was exchanged for 500 pounds, or about 2 shillings 3 pence per square mile. If the actual coal land alone is considered, each of the 484 square miles of coal cost a little over a pound. The coal fields are located in what is now northeastern Pennsylvania, in an area encompassed by nine counties. The four distinct fields are the Northern, or Wyoming (176 square miles); Eastern Middle (33 square miles); Western Middle (94 square miles); and the Southern, or Schuylkill (181 square miles).[4] Three distinct coal regions developed according to geographic features and the politics of the counties in which they lay: the Wyoming, the Lehigh (including the Eastern Middle region and the east end of the Schuylkill field), and Schuylkill (the Western Middle field and the remainder of the Schuylkill field).

The existence of anthracite deposits was known at the time of the English purchase of the coal region. Legend has it that some of the Indians living in the area were aware that the black stones would burn. The difficulty of igniting and maintaining a flame probably made the coal more a curiosity than a resource; nonetheless, in 1763 the Susquehanna Company reserved coal and iron mining rights on the lands of the eight townships it was settling in the Wyoming Valley. The reservation was likely more in anticipation of discoveries of soft coal than in hopes for anthracite.

The earliest use of anthracite was industrial. Although gunsmiths are reported to have burned hard coal for their metal work as early as 1755, the first documented use took place in 1769, when the blacksmith Obadiah Gore of Wilkes-Barre (on the Susquehanna River, where it flows through the heart of the Wyoming range) demonstrated the high heat-generating quality of the coal under the forced-draft conditions of a forge. Blacksmiths within inexpensive hauling distance of the anthracite deposits adopted the fuel as their principal heat source. Transportation conditions were primitive, however, so the market for the coal was limited. Until the coal became a household fuel, the demand for anthracite was too restricted to encourage investments in the internal improvements that would have been necessary to transport it cheaply to centers of population.

Several experimenters are credited with the first successful use of anthracite in a home fireplace. Jesse Fell of Wilkes-Barre usually receives that distinction for burning anthracite on a specially constructed grate in 1808. Fell advertised his finding widely, guaranteeing himself a place in the sequence of recorded events that led to the widespread use of the coal as both a domestic and an industrial fuel. George Shoemaker of Pottsville helped spread the word about the effectiveness of anthracite as a fuel. In 1812 he hauled nine wagons loaded with coal to Philadelphia, a natural market for the Schuylkill field. He succeeded in selling two of the loads and giving away the remaining seven. Although he left

Philadelphia with the reputation of a fraud, his early attempt at selling anthracite eased the marketing difficulties of those who followed him.

The natural market for the Wyoming coal was in Baltimore and New York. Although hard coal was shipped to those markets in respectable quantities in the years before 1820, that year is usually regarded as the watershed date for the New York market, for it marks the beginning of serious efforts to improve transportation by building canals. The Delaware and Hudson Canal Company was formed in 1825 to construct 16 miles of gravity railroad from the mines at Carbondale, Pennsylvania, to Honesdale, and 108 miles of canal from Honesdale to Rondout on the Hudson River. The heavy expenditure required to construct and maintain the transportation facilities for moving anthracite from mine to market helps explain the tendency of firms to grow large enough to dominate the industry. The firm that controlled transportation held an advantage over competitors in terms of rates and system availability. Furthermore, the firm carrying the expense of a canal project was forced by that financial burden to develop the scale of mining to support and pay for the canal. The Delaware and Hudson Canal, for example, cost a total of $2,305,599.[5]

Coal from the Lehigh field had a geographically favorable market in Philadelphia. The fuel was not quickly accepted, however. Prejudice against the black stones combined with the availability of wood, charcoal, and Virginia bituminous to thwart enterprising operators who were trying to sell Philadelphians anthracite. The disruptions to trade accompanying the War of 1812 helped open the Philadelphia market and provided a stimulus to those interested in improving the means of shipping coal there. In 1818 the Lehigh Coal Company was chartered to build a road from the mines leased from the Lehigh Coal Mine Company. In the same year the Lehigh Navigation Company was formed to improve navigation on the Lehigh River. Both projects were carried to completion in 1819. The two companies merged and in 1821 became the Lehigh Coal and Navigation Company.

The Wyoming field was dominated by a large firm from its earliest development. The Delaware and Hudson Canal Company owned the only economically feasible route to market. It also owned and operated coal mines and held title to coal lands not in use. The Lehigh field was dominated by the Lehigh Coal and Navigation Company, an organization charged with setting extremely high tolls for use of its canal. High tolls discouraged other operators from entering the anthracite competition. But the Schuylkill field was different. Here the independent operator was king. When the Schuylkill Navigation Company was chartered in 1815 by the State of Pennsylvania, coal was not a consideration. The company expended about $3 million to construct a 108-mile-long canal from Pottsville to Philadelphia with an eye to hauling agriculture and forest products to tidewater markets. The company neither sought nor received mining privileges in its charter. By the completion date of the canal, 1825, anthracite was already the main product bringing toll income to the company (part of the canal opened to navigation in 1822).

The Schuylkill region was developed and dominated by independent operators until the 1870s. The canal company had every reason to encourage new operators and thereby increase its haulage. Schuylkill County became famous for and proud of its status as the home of independent mine operators (although coal land ownership was quite concentrated). As early as 1833 there were at least forty-seven operators shipping coal over the canal.[6] Until the mid-1860s Schuylkill mines shipped more coal than did the mines in the Wyoming or Lehigh fields.[7] Schuylkillians attributed the mining success of their county to the uninhibited enterprise permitted by their freedom from domination by large transportation companies. So convinced were they of this advantage, and so aggressive were they in protecting it, that the Pennsylvania statute of 1869 permitting coal land ownership by railroads excepted Schuylkill County.[8]

Although independent mining enterprises were probably responsible for the Schuylkill lead in the race to extract coal, the large number of independent operators rushing to capitalize on their coal-land leases concentrated on maximizing returns in the short run. An independent leaseholder with three years to ravage the land was not going to concern himself with the long-run best interests of the owner. In a pell-mell effort to meet quotas and hold down costs, the easy-to-mine outcrops were exploited at the expense of often richer veins. Leases usually demanded that improvements pass to the owner at the end of the lease period, so improvements were kept to a minimum. All in all, the system of many independent mine operators working leased lands ultimately led to the rise of a dominant force in the Schuylkill field, exactly what the people of the county had hoped to prevent by maintaining the competitive system.[9]

From 1820 to 1850 the anthracite industry developed around the canal systems of transportation. At the same time, however, the groundwork for a shift to railroads was being laid. Even before steam-powered locomotives were available to haul coal, the mining companies (often the same as the canal companies) were building gravity railroads from mines to canals. Gravity power was gradually superseded by steam locomotives, and lines from mines to canals were supplemented by an extensive system of feeder lines among mines and between mines and local markets. These rail facilities extended the workable area of the anthracite fields because they linked up with the canals. Later, however, the rails would replace the canals.

The creation of competitive rail systems dependent on anthracite tonnage for profits swept independent mine operators into several large combinations that were themselves eventually forced to combine. The process began in the Wyoming and Lehigh fields, where competition had been limited by the dominant canal companies since the beginnings of the industry. The Pennsylvania Coal Company, chartered by Pennsylvania in 1838, began building gravity-railroad connections in 1850 from its mines to the Delaware and Hudson Canal and quickly grew into a major producer. The Delaware, Lackawanna and Western Railroad Company, originating from an 1849 Pennsylvania charter, began accumulating coal lands in 1851. By 1870 it had acquired 17,000 acres through purchase and merger, especially merger with the Nanticoke Coal and Iron Company, itself the product of the merger of several companies. The Delaware,

Lackawanna and Western (DL&W) did not ignore its rail system at the expense of coal lands but instead constructed a line from the New York-Pennsylvania border southeast to the Delaware River, then connected it to tidewater by leasing access in 1856 to Central Railroad of New Jersey tracks. The DL&W arranged an independent tidewater outlet by leasing the Morris and Essex Railroad in 1868 and then leased the Oswego and Syracuse Railroad in 1869 to gain access to the Great Lakes connection; within the coal fields, DL&W had, by 1873, added the Lackawanna and Bloomsbury Railroad. Through its combination of landholdings and railroad connections, the DL&W would become an important anthracite competitor.

The Lehigh Valley Railroad Company (LVRC) grew much like the DL&W, arranging outlets to tidewater and the Great Lakes with leases, agreements, and mergers; but its charter did not include mining rights, so the company bought mining companies and merged them into the LVRC-controlled Lehigh Valley Coal Company. The Pennsylvania Railroad, the Erie Railroad, and the Central Railroad of New Jersey used the same technique to gain control of anthracite acreage and rail lines from the mines to their markets. The Delaware and Hudson Canal Company (DHCC) did not let the railroads seize the coal tonnage without a struggle. The DHCC built its own feeder lines and bought coal lands and mineral rights, and by 1872 the canal itself was a negligible asset of a mining and railway company. The canal was abandoned in 1899, and the firm dropped the word *canal* from its title to become the Delaware and Hudson Company.

When the Reading Railroad joined the competition in the Schuylkill field in 1842, it did little initially to change the independence of Schuylkill mine operators, except to end the monopoly enjoyed by the Schuylkill Navigation Company.[10] Competition between canal and railroad grew so intense that by the end of the decade a working agreement to share tonnage was negotiated to avert financial disaster on both sides. Monopoly once again threatened Schuylkill transportation when the Reading leased the canal in 1870. Like the other anthracite canal companies, the Schuylkill Navigation Company was overwhelmed by rail competition in the years after the Civil War. The Reading could not secure a monopoly in Schuylkill because other railroads in search of tonnage were laying tracks into the region. The Northern Central Railroad (held by the Pennsylvania Railroad) extended into Schuylkill from the west, and the Lehigh Valley Railroad penetrated from the east. Moreover, the heart of the Schuylkill region was opened by the Union Railway Company, a joint property of the Lehigh, the Lackawanna, and the Central of New Jersey.

The Reading management responded to growing competition for anthracite tonnage by destroying the independent operator system that had characterized the Schuylkill since hard coal had first been mined there. By 1870 Schuylkill landowners were willing to cooperate with the Reading. Fifty years of mining by independent operators with little capital for long-term improvements had retarded Schuylkill development and allowed the other fields a competitive advantage. In 1829 the Schuylkill region provided 71.35 percent of the total anthracite shipped to market, but by 1870 the region's contribution had fallen to 30.70 percent. Although the 1829 figure is the peak contribution and the 1870 percentage was lower than that for the year before or the year after, the long-run tendency was for Schuylkill to produce and ship a smaller and smaller percentage of total anthracite tonnage. The Reading offered all the advantages of a large business that could invest what was necessary to make Schuylkill mines competitive with Wyoming and Lehigh mines.

The Reading's charter did not grant the company rights to buy coal lands, so in 1871 Reading chartered another corporation, the Laurel Run Improvement Company, and acquired anthracite properties in its name. The Laurel Run charter stated that the firm could be purchased by a railroad company, but only if that company held a Pennsylvania charter. The Reading acted on its right to buy and renamed its new firm the Philadelphia and Reading Coal and Iron Company. Through its coal and iron company, the Reading acquired 70,000 acres of coal land by the end of 1871 and over the next few years increased total holdings to 1,000,000 acres—about a third of the Pennsylvania anthracite acreage.

Reading's management invested heavily in coal properties to discourage other carriers from extending into its territory and in that way strengthened the company; but the land purchases were made with borrowed money from bonds, and that indebtedness weakened the road financially. Moreover, because the Reading was buying more anthracite acreage, competitors were compelled to also buy more to protect their positions. With Reading and its competitors buying coal land and pushing up demand, prices rose concomitantly and everyone's cost of expansion was driven higher with each incremental purchase. Reading purchased its mineral lands with debt instruments rather than with stock. So when Reading and its competitors expanded production to generate returns on their mineral investments, they flooded the market, prices plummeted, and Reading defaulted on scheduled debt payments. Under normal market conditions, the Reading could have rolled over its debt; that is, it could have borrowed more money (sold more bonds) to pay off earlier debt. But when falling coal prices coincided with a business panic—in 1873, for example—banks were reluctant to loan a financially troubled company money, and the Reading's bonds were hard to sell in a depressed economy. The Reading's bankruptcy in 1880 worsened competitive conditions in anthracite because while Reading was temporarily freed of its debt obligations, competitors were not freed of theirs.

The emergence of giant carrier-mining operations in the anthracite coal industry fostered great advances in production. Each firm had a high fixed-cost investment in land, mining improvements to the land, mining equipment, rail right-of-way, rail lines, and railroad hardware. The larger the coal output, the thinner the spread of fixed costs. Moreover, because the mines and the carriers usually belonged to the same firms and independents were encouraged to join in carrier combinations, conflicts were reduced to battles between capital and labor. As the ownership of the mines became more and more concentrated, miners were forced to rely increasingly on their own institution for concentrating power—the union. The anthracite coal fields were the venue for some of America's most violent labor-management conflicts.

The press to increase tonnage is evident from the figures on total production for shipment. In the 1860s, the largest annual output was the nearly 14 million long tons produced in 1869; in the 1870s, the largest was the more than 26 million long tons produced in 1879, an increase of over 88.5 percent for the decade.[11] Prices were affected as the growth of coal shipments overwhelmed the growth of demand. The estimated average annual wholesale price per long ton for all sizes of coal (hereinafter referred to simply as the price) was about $5.38 in 1869 but only $2.34—or more than 56 percent less—in 1879.

Overproduction of anthracite in 1866 was followed by a drop in price, but the fiercely independent Schuylkill operators were not inclined to limit production. Determined to share their financial problems with labor, the numerous producers cut wages but met organized resistance from the Workingmen's Benevolent Association. The union refused wage cuts, ordering shutdowns instead whenever supply outstripped demand and forced prices down. Carrier-producers were not satisfied with an industry controlled by a strong union. The emergence of the Reading as a dominant authority in Schuylkill by 1871 made it easier for the now few but powerful carrier-producers to limit production and wages to control the market price of coal and the costs of production.

In late 1872 five of the six major carrier-producers established a working agreement to pool the market. Representatives of the companies agreed that about 16 million tons on the market would provide a market price satisfactory to the sellers (capacity was about 21 million tons). Each participant in the pool was assigned a percentage of the agreed-upon tonnage according to the capacity of the mines shipping coal over its lines.[12] Although various logistical details were addressed by the formal agreement, it was essentially a simple carrier pool designed to limit sales and prop up prices.

The 1872 agreement functioned adequately, if not perfectly, from 1873 to 1875. Prices rose above $5 in 1875, but violations of the agreement had begun to erode the confidence of participants. To prevent further cheating, carrier-producers established a new pool in 1876. For every ton of coal sold over and above its pool-specified limit, a carrier-producer was required to pay $1.50 into a compensatory fund. The money accumulated was to be paid out to member producers suffering from the effects of cheating within the pool. The fine was unfortunately not legally enforceable and was probably not collected. The 1876 accord did not survive the year but rather was dissolved in August. With the dissolution, prices fell in one month from $5.18 to $2.91. Pressure for a new agreement took immediate root but required sixteen months to bear fruit.

No accord was forthcoming in 1877, but conditions in the industry that year were sufficient to encourage one: the average price received was $2.70. A new pool established for 1878 varied in sundry details from the others but generated just as much dissatisfaction. Despite limited success—the price rose by almost a dollar—the pact was not renewed at year's end. Not surprisingly, unrestricted competition in 1879 pushed prices down to record lows (some shipments were sold for less than two dollars). By 1880, however, the national economy had begun recovering from depression conditions dating back to 1873. The surging recovery years of 1880–84 permitted a prosperous anthracite industry without any formal pooling contract. Instead, firms in the industry worked together under an informal agreement that exacerbated the overproduction problem of the giant firms competing for the market.

The informal agreement was a response to the failure rate of formal accords and the rising tide of public dissatisfaction with combinations designed to increase prices. The anthracite industry was one of many American industries suffering the woes of competition between giants whose combined capacity greatly outstripped market demand. The aim of setting prices or percentages ,or both, for each competitor was surrendered in the days of informal combination in favor of an industrywide restriction on output. When carrier-producers found their supply too great to sell at established prices, their representatives worked out details for production stoppages to reduce industry output. Mines that were normally operated constantly were closed 88 days in 1880, 48 in 1881, 49 in 1882, 60 in 1883, and 107 in 1884. The closings were a short-run solution but a long-run problem, for they encouraged the expansion of anthracite mining capacity. Outright cheating—mining coal on restricted days—hurt the pool, but it was the violations of the spirit of the restriction program—opening new mines and expanding the capacity of old ones to increase output on production days—that made the continued success of informal pools improbable. The industry shipped 23.4 million tons in 1880 and 31.7 million tons in 1883.

In 1885 another formal pool was established along the lines of the earlier ones. Although prices fell and cheating prevailed, the agreement was renewed in 1886 and permitted to lapse at year's end. The effects of the Interstate Commerce Act (1886) were yet to be determined, but anthracite companies (carrier-producers) were sufficiently alarmed at the apparent extension of government regulation to avoid formal pools. In the years following the end of the 1886 pact, the industry returned to informal and generally ineffective pooling. Shipments rose from the 34.6 million tons of 1887 to over 40 million tons in 1891 while falling prices approached three dollars a ton.

The Reading Railroad made a heroic attempt to consolidate the anthracite industry in 1892. Using leases, agreements, and communities of interest in anticipation of the eventual solution of the industry's problems, the Reading gained control of about 70 percent of the total shipments of anthracite. The plan, and the Reading, failed the following year as the industry and the nation entered the depression of 1893. The reasons for failure were many. The Reading had spread its credit thin to pull carriers and producers into its web of operations, and the panic of 1893 made continuation of that credit difficult. The company may have mismanaged its infant empire by pushing prices up too high, too fast. Public and private opposition to the consolidation brought the Reading under fire from several directions, fire that began picking the structure apart with court orders.

After the Reading debacle, the industry tried again to restrict production to hold down output and push up price. Restrictions worked no better than they had earlier: output topped 46.5 million tons. Formal allotments were attempted again in 1896 but were given up once more for informal restriction in 1897. Efforts at stabilizing the industry with pools and restrictions had failed several times by 1898, when participants moved again in the direction opened by the Reading in 1892. Serious industrywide consolidation emerged as the sole workable solution to overproduction by the anthracite carrier-producers.

Because anthracite holdings were in the possession of the railroads, competition could be controlled through consolidations and communities of interest between and among the railroad companies. The process got under way early in 1892, when the Erie Railroad acquired control of the New York, Susquehanna and Western Railroad. The Susquehanna had been established ten years earlier to carry coal for independent anthracite operators. By 1892 it had completed its connections from coal fields to market and attracted freight (anthracite) by offering rates below those of the already established roads. The Susquehanna had cut into the coal tonnage of the Erie Railroad by competing for output from Pennsylvania Coal Company mines and Delaware and Hudson Company mines. Upon acquisition, the Erie brought the Susquehanna under its management, although the railroad remained a separate entity. The two roads shared the same basic board of directors, and the Susquehanna's coal company also shared directors with Erie's coal company.[13]

The Reading management, in keeping with its record of efforts to consolidate the anthracite industry, was a leader in the 1898 changes. The company's leadership was now ensconced in a holding company (the Reading Company) that directed the Philadelphia and Reading Railway Company (reorganized from the railroad company) and the Philadelphia and Reading Coal and Iron Company. The Reading's goal of controlling the Central of New Jersey, thwarted twice before (by bankruptcy in 1883 and court action in 1892) was realized in 1901 through direct purchase of over 53 percent of the company's stock (145,000 shares at $160 per share).[14] The attractions of the purchase were that (1) combined, the two companies controlled over 30 percent of current coal shipments; (2) together the companies owned and controlled over 60 percent of the Pennsylvania coal reserves; and (3) the combined company held excellent routes and terminal facilities.

The purchases by the Erie Railroad and by the Reading were distinctive examples of the consolidation movement. Additional, if less impressive, stock purchases were taking place during the same time period. In 1901, for example, five anthracite railroads (the Lake Shore and Michigan Southern, the Reading, the Central of New Jersey, the Lackawanna, and the Erie) made a combined purchase of Lehigh Valley stock. The total cost was $12 million and the smallest share, $1 million. The acquisition by competitors of ownership in the Lehigh eliminated that road from disruptive competition and gave the six companies a common interest that was extended through a series of shared directors. A complicated web of interlocking directorates provided each road with fairly direct communications with the ruling bodies of the other roads in the creation of an effective community of interest.[15] Once the carriers were so combined, they set out to eliminate the last competitive element in the anthracite industry, the independent operators.

The anthracite railroads owned large coal reserves and controlled the shipments from independents by contracts. So long as the carrier-producers struggled amongst themselves, the independents held some competitive power by playing the railroads off against one another. Independents contracted with railroads to haul their coal, and the contracts generally lasted seven years. The life of the contracts was short enough to give the independents an opportunity to shop regularly for better freight rates. That opportunity was lost with the success of the carrier combination. The combined railroads determined to effect life-of-the-colliery contracts and 40 percent (of tidewater price) rates on the independents, thereby eliminating competitive pressure from that direction. For their part, the independent operators determined to fight the carrier combination.

In 1898 the Anthracite Coal Operators Association (an organization of independents) reacted to the tightening control by the carrier-operators by chartering their own railroad, the New York, Wyoming and Western Railroad Company. A right-of-way was secured, rails purchased, and tonnage contracted, but the project was stopped by the carrier combination. (The terms *carrier-operators* and *carrier combination* are used interchangeably at this point because the carrier combination was a combination of carrier-operators.) The Temple Iron Company was purchased by the combination and used as a device through which the carrier combination bought out the independent anthracite firm of Simpson and Watkins. This action eliminated 500,000 tons pledged to the proposed railroad and at least 800,000 tons that would eventually be pledged once previous contracts expired. Both Simpson and Watkins were shareholders in the proposed railroad and were on the board of directors.

The New York, Wyoming and Western Railroad was not to be, but the independent operators struggled on against overwhelming odds. Another try at their own rail outlet was made in 1899. The Pennsylvania Coal Company, the largest independent, proposed the extension of the Erie and Wyoming Valley Railroad to tidewater. Controlled by the Pennsylvania Coal Company, the Erie and Wyoming Valley Railroad was a gathering line, connecting the company's mines to Erie Railroad lines. The Erie stood to lose a large customer if the project were carried out, so the firm of J. P. Morgan was contracted to buy control of the Pennsylvania Coal Company. The Erie paid $32 million for the coal company and its railroads (Morgan received $5 million in first preferred voting trust certificates).

Only purchases of the major independents are chronicled here. The railroads of the carrier combination routinely bought up independent coal companies either directly or indirectly through their own coal companies. Those independents not purchased came under the control of the combination when contracts for the life-of-the-colliery were sold to them in return for a 35 percent freight rate.

The railroad combination attained control over more than 90 percent of the anthracite trade with its mine ownerships and lifetime contracts.[16]

The giant carrier-operators of the anthracite coal region functioned as a monopoly, although their outward appearance was one of many separate and distinct railroad companies and mining companies. Public attention was directed toward abuses charged to trusts, monopolies, and giant business enterprise in general in the 1880s (Interstate Commerce Act, 1886) and 1890s (Sherman Antitrust Act, 1890); in the first decade of the new century (commodity clause, Hepburn Act, 1906); and again in the second decade (Clayton Antitrust Act, 1914). The anthracite industry attracted its share of the antimonopoly interest with its elimination of independent operators and its labor difficulties. It was not obvious exactly how the industry was monopolized. Many of the various stock purchases and combination agreements were industry secrets, but the public was aware (and made aware by the press) of the ability of the carrier-producers to set and maintain a price. During the years of faulty accords and pools, buyers could count on the failure of the pool and the collapse of price if they waited long enough. After 1898, however, the combination did not falter.

The anthracite industry was the center of several labor conflicts in the post–Civil War years. As the employing companies grew in power and the distance between owners and workers increased, the labor difficulties became increasingly bitter and severe. The workers' concerns mattered little to giant capitalists intent on building ever larger empires and fortunes. In the bitter strikes of 1900 and 1902, organized miners fought closings and consolidations of mining operations undertaken by the combination. Anthracite management instituted changes to bring efficiency to an industry overdeveloped from years of extreme competition, but the hardships such changes wrought on the miners were ignored. The 1902 strike was settled through government intercession. The wage increases ordered by the arbitrators were granted by the companies, but the price of coal was promptly increased to protect profits. In response to these events, the publisher William Randolph Hearst sought the dissolution of the anthracite combination by filing a petition with the Interstate Commerce Commission (ICC).

The investigation stemming from the Hearst petition began in 1903 and was finally dismissed in 1914, being superseded by more complete proceedings. The ICC hearings, however, combined with other events to put pressure on the anthracite interests and eventually led to action by the U.S. Supreme Court. The New Haven decision rendered by the high court in 1906 held implications for the combination even though the case targeted bituminous coal. The court ruled that a railroad company was not permitted to buy and sell goods it hauled without regard to published tariffs. If the difference between the price the railroad paid for coal and the price it received for the delivered coal was less than the published hauling rate, the railroad was in violation of the Interstate Commerce Act. The decision meant that railroads could not sell their own coal for prices that did not cover published hauling rates, and railroads that owned coal mines had been undercutting competitors by selling their coal at prices that did not cover the published hauling rates charged the competitors. Then in June of 1906 Congress passed the Hepburn Act with a commodities clause that made it unlawful for railroads to haul, in interstate commerce, goods they produced (lumber and forest products were excluded to protect lumber companies with rails constructed for the express purpose of hauling their products from forest to mill, mill to market, and so on, when these rails crossed state lines). The clause struck at the heart of the anthracite combination.

Some of the railroads in the combination mined their own coal; others owned the companies that mined the coal they hauled. The Reading Company owned a railroad and also the mining companies providing tonnage for the railroad. The companies of the combination did not move to alter their structures because it was generally believed that the commodities clause would be held unconstitutional. But on May 1, 1908, the clause went into effect, and in June the government filed a case in circuit court against anthracite carriers.

The government lost its case in circuit court and appealed to the Supreme Court. The Court did not declare the clause unconstitutional, and this 1909 decision introduced confusion on the issue of the railroads' interest in the products they hauled. Apparently railroads needed only to separate themselves legally from their mining operations: they could still own and control these and remain within the law. Roads already operating separate mining companies appeared to be safe. Those doing their own mining set up separate companies to own and operate the mines.

The government also attacked the anthracite combination through the Sherman Antitrust Act. The suit was filed in 1907 and a decision handed down in 1910. The Temple Iron Company was ordered dissolved, and lifetime contracts between railroads and collieries were banned. The Supreme Court upheld those circuit court decisions (1912) but did not find evidence of a general combination. In 1915 the Court decided against the legality of separate coal sales companies controlled by the railroads. The coal company device was held in violation of both the Sherman Act and the Hepburn Act, and again in 1920 the high court ruled against the combination by forbidding the railroads to own the stock of the coal companies. Segregation of railroads and coal companies was ordered.

By World War I the anthracite industry had developed into a series of giant firms that operated as a monopoly through direct combinations and communities of interest. Although the courts had reduced monopoly power when they dissolved the combinations and eliminated the perpetual contracts used to control competition, they had not altered the basic character of the industry. There would be no return to a competitive environment featuring large numbers of small operators. The economies of mining had created the giant firms, just as they had prevented a return to destructive competition with the court-ordered segregation. The anthracite industry had adopted the same code of oligopolistic competition as other industries dominated by giants.

Unlike the anthracite industry, the bituminous coal industry did not develop into a battleground for giant competitors. Whereas anthracite coal resources are concentrated in a small segment of Pennsylvania, bituminous reserves are much greater and are widely dispersed. The anthracite industry supported giant firms and eventually near-total monopoly because the coal was concentrated: one firm could control a large percentage of the anthracite industry by buying, leasing, and contracting available mines and mine sites. But if one firm had corralled as much as 484 square miles of bituminous coal lands (the estimated pre–World War I size of the total Pennsylvania anthracite reserve), that enterprise would have had nothing near a monopoly in the industry. Although giant firms did mine bituminous coal, the problems in that industry were more closely related to the large number of small producers. Bituminous production throughout the period between the Civil War and World War I (and beyond) was similar to anthracite production in the Schuylkill region in the years before the Reading Railroad began buying, leasing, and contracting coal reserves. Free enterprise avoids some of the pitfalls of oligopoly and monopoly but holds other perils.[17]

Copper mining also spawned giant firms in the United States in the years between the Civil War and World War I. The use of copper dates back to the ancient world, where it effected so great an impact on mankind that two millennia of history are recognized as the Copper Age. Native ore that yielded above 90 percent copper was the first choice of metal workers. When pure copper ran out, high-grade ore deposits attracted miners who roasted the ore (smelting) to extract matte copper, a product containing about 50 percent pure copper. For most of the 5,000 years mankind has made use of this soft metal, matte copper was essentially the final product of the miner-processor. Weapons, cookware, jewelry, and other goods manufactured from copper used matte or pure copper as raw material. The craftsmen heated the copper and beat it into the desired shape. When hotter furnaces were developed, casting became a possibility, but copper's malleability is so great that casting was not particularly attractive. Hotter furnaces permitted use of harder metals and production of alloys (iron in the first instance, bronze in the second) that displaced copper as the most important metal of civilization. As the age of copper gave way to the Bronze Age and then the Iron Age, copper fell in importance as a metal essential for civilization, but it maintained a stable position as a minor input for the manufacture of decorations and other more or less nonessential items used by society. Copper held that station until the late nineteenth century (the study period for this work), when the expansion of plumbing and the revolution in communications created a new age of copper.

Large-scale exploitation of copper deposits in the United States dates from the 1840s and the discovery of exceptionally rich ores in Michigan. Earlier U.S. experience with copper comprised many small operations in several states along the Northeast coast. The Ely mine in Vermont was the largest mine in the country during many of those years. In the pre–Civil War years, world copper production was dominated by Wales and Cornwall in Great Britain, where even large quantities of American ore were shipped for processing. The American role in the industry grew quickly with the development of copper resources in the Lake Superior region of Michigan in the mid-1840s.

The Pittsburgh and Boston Mining Company was formed as an association in 1844 (changed later to a corporation) to work the Cliff mine at Lake Superior. The successful Cliff mine marked the first surge in Michigan copper production and heralded the long period of Michigan's domination of copper mining in the United States. The 1845 national output of copper was only 112 short tons. That total had increased by more than six times by 1850 (728 tons), and the 1860 output was eleven times that of 1850.[18] Despite increases in demand and price (from 22 cents per pound in 1859, to 34 cents in 1863, to 47 cents in 1864), Michigan copper production stabilized during the Civil War years. National output increased somewhat (the maximum national war-years production of 10,580 tons in 1862 was only a 31 percent increase over the 1860 figure), however, as old copper districts came back to life and new ones were staked out in Tennessee, Virginia, North Carolina, and the Western territories. The Planet mines on the Colorado River produced ores with as much as 60 percent copper content—a hint of the future of copper in the United States during the nineteenth and twentieth centuries.

The Calumet and Hecla Mining Company—formed in 1871 with a merger of the Calumet, Hecla, Portland, and Scott mining companies—became one of the first giants in the copper industry. The Calumet conglomerate was discovered in 1864 and brought into production by the Calumet and Hecla companies by 1866. Under the leadership of Alexander Agassiz (1867), the companies combined and later became the largest copper operation in the United States. By 1886 the firm was producing 25,000 tons of copper annually, more than the entire national output in every year before 1879 (and more than the total national output for the years 1845–57). Between 1871 and 1886 the operation produced 228,000 tons (more than the total national output for the years 1845–74). Large-scale mining paid off: using a paid-in capital of $1.2 million, Calumet and Hecla generated extensive improvements in its plant and equipment and paid dividends of $27.7 million over the years 1871 to 1886.[19]

Calumet and Hecla was almost a monopoly in the 1870s. Michigan dominated copper production and sales in the United States, and Calumet and Hecla dominated copper in Michigan. Moreover, a number of Michigan's smaller copper producers formed a pool in that decade and designated Calumet and Hecla as the seller for the pool's products. When the world demand for copper fell, U.S. producers lobbied for tariffs to protect the domestic market.[20] International competition was held at bay temporarily by consequent legislation enacted in 1869. The exclusion of foreign copper combined with the concentration of market control in the Calumet and Hecla to produce higher prices (higher than would be forthcoming under competitive conditions) and market stability. The copper industry had attained in 1870 the concentration, control, and stability that other industries would not find for another half century, but those conditions were not durable. Copper did not avoid the traumas of the period, and Calumet and Hecla lost its near monopoly.

The stability of the Lake-controlled copper industry was shattered by ore discoveries in Arizona and Montana in the 1870s, discoveries that led to producing properties in the 1880s. Copper had been uncovered at earlier times in the Western territories, but transportation facilities had been too primitive to permit profitable exploitation. The 1871 discovery in eastern Arizona, the Clifton-Morenci district, revealed deposits rich enough to warrant production despite the 700 miles separating the camp and the nearest rail connector. The Lezinsky brothers, storekeepers, developed the Longfellow mine and then sold out to Scottish investors who continued the work with their Arizona Copper Company. Another property in the same district, operated by the Detroit Copper Company (organized by William Church), was associated with Phelps Dodge's first ventures in copper.[21]

Anson Phelps, William Dodge, and Daniel James (Phelps was the father-in-law of both Dodge and James) began an export-import firm in 1834, when Dodge and James joined Phelps's enterprise after the death of an earlier partner. Two partnerships were formed: Phelps Dodge and Company in the United States and Phelps James and Company in England. Phelps Dodge shipped cotton to England, and Phelps James shipped English products, principally metal ingots, to the United States. In addition to their commercial business, Phelps and partners began manufacturing metal products from the imported copper, brass, and tin and investing in railroad construction, coal mining, and lumbering. The partnership was soon associated with the Erie Railroad; the Delaware, Lackawanna and Western Railroad; and the Central of New Jersey and eventually with other roads. The Lackawanna Coal and Iron Company was a Phelps Dodge interest in the anthracite industry. The partners also participated in large-scale lumbering in both Pennsylvania and Georgia, where they constructed giant mills and towns to accompany them. By 1880 Phelps Dodge had succeeded in several giant enterprises, but the firm's impressive expansion into copper mining lay ahead.

In 1881 William Church traveled to New York to find financial backing to maintain his Arizona copper property. A likely investor was Phelps Dodge, a company prosperous after nearly half a century of successfully importing metals, manufacturing metal products, and occasionally investing in mining enterprises. (True, it had lost money in tin mining, but that had been an exception for a company widely known as a model of competent business.) When Church approached Phelps Dodge, the partners were already considering building a smelter to process copper ore. They made no commitment to Church but followed up on his request for funds with an investigation of his properties and eventually an investment of $30,000 in the Detroit Copper Company.

James Douglas was also responsible for Phelps Dodge's move into copper mining. A Scot recognized for his expertise as a metallurgist and mining engineer, Douglas was between inspection trips to the Western territories (for clients other than Phelps Dodge) when consulted by Phelps Dodge on the advisability of the smelter project. Douglas anticipated the development of smelters in the mining regions of the West where ore deposits were large enough and rich enough to support—in fact to demand—on-site processing. On his recommendation, the New York smelter project was dropped. Douglas was preparing for another Arizona inspection trip at the time of his conference with Phelps Dodge. Dodge and James, partners directing the company since the death of Phelps in 1853, commissioned Douglas to investigate and evaluate the Morenci property of Church's Detroit Copper Company as part of his planned Arizona trip.

Douglas examined Church's holdings and recommended the investment to Phelps Dodge. Douglas was also impressed with the potential of the Bisbee camp, the site of the well-known Copper Queen mine. In fact, so much was Douglas taken with Bisbee that he secured an option on the adjoining Atlanta claim. He discussed the Atlanta with Dodge and James, then returned to Arizona to explore the area again before finally recommending a purchase. The Atlanta was bought by Phelps Dodge in 1881. The expected copper lode was discovered in 1884 after three years of expensive and exasperating searching. At least parts of the vein, however, ran under Copper Queen land. In an action taken to avoid litigation over ownership of the copper claim, Phelps Dodge bought out the largest owners of the Copper Queen. The Queen, the Atlanta, and several smaller claims were merged in 1885 to form the Copper Queen Consolidated Mining Company. Shortly after the giant copper producer was established, James Douglas, a part owner of the Atlanta as payment for his technical work, became its president.[22]

The years between the establishment of the Copper Queen Consolidated and the end of the nineteenth century were financially difficult. The price of copper began falling after 1882, reaching levels around 10 cents a pound (from the 1882 price of 18.5 cents) and remaining there, with one major exception, until the end of the century. The beginning of the twentieth century brought a rise in demand for copper wire in the rapidly expanding electrical and communications industries which absorbed the increases in supply accompanying the development of the new Western states copper industry. The exceptional year, 1888, can be explained by the Secretan copper syndicate's attempt to corner the world copper market. The corner collapsed after about eighteen months of operation, however. The price set by the syndicate was too high to permit market clearing, and copper stockpiles grew to levels beyond support by the speculators involved. The high prices received by the Copper Queen helped the company over the years of lower prices. During the last years of the nineteenth century, the company paid off the cost of its large new smelter and expanded claim holdings by exchanging Copper Queen stock for titles to nearby properties. Through expansion the smelter was kept busy and capital costs were spread over a broader output. Over the years 1885 to 1908, the Queen produced more than 365,000 tons of copper and paid dividends in excess of $30 million.

The Detroit Copper Company property at Morenci was not as successful as the Copper Queen. Output was respectable, ranging from 750 tons to 2,500 tons a year between 1881 and 1895, but the growing expense of finding and extracting ore prevented the payment of any dividends in those years. In 1897 William Church sold his share in the company to Phelps Dodge. The partners built a new smelter at Morenci, made improvements in the old camp, and increased output to 9,000 tons by 1902 and 12,000 tons by 1908. This expansion allowed the company to pay dividends. Phelps Dodge also expanded by buying the Mocte-zuma Concentrating Company in Nacozari, Mexico, from Guggenheim interests and developing the property into a valuable addition to the firm's copper hold-ings. By the beginning of the twentieth century Phelps Dodge, though still a trading company based in New York, owned three valuable Western copper properties and stood ready to become a giant in the copper industry.

Phelps Dodge built houses for its workers, schools, company stores, rail lines, and other social overhead capital to guarantee a reliable supply of labor and materials to work their copper properties. (The company had done the same to support its lumber enterprises east of the Mississippi.) In 1900 Phelps Dodge created a new town at a site some twenty miles east of Bisbee, where it built a smelter large enough to process ores from the Copper Queen and its Mexican mines as well as those from independent mining companies. The town was named Douglas after the Copper Queen president who had taken the lead in building a community with many of the amenities of a comfortable life, like wide streets, electricity, gas, a water works, a sewerage system, an ice plant, and a telephone system.

Travelers reached Douglas via Phelps Dodge's Arizona and Southwestern Railroad, a line built to provide rail service between points not connected by the two major roads in the area, the Santa Fe and the Southern Pacific. The first link opened in 1889 was a thirty-mile standard gauge line connecting Bisbee with the Santa Fe at Fairbank. Later the line was extended to Benson, Arizona, to connect with the Southern Pacific. When Douglas was established, the railroad was ex-tended to the new town and southward to connect the Phelps Dodge properties in Nacozari. In 1903 Phelps Dodge completed its El Paso and Southwestern Railroad from Douglas to El Paso, over 200 miles. The company was extending its trans-portation system to guarantee access to Eastern markets. Shortly thereafter the El Paso and Northeastern Railroad was purchased to provide transportation for coal to the smelter at Douglas. By the opening of World War I, Phelps Dodge was operating, as subsidiary companies, over 1,000 miles of railroad to carry raw materials to, and finished products from, company mines and processing plants.

Phelps Dodge replaced its partnership in 1908 with the Phelps Dodge Com-pany, Incorporated. Established as a holding company with a capital of $45 million, Phelps Dodge continued to mine, smelt, and haul copper. The 721.5 tons produced by the company in 1882 had increased to 76,500 tons a year by 1913. In 1917 the firm employed 8,800 people and did a volume of business valued at $62,262,000. Phelps Dodge had grown from a modest export-import business in 1834 to one of the giant copper producers of the United States by World War I. It was not a monopoly but an oligopoly in competition with other giants. Phelps Dodge was neither the largest nor the most important of the copper giants during the Civil War to World War I years, but the firm's long and varied existence holds particular interest for business historians. The colorful firm, rooted in early U.S. history, remade an export-import commercial enterprise into a profitable ex-tractive enterprise. Fellow copper giants were memorable in their own ways.

In the 1870s new mines in Arizona and Montana contested the control of U.S. copper held by Michigan producers. Butte, Montana, had attracted gold prospectors as early as the Civil War. The discovery of rich copper lodes was not exciting to those seeking gold, but the development of copper properties was encouraged by the erection of a smelter in Butte in 1879 and a rail connection in 1881. The Anaconda mine in Butte was the largest producer of copper in the United States by 1887, and Butte led the nation in copper with an output of 40,000 tons (total U.S. output was 90,000 tons that year). By 1890 Michigan (39 percent), Arizona (13 percent), and Montana (44 percent) combined to produce 96 percent of the U.S. copper output, a total that had increased by more than 50 percent since 1885. With the increases in output came price declines and pressure to combine already large mining operations into giants that could better maximize economies of large scale associated with the new technology of the 1880s and 1890s.

The Bessemer process was as beneficial to copper refining as it was to iron manufacturing. Bessemer converters permitted production of copper at costs low enough to make copper profitable even at the low prices in the last decade of the nineteenth century. Final refining by electrolysis produced very pure copper inexpensively and almost completely recovered any precious metals accompanying copper in the ore charges. The supply of copper grew rapidly between 1870 and the end of the century as production at Lake Superior increased, large discoveries were made in Arizona and Montana, and new sources were located in California and Utah. The price of copper was depressed at least partially as a consequence of the huge increases in output. Demand increased as the electrical products industry came into its own, wire telegraphy expanded, electric railways became a growing national phenomenon, and the world powers were building new and larger navies. High demand was stimulated by the low selling price of copper. Under such conditions, copper firms able to mobilize the new processing technology not only survived but prospered as well.

The twentieth and twenty-first centuries are part of a new era in copper, perhaps an age in which the ancient metal is as strategic a part of civilization as it was in the Copper Age. Early twentieth century technology demanded copper and increased the recoverable supply. Massive copper deposits in the form of sulphides making up minute proportions of porphyritic rock became economically feasible for development if huge quantities of the ore were ground and treated to isolate its copper component. The Jackling porphyries—named for D. D. Jackling, who encouraged the development of the technology necessary to exploit them (also called Hayden-Stone-Guggenheim coppers for those who financed the development)—were by necessity giant operations. Thousands of tons of ore must be processed daily if the high cost of capital in processing facilities is to be spread over enough copper to keep cost below market price. The two pioneer firms in porphyries, the Utah Copper Company and the Boston Consolidated Gold and Copper Mining Company, Ltd., merged in 1910 to achieve a profitable scale of production.[23] By 1916 the six porphyry copper mines in the United States were producing a combined output of 300,000 tons of copper, more than 30 percent of total national copper production.[24] About 95 tons of ore had to be processed to gain each single ton of copper. A large financial investment was required to bring these giants into production, but the investment was profitable, even in years of low copper prices.

Extremely large operations were not confined to porphyry exploitation. The richness of copper resources, and the profit to be had if the ores were treated with state-of-the-art technology, attracted the attention of entrepreneurs able to capitalize on those conditions. Butte became the home of several giant operations. The Anaconda was the largest, but its competitors were by no means small. Its major competitor was the Boston and Montana Consolidated Copper and Silver Mining Company. As part of the Bigelow-Lewisohn group (Joseph W. Clark and Leonard Lewisohn) holding properties in Michigan, Montana, Arizona, and Tennessee, the Boston and Montana Consolidated was a contributor to a total copper output of almost 54,000 tons (Michigan and Montana holdings only).

When World War I began in Europe in 1914, the Anaconda Copper Mining Company stood ready to become the largest U.S. copper firm. Starting in 1899 with the formation of Amalgamated Copper, a holding company, leading financiers began constructing a copper empire by exchanging stock of Amalgamated for stock of firms horizontally and vertically related to Anaconda, the property they used as a foundation. Through their ownership of Amalgamated stock (over $150 million was issued), men like William G. Rockefeller, Henry H. Rogers, James Stillman, and John D. Ryan were associated with the Anaconda, the Washoe Copper Company, Colorado Smelting and Mining, Diamond Coal and Coke, Big Blackfoot Milling, Hennessy Mercantile, the Boston and Montana, and the Butte and Boston. In addition to the copper empire constructed through Amalgamated, a community of interest magnified the influence of the participating financial group.[25]

The Butte properties controlled by Amalgamated were plagued by the operations of F. Augustus Heinze. Starting in the mid-1890s, Heinze purchased claims in the Butte district and used them as a basis for bringing suits against his giant neighbors. Under the "rule of the apex," a vein of ore belongs to the mine owning its peak, or apex—even if parts of the vein run into the claim lands of others. (Not all Western mining districts applied the apex rule. In Bisbee, for example, Phelps Dodge agreed with its giant competitors to use standard boundary lines to determine ore ownership.) Heinze claimed to be suffering from violations of the apex rule and went to court for satisfaction. His Butte neighbors took similar positions and countersued Heinze for taking their ore. More than a hundred suits were pending between Heinze and his competitors at various times after Heinze went into business. In 1902 he established the United Copper Company, a New Jersey corporation, as a vehicle to hold his properties.

In 1906 the Butte Coalition Mining Company was formed by financial interests friendly to the Amalgamated. John D. Ryan was a director of the Coalition as well as managing director of Amalgamated. There was a business relationship between

Ryan and Thomas F. Cole, the president of the Coalition. Butte Coalition was a holding company for properties bought from Heinze, and the Red Metals Mining Company was set up to operate those properties. As Heinze mines were taken into Butte Coalition and Red Metals Mining, the growing community of interest was used to eliminate obstructive law suits and to permit cooperative development of the vast resource base at Butte.

Amalgamated sold copper products through the United Metals Selling Company it chartered in New Jersey in 1900. Again, a company not directly belonging to Amalgamated served its interests through an expanded community of interests. United absorbed the selling business formerly run by the Lewisohn brothers and expanded into production by purchasing the Raritan Copper Works Refinery in New Jersey. United sold all the copper produced by Amalgamated firms and refined a portion of it. Rather than restrict its business to Amalgamated, United refined and sold copper for allied and friendly companies as well.

Amalgamated interests became involved in porphyries copper in 1908 with the formation of the International Smelting and Refining Company (New Jersey). The new firm proposed construction of a smelter to treat ores from the Utah Consolidated and others and began with a $10 million stock issue. The extent of the community of interest with Amalgamated is revealed by the names of some of the the new company's first directors: Urban H. Broughton, President of Utah Consolidated, Director for United Metals, and son-in-law of Henry H. Rogers; Thomas F. Cole, President of the Butte Coalition; John D. Ryan, Managing Director of Amalgamated; Adolph Lewisohn, President of United Metals. Once the smelter construction was under way, International integrated vertically by forming the Tooele Valley Railway Company to build a connecting line between the smelter and existing lines. It also sold $500,000 of its own stock to Utah Consolidated, its principal customer.

By 1910 Amalgamated interests began shifting properties from the holding companies to Anaconda, the operating company. Through an exchange of stock, the Anaconda added control of Butte mining and smelting properties formerly held by Amalgamated and Butte Coalition. It also gained support firms for the supply of fuel and mining timber. As Anaconda added mining and refining properties, the original companies were dissolved and their operations absorbed by Anaconda (under Amalgamated, Butte Coalition, and others; companies taken in had continued to operate independently). In preparation for further consolidation, Amalgamated absorbed United Metals, the selling arm of the mammoth copper business assembled by common financial interests.

While Amalgamated was shifting properties to Anaconda and acquiring others, International Smelting and Refining was expanding and preparing for a similar shift. In 1912 the Inspiration Consolidated Copper Company was established to take over the Inspiration Copper Company and the Live Oak Copper Company, both porphyry operations located in Miami, Arizona. Amalgamated interests had not served on the boards of either of the acquired firms, but they did sit on the board of Inspiration Consolidated. Amalgamated purchased a large block of shares in Inspiration Consolidated, and International Smelting built a smelter in Miami to treat ores from the newly acquired mines. International also constructed a lead smelter to complement its copper smelter in Tooele, Utah; established the International Lead Refining Company as a subsidiary to run a lead refinery constructed in East Chicago; and increased the capacity of its Raritan Copper Refinery in Perth Amboy, New Jersey.

International Smelting and Refining sold out to Anaconda in 1914 for about $10 million. Anaconda formed the International Smelting Company (Montana) to hold the properties at Tooele and Miami while Anaconda retained the stock of the new firm. The other companies gained in the transfer were held directly by Anaconda. In 1915 Anaconda issued $16 million of 5 percent two-year notes. Some of the funds thus received were used to purchase copper company stocks from Amalgamated. Six million dollars bought United Metals, which was dissolved and replaced by a wholly owned subsidiary of Anaconda, the United Metals Selling Company of Delaware. Anaconda now owned and operated mines, smelters, and refineries, as well as its own selling organization. That same year brought an end to Amalgamated, as the shareholders voted to exchange their stock for shares of Anaconda, a vertically integrated operation—the most completely integrated in the American copper industry.[26]

Although it took a different route, the copper industry became an oligopoly about the time the anthracite coal industry did. Copper did not pass through a monopoly phase, although Calumet and Hecla did maintain a near monopoly in the 1870s. The industry did not become an oligopoly through the division of a monopoly, however. The largest part of the industry controlled by any one firm was that held by United Metals (approximately 50 percent of sales). The financial interests behind Amalgamated may have had monopoly in mind at the onset. They were perhaps deterred by decisions to break up other monopolies—or perhaps they sought the competitive security of oligopoly. When World War I began, the U.S. copper industry had evolved from scant beginnings predating the Civil War to an oligopoly ruled by giant firms already integrated and competing along lines that were rapidly becoming the norm for American business.[27]

NOTES

1. Howard Nicholas Eavenson, *The First Century and a Quarter of American Coal Industry* (Pittsburgh, PA: Blatimore Weekly Press, 1942), table 3, 32–34.

2. Ibid., table 4, 35–36.

3. Alfred D. Chandler Jr., "Anthracite Coal and the Beginnings of the Industrial Revolution in the United States," *Business History Review* 46 (Summer 1972): 141–81.

4. Hudson Coal Company, *The Story of Anthracite* (New York: Hudson Coal Company, 1932), 13; and David O. Whitten, "Anthracite Coal," in *Extractives, Manufacturing, and Services: A Historiographical and Bibliographical Guide*, vol. 2 of *Handbook of American Business History*, ed. David O. Whitten and Bessie E. Whitten (Westport, CT: Greenwood Press, 1997), 105–21.

5. Eliot Jones, *The Anthracite Coal Combination in the United States: With Some Account of the Early Development of the Anthracite Industry*, Harvard Economic Studies, vol. 11 (Cambridge, MA: Harvard University, 1914), 10. For a detailed description of the impressive features of the Delaware and Hudson Canal, see Hudson Coal Company, *Story of Anthracite*, 59–72.

6. Jones, *Anthracite Coal Combination*, 19.

7. Ibid., chart 103.

8. Jules Irwin Bogen, *The Anthracite Railroads: A Study in American Railroad Enterprise* (New York: Ronald Press, 1927), 226.

9. Clifton K. Yearley Jr., *Enterprise and Anthracite: Economics and Democracy in Schuylkill County, 1820–1875*, Johns Hopkins University Studies in Historical and Political Science, ser. 79, no. 1 (Baltimore, MD: Johns Hopkins Press, 1961).

10. Chester Lloyd Jones, *The Economic History of the Anthracite-Tidewater Canals*, Series in Political Economy and Public Law, no. 22 (Philadelphia: University of Pennsylvania, 1908).

11. Jones, *Anthracite Coal Combination*, app., table 1, 223–25.

12. The percentages were Philadelphia and Reading, 25.85; Central of New Jersey, 16.15; Lehigh Valley, 15.98; Delaware and Hudson, 18.37; Delaware, Lackawanna and Western, 13.80; and Pennsylvania Coal Company, not formally in the pool, but allowed for with 9.85. George O. Virtue, "The Anthracite Combinations," *Quarterly Journal of Economics* 10 (April 1896): 302.

13. The Susquehanna held the New York, Susquehanna and Western Coal Company, and the Erie held the Hillside Coal and Iron Company. Jones, *Anthracite Coal Combination*, 60–61.

14. For details of financial arrangements, see ibid., 62.

15. For details, see ibid., 72–73.

16. Ibid., 59–97.

17. Walton H. Hamilton and Helen R. Wright, *The Case of Bituminous Coal*, Investigations in Industry and Labor (New York: Macmillan in association with the Brookings Institution, Institute of Economics, 1926); Walton H. Hamilton and Helen R. Wright, *A Way of Order for Bituminous Coal*, Investigations in Industry and Labor (New York: Macmillan in association with the Brookings Institution, Institute of Economics, 1928); Carroll L. Christenson, *Economic Redevelopment in Bituminous Coal: The Special Case of Technological Advance in United States Coal Mines, 1930–1960*, Wertheim Publications in Industrial Relations (Cambridge, MA: Harvard University Press, 1962); and Jennings B. Marshall, "Bituminous Coal Mining," in *Extractives, Manufacturing, and Services: A Historiographical and Bibliographical Guide*, vol. 2 of *Handbook of American Business History*, ed. David O. Whitten and Bessie E. Whitten (Westport, CT: Greenwood Press, 1997), 93–103.

18. U.S. Bureau of the Census, *Historical Statistics of the United States, Colonial Times to 1957* (Washington, DC: U.S. Government Printing Office, 1960), ser. 225, 368.

19. F. Ernest Richter, "The Copper Mining Industry in the United States, 1845–1925," *Quarterly Journal of Economics* 41 (1926–27): 236–91 and 684–717.

20. Robert B. Pettengill, "The United States Copper Industry and the Tariff," *Quarterly Journal of Economics* 46 (November 1931): 141–57.

21. Robert Glass Cleland, *A History of Phelps Dodge, 1834–1950* (New York: Knopf, 1952).

22. Douglas and heirs were a driving force behind Phelps Dodge, but Douglas's ownership and management remained with the operating copper corporations, not the parent partnership.

23. Richter, "Copper Mining Industry," 267.

24. Utah Copper, Nevada Consolidated, Chino Copper, Ray Consolidated, Miami Copper, and Inspiration Consolidated.

25. F. Ernest Richter, "The Amalgamated Copper Company: A Closed Chapter in Corporation Finance," *Quarterly Journal of Economics* 30 (February 1916): 387–407.

26. Ibid., 404.

27. Charles K. Hyde, "Metal Mining," in *Extractives, Manufacturing, and Services: A Historiographical and Bibliographical Guide*, vol. 2 of *Handbook of American Business History*, ed. David O. Whitten and Bessie E. Whitten (Westport, CT: Greenwood Press, 1997), 69–90; and Andrea C. Dragon, "Zinc," in *Infrastructure and Services: A Historiographical and Bibliographical Guide*, vol. 3 of *Handbook of American Business History*, ed. David O. Whitten and Bessie E. Whitten (Westport, CT: Greenwood Press, 2000), 15–28.

PART IV

Industrial Giants: The Manufacturing Titans

CHAPTER 11

Standard Oil Corporation

The modern petroleum industry has roots extending to the seedbed of recorded history. From asphaltic bitumen, ancient Mesopotamians developed petroleum products that for three thousand years served essential roles in their industry, arts, crafts, medicine, and religion. When the focus of Western civilization shifted from Mesopotamia to the Mediterranean Sea, the petroleum technology of several thousand years was surrendered, not to be rediscovered until the middle of the nineteenth century A.D.

Early in the nineteenth century, when anthracite coal deposits were gaining attention as an oddity in eastern Pennsylvania, crude oil seepage in the western portion of that same state was the object of entrepreneurs seeking a panacea. Just as anthracite was at first disdained as an unsatisfactory fuel, crude oil was not recognized as a useful source of illuminating oil. The market for a low-cost illuminant and the attraction of the profits it offered combined with the medical interest in crude oil to prepare the way for Edwin L. Drake's successful oil well in 1859.

Affluent Americans of the 1850s illuminated their homes with manufactured gas, sperm oil lamps, and sperm candles. Most citizens depended on tallow candles and lamps fueled with lard oil or camphene (distilled turpentine and alcohol). Camphene produces a bright light but has a foul odor and is highly flammable. Production of sperm candles and sperm oil was restricted by the limitations of the whaling industry and offered little or no promise as a fuel for a mass market—and a mass market was waiting. Manufactured gas served well as a source of light but was expensive to produce and difficult, even dangerous, to transport. Gas manufacturing nevertheless contributed to another illuminant, coal oil.

Manufactured gas is the product of heating coal to temperatures of about 1600° Fahrenheit. A residual of this process, coal oil, is a petroleum-like substance. If the temperature in the retort is reduced to about 800° F, gas production declines but the coal oil expands and assumes properties similar to those of crude oil. Coal oil can be distilled into a variety of lighter and heavier oils. One of the lighter oils, suitable for burning in camphene lamps, was marketed in 1856 as kerosene. A market for coal illuminating oil developed and attracted entrepreneurs into refining. The coal oil refining industry eventually provided expertise and market outlets for the crude petroleum that arrived in surplus in the 1860s.

The profitable markets for kerosene and petroleum-based medical products encouraged entrepreneurs to expand the refining industry and stimulated the search for crude oil. Efforts to attract investors to underwrite exploitation of an oil seepage near Titusville, Pennsylvania, led to the publication in 1855 of the now famous Silliman Report. For a fee of $526.08, Benjamin Silliman Jr. provided his professional views on the many possibilities for turning rock oil (petroleum) into materials useful to mankind.[1] Although original expectations centered on medical products, Silliman revealed the illuminating potential of crude, thereby generating additional interest in the oil. Investors, however, were not eager to put money into developing a resource feared to be too scarce to compete with coal oil; even after Drake's successful well at Titusville, investors and refiners remained reluctant to develop oil for fear that it would be quickly exhausted.

Salt drilling was an important, if unlikely, contributing factor in the creation of the early oil industry. When Edwin L. Drake traveled to Titusville to develop holdings of the Seneca Oil Company of Connecticut, he planned to gather oil from the seepage, but too little lay within reach to make a profitable return on the investment in land and his salary. Drake took credit (others made similar claims) for the idea of drilling into the seepage to find pooled oil belowground, a commonplace idea today but alien in 1859. Not far from Titusville, in Ohio, salt well drilling was an established industry that provided the salt essential for the state's extensive pork packing business. Drake hired W. A. Smith, an experienced driller, and on August 28, 1859, Smith ladled oil out of a well he had pushed down to a little over sixty-nine feet. A pump was added, and the modern oil industry was born.

News of Drake's success set off a wave of drilling by men chasing sudden wealth. The year was 1859, only a decade after the discovery of gold in California touched off the Gold Rush of '49, and the country was alive with the get-rich-quick spirit. Promising sites around Titusville were immediately leased and drilled in a gold-rush atmosphere. The potential market notwithstanding, producers of crude oil did not find ready money for their output. In crude form the oil was of interest only to a refiner, and existing refining equipment was devoted to processing coal oil. Refiners were unwilling to convert their facilities to accommodate petroleum for fear the oil would be used up and they would be left to reconvert for coal oil. Geologists knew too little about this mineral to allay fears of its sudden exhaustion. From the early days of the modern industry to the present, creditable experts have predicted the impending demise of natural oil stores.

The gap between crude oil stores and the market for inexpensive illuminating oil was partly bridged by entrepreneurs who distilled crude oil with a couple of hundred dollars' worth of equipment. Like moonshiners, these "refiners" heated the crude, usually in batches of about five barrels, to cook off the gases and very light fractions and to separate, through condensation, those that could be sold for illuminating oil. The heavy oils remaining after distillation were discarded. A five-barrel batch could be worked in about ten hours. The illuminating oils output was exaggerated by the broad range of oils acceptable for sale to consumers. By 1862 coal oil refiners were shifting to crude oil and driving distillers from the market. Economies of scale in refining, the efficiencies in close fractional refining (rather than waste various oils, refiners tried to maximize production of the more marketable products and to offer the remainder for specialized uses), and the superior products from the refining processes combined to give refiners a strong competitive advantage over small-scale distillers. Coal oil refiners also enjoyed established distribution networks, whereas the small-scale refiners had to find markets.

Storage facilities and transportation networks had to be developed before entrepreneurs could begin building a market for crude oil. When drillers opened wells and pumped oil to the surface, they had to either store it or move it along to a refiner or distiller. There were no pipelines in the first few years of oil production, so even oil with an immediate destination was shipped in a container. Pressed by unexpected numbers of orders, barrel makers responded by producing inferior containers that leaked during shipping—yet they failed to meet the demand for barrels. Oil was dumped into ditches, stream beds, or any other natural or man-made container to save as much as possible. Oil brought to the surface was not measured, so there is no way of knowing how much was wasted at the wellhead and in shipping. An accepted estimate of production in 1860 is a half million barrels of oil, but much of that was lost. By 1861 drillers had discovered that some wells would push oil to the surface without pumping. Harnessing such flowing wells increased output, the demand for storage containers, and waste.

Pipelines reduced the problems of shipping crude oil in bulk. Before 1865 producers had loaded barrels of oil onto wagons or barges en route to railheads, for in the early years of the industry, rail lines did not extend into the oil-producing regions. Many other nineteenth-century developers of raw materials used to make final consumer products faced similar transportation problems. Miners of anthracite coal, bituminous coal, copper, iron, and other minerals depended on long overland hauls until rail lines could be extended to outlying areas. Loggers used streams to float their timber to mills, and cut lumber was often floated on to market. Perhaps the most memorable solution to such transportation problems was that of the cattlemen, who hired drovers to move their livestock to the railheads and, in the process, limned a backdrop for hundreds of movies.

Oil producers' handling problems did not disappear at the rail lines. Before the advent of tank cars, barrels of oil were loaded onto flatcars for the trip to market, with oil lost at every point in the shipping process. Barrels leaked or broke open under the stress of loading and unloading and as they jostled along in wagons and on rail cars. Barge travel was not much easier on the barrels. A barge loaded with barrels of crude oil often broke up in rough water or on impact with a snag or another barge. Only with the introduction of effective piping from wells to rails after 1865 and the growing availability of the horizontal boiler type of iron tank car after 1866 could producers of crude send bulk shipments to refiners with minimum losses through breakage and leakage. Pipelines effected gains in efficiency, and the power over oil shifted from those who took it out of the ground to those who owned the facilities to move it about.

The technologies for drilling oil, piping, storage, rail shipment, refining, and selling were established during the decade from 1865 to 1875. Although the oil industry itself was characterized by instability, its technological base was sound. Accommodation lines brought crude from the tanks (wooden tanks gave way to iron ones in the course of the technological development of the industry) owned by drillers to those owned by pipeline or storage companies. Gathering lines extended from the storage tanks near the oil fields to the storage tanks at the railhead. Tank cars carried the oil to refineries. The products of the refineries, usually packaged in containers suitable for the purchaser, were sent by rail or by ship to ready markets.

Instability in the oil industry stemmed from the freedom of entry into drilling and refining. Anyone with a few thousand dollars and a lease on or ownership of prospective oil lands could be the owner of an oil well or a dry hole in the ground. Drillers were driven by the prospect of a quick fortune and had little incentive to stop drilling and pumping when the market for crude oil flooded. The "rule of the apex" in copper mining (whoever owned the peak, or apex, of the vein of copper laid claim to the entire vein, including those parts that extended under the land of others) had its parallel in the "rule of capture" in the oil industry. Crude oil producers were aware that many of them were pumping oil from the same source, even if each had a right on a separate plot with a separate lease, but the owner of the oil was the one who brought it to the surface—the rule of capture. If two drillers pumped from the same pool, the one with the more powerful pump would get a larger share of the available oil. The driller with the weaker pump was encouraged to secure a stronger pump or sink yet another well. As a result, all the drillers on a single pool had an incentive to sink as many taps as possible and get the oil before someone else did.

Landowners stimulated the drive to pump as much oil as possible as quickly as possible. Leases usually stipulated a time period in which wells were to be sunk and oil pumped or the lease would be revoked. Each owner of land over an oil pool had every reason to want to retrieve as much crude as possible before someone else took it. If drillers and landowners wanted to slow down the pumps until prices became more attractive, they faced the task of convincing everyone with access to the pool to stop pumping at the same time. Persuading perhaps hundreds of drillers and owners to control withdrawal of oil was nearly impossible. Neither the drillers nor the landowners knew which drills were drawing on a particular oil pool, so organization was additionally complicated by their not knowing exactly whom to organize.

Investors also pressured for rapid oil extraction, with an eye to repayment of the financial backing for a well. Few investors were willing to forgo immediate returns in the hope of higher future prices, especially in a period of falling prices. As prices tumbled, landowners, drillers, and investors pressed to sell as much oil as possible before prices fell further. Although one well could not cause the market to respond with a price reduction, when the producers acted in concert, the supply did increase and prices did fall. The barrel of crude oil that sold for an estimated $18.50 to $20 in January of 1860 was bringing $4 at year's end. In 1861 prices ranged from a high of $10 to as low as $2.[2] As the market for crude developed, transportation and storage facilities were established to handle it; yet prices continued to fluctuate: $8 in 1864, under $4 in 1867, over $5 in 1869, and below $2 in 1873.[3]

By 1862 the oil industry had attracted the attention of John D. Rockefeller. At twenty-three, Rockefeller was well on the way to making his fortune. When he was twenty, Rockefeller and Maurice B. Clark had established a partnership as produce merchants. It was 1859—the year of the Drake oil strike—and the location was Cleveland, Ohio (Rockefeller was born in New York, but his family moved to Cleveland in 1853). Throughout the Civil War, the demand for produce, rising prices, and the shift in commerce to Cleveland from Southern cities closed by hostilities provided the youthful partners with wealth and business experience.

Samuel Andrews, a successful oil refiner, approached Rockefeller and Clark for financial backing to construct a refinery in Cleveland. The Excelsior Works, built by the partnership of Clark, Andrews & Company, began operations in 1863. Rockefeller and Clark continued their rewarding produce business and left Andrews to run the refinery. In 1865 Rockefeller and Clark dissolved both their produce and petroleum partnerships. Rockefeller continued in the oil business with the Excelsior Works under the partnership of Rockefeller and Andrews, establishing a new firm—Rockefeller & Company—to construct a second refinery in Cleveland. William Rockefeller, John's younger brother, was employed to establish and manage an office in New York to handle export sales for the family oil businesses.

John D. Rockefeller was aware of the human and financial capital necessary to acquire a secure position in the insecure oil industry. He attracted managerial experience into his business in the person of Henry M. Flagler, a veteran in grain and produce. Flagler brought money with him by persuading his wealthy father-in-law, Stephen Harkness, to invest in the Rockefeller ventures. Although Rockefeller and his various partners had been in the oil business only a few years before they incorporated the Standard Oil Company of Ohio in 1870, their operations already showed signs of vertical integration.[4] Capitalized at $1 million, Standard held land and two refineries in Cleveland, a barrel-making plant and timberlands to supply the barrel staves, tank cars, warehouses both in the oil-producing areas and in New York, facilities on the Great Lakes, and lighters that operated in New York Harbor.

Rockefeller created Standard Oil as a refining company then began expanding vertically: backward to crude to keep the refineries operating and forward to markets for refined products. To successfully integrate from crude oil wells through refineries to retail sales of petroleum products, Rockefeller had to guarantee transportation facilities. If he could gain advantageous transportation contracts, Rockefeller could increase his profit margin, overpower and absorb his competitors, and use the yet larger Standard to secure even better shipping rates.

Rockefeller was one of many grasping robber barons determined to force advantageous discounts from the railroads. In fact, the railroads were locked in competitive struggles with each other at that time. As more cargo was shipped over a company's lines, high fixed costs per unit shipped fell faster than added costs rose, so the railroad with the most tonnage enjoyed the lowest rates. Shippers expected to be courted for their cargo: the more cargo at stake, the harder the negotiating and the better the deal for the shipper. Able to guarantee heavy shipments, Standard Oil demanded and received lower rates than those charged its smaller competitors. In due course, the rate advantage helped Standard grow and gain ever stronger bargaining power as competitors joined the leviathan to share its low rates.

Large size was especially important for survival in the refining business after 1870. Railroads in trunk-line territory were heavily capitalized, and oil refiners (most of whom were operating in that territory) were similarly overexpanded—refining capacity was approximately twice the market demand for refinery products. The South Improvement Company scheme was devised to alleviate overexpansion for some of the refiners and railroads. South Improvement itself belonged to the Pennsylvania Railroad: Participating companies (Standard was one) were issued stock, and South Improvement acquired revenue through the pooling agreement between the railroads and the refiners. Rates were increased for everyone shipping oil, and South Improvement served as the regulating agent for the shipments. The railroad pool included the Pennsylvania, the Erie, and the New York Central: 45 percent of the oil was to be shipped by the Pennsylvania and 55 percent was to be evenly divided between the Erie and the New York Central.

South Improvement divided oil shipments and served as a repository for rebates and drawbacks. Rebates were paid to South Improvement on every hauling fee paid by members of the pool. These rebates varied according to the product and the shipping route but were substantial, ranging as high as 50 percent. Drawbacks were rebates on oil shipped by companies that were not part of the agreement. Member companies owned stock in South Improvement; hence, they would ultimately be repaid in some measure for the higher freight rates they were charged and would also receive a portion of the higher rates charged their competitors.

Had South Improvement been successful, member companies would doubtless have driven nonmembers from the business. But the public outcry from indignant crude oil producers brought South Improvement to a precipitate end. The struggle to gain competitive advantage, however, did not cease with the demise of the South Improvement Company pool; Standard Oil simply sought other ways of taking control of the industry.

By the time Rockefeller moved to dismantle the South Improvement Company, Standard Oil had engulfed more than a quarter of the refining industry in the United States. Using its size and influence in conjunction with the industry's low profit margins and losses in the immediate past, the Rockefeller organization encouraged competitors in Cleveland and New York to either join with Standard Oil through an exchange of stock or sell out for cash. The Rockefeller plan was no different from those employed to reduce competitive waste in other industries. If competitors would not cooperate, then the next step was to create one firm large enough to dominate the industry. Competing firms were forced to surrender wasteful practices as they were drawn into a common company and organized into rationalized, integrated units for the profit of all; but the common profit was not necessarily the commonweal, and the expansion of Standard according to the Rockefeller plan was accompanied by public protests.

Even while the South Improvement scheme was in the making, Rockefeller's plan was being applied to the refining industry in Cleveland to accomplish on a microscale the reorganization that would be effected nationally. By the spring of 1872 Cleveland was nearly a Standard refining monopoly:. with few exceptions, competing firms were purchased by Standard or absorbed into the company. Rockefeller delayed application of his plan to the national industry until less obtrusive efforts—South Improvement, for example—had been attempted. The failure of South Improvement was followed by another pooling agreement: the National Refiners' Association.

National Refiners' managed the oil business of its members. Firms signing the agreement accepted oil purchased by the association, refined the share allotted to them, and abided by price decisions and transportation rates set by the fifteen-member committee established to run the pool. Profits were divided according to the value of the member firms. The National Refiners' Association enjoyed a tenure similar to that of pools in other industries. It began by inciting fear in the sellers of crude oil and the buyers of refined products; a pool capable of setting prices for raw materials and finished goods was formidable. Producers of crude retaliated by reviving their own pooling organization. The specter of pool-versus-pool pricing generated an agreement between the two ostensibly powerful organizations. In 1873, less than a year after the creation of the National Refiners' Association, both pools and their joint pact had collapsed from their inability to enforce compliance from members. Rockefeller's plan alone stood as a rational prospect for the overextended, unstable oil industry.

By 1873 Standard's facilities in Cleveland and New York were selling about 40 percent of the output of American oil refineries. Despite its size and power, Standard was operating at less than 70 percent capacity—a measure of the overcapacity of the refining industry. Standard's position was by no means secure: if refining profits were attractive, nothing could prevent new firms from entering the industry, expanding capacity, and pushing down prices and profits. The Rockefeller plan was implemented to prevent, or at least forestall, the consequences of easy entry.

Rockefeller and the Standard Oil executives were aware of the bargaining position their firm enjoyed with transportation companies. Standard was large enough to guarantee sufficient freight to make their business essential to the railroads; moreover, the favorable rates the transit companies offered Standard made the firm even more powerful and therefore attractive to competitors who might consider joining the Standard family. With these points in mind, Rockefeller moved toward control of the oil industry on two fronts: rail transportation and trunk pipelines. While Standard executives secured control of strategic terminals in New York and gathering lines in the oil-producing regions to increase pressure on the railroads for ever lower rates, other of Rockefeller's officers were allying the company, in secret if possible, with large independents. These new allies, operating independently (or so the public was meant to believe), were to expand Standard by absorbing, buying, and allying with other independents.

The Rockefeller plan was not without opposition, however. The Empire Transportation Company of the Pennsylvania Railroad, for example, attempted to block Standard Oil's drive for control of refining. Despite extensive and costly maneuvering, Empire succumbed in 1877 to Standard's machinations. By the end of 1878 Standard controlled 90 percent of the refining industry in the United States. The horizontal refining combination was supported by a weak vertical network of transportation facilities and marketing connections. Standard's next goal, then, was to strengthen its vertical structure.

Rockefeller was hesitant to involve his organization in the construction of trunk pipelines, the new front in the war for petroleum profits. Despite their success in piping oil from wells to gathering points and on to tank farms for storage, many oilmen regarded the long-distance line as technically infeasible. For Standard, the long-distance line held no attraction. The favorable rate structure Standard had negotiated with the railroads warranted no interest in a new system of transit, even if that system were more efficient: Standard was a near monopoly with a vested interest in the established gathering line–to-railroad transit system.

Change came from less well placed competition in the form of the Tidewater Pipe Company, Ltd., founded in 1878. Tidewater constructed and successfully operated a 100-mile line in Pennsylvania from Coryville to Williamsport beginning in the spring of 1879. The line was eventually extended to Bayonne, New Jersey, but the impact of the first segment was enough to shake Standard out of its lethargy and into the trunk pipeline war.

Once Standard undertook to construct pipelines, it did so on a grand scale. Funds were no obstacle to the powerful company. By the end of 1879 a 100-mile line from Standard tanks in Pennsylvania to Standard refineries in Cleveland was under way. Early in 1880, construction began on a 400-mile pipeline from Olean, New York, to Bayonne, New Jersey. An arrangement with the Erie Railroad allowed Standard to lay its pipe on the Erie right-of-way. This agreement at once erased the problems usually associated with establishing a pipeline right-of-way and made it possible for Standard to use portions of the line before it was completed. Easy access to the Erie allowed Standard's shipments to run the distance of the pipe and then be transferred to tank cars. By building from both terminal points toward a junction at some intermediate point, Standard reduced construction time.

In 1881 Standard reorganized its pipeline holdings under the National Transit Company. National Transit soon absorbed United Pipe Line, its 3,000 miles of gathering lines, and its more than 30 million barrels of storage-tank capacity, making it the largest unit in the Standard Oil holdings. With the exception of the competitive Tidewater line and a few gathering lines, National Transit controlled for Standard all the oil pipelines in the U.S. oil industry. Late in 1883 even the Tidewater line came under Standard control. Although it did ship oil for independent refineries, the Standard organization alone enjoyed the advantage of the lowest rates. The prospects for potential competitors were bleak but clear: to compete with Standard Oil, a firm must attain the vertical integration that gave Standard its advantages.

The strength of Standard Oil derived from its near monopoly in pipelines. Independent refineries continued to operate. Standard held no monopoly in distributing petroleum products on either the domestic market or the foreign market (foreign markets were shared increasingly with the emerging Russian oil industry), and Standard did not produce much crude oil. When Standard was referred to as an oil monopoly at this time (1880s), the reference was either an error or an exaggeration of the pipeline monopoly to the entire industry. During the 1880s, Standard cooperated with the independent producers in the established oil regions of Pennsylvania and the Appalachian area in general. Coincidently the company was entering production in the Ohio and Indiana "Lima fields."

Cooperating with producers served Standard Oil's economic interest. The average output per well in the 1880s was on the decline, and the percentage of dry holes drilled was on the rise. The new Lima fields of Ohio and Indiana looked promising for the industry, but expansion awaited a technological breakthrough to permit efficient refining of Lima's sulphur-heavy crude. Moreover, the price of crude was below a dollar a barrel (Lima crude was selling for 15 cents), giving drillers little incentive to seek new oil. The future of Standard Oil rested on the availability of huge quantities of crude, and its supply was a function of the price it brought. So when the representatives of the Producers' Protective Association approached Standard Oil in 1887, they found executives willing to do their part to push up the price of crude oil.

In November of 1887 an agreement was signed by the Producers' Protective Association and Standard Oil. Members of the association agreed to hold production to about 70 percent of the 60,000 barrels a day being produced. For its part, Standard was to hold 5 million (later increased to 6 million) barrels of oil purchased at the current price of 61 cents. Reducing production was expected to increase the price of crude oil. Beyond the higher price they would receive for their oil, the producers' payoff would be the proceeds from the sale of 4 million of the 6 million barrels when those were marketed at the end of the one-year reduction contract. Proceeds from the sale of the remaining 2 million barrels sold at 62 cents a barrel were to be divided among workers unemployed because of the cutback.

The 1887 agreement worked: Output fell, asdid inventories, and the price of crude oil rose to about 90 cents. Although continuations and renewals of the agreement were considered and even rumored, it was permitted to expire on schedule. Standard had achieved its objective of increasing oil prices and stimulating drilling activity. And Standard was registering success in the Lima fields. By the time the agreement on crude oil reduction had expired, Standard had developed a refining technique that would make Lima crude not only competitive but profitable. Abandoning its guise of cooperation with producers, Standard now concentrated on producing in its own right. The producers, in turn, concentrated on creating a competitive alternative to Standard: the Pure Oil Company.

Once the beneficial prices of the agreement period began to fade, the members of the Producers' Protective Association moved to create their own company, the Producers' Oil Company. Producers' Oil constructed a short gathering-line system and purchased fifty tank cars. These small holdings did not improve the profit position of the associated firms, but the new company was the beginning of a larger, if slow-moving, development. Producers' Oil arranged for sale of its members' oil abroad through a New Jersey firm, the Columbia Oil Company. In a move to guarantee a flow of crude to the independent refiners associated with Producers' Oil, another company was established—this one designed to attract producers of crude. The Producers' and Refiners' Oil Company added pipeline to that already laid by Producers' Oil and, by providing administrative machinery for their mutual support, improved the independents' position in both refining and producing.

The independents' transportation needs were to be met with a new pipeline to the coast. Lewis Emery, an independent refiner, was an innovator as well. His United States Pipeline Company was underwritten by many of the firms associated with the Producers' Oil Company and the Producers' and Refiners' Oil Company. Although crude oil was a regular pipeline product, popular belief was that refined oil would deteriorate in a pipe shipment. Emery's pipeline for shipping refined products disproved that misconception; but his innovation had little impact on the industry, for most refined oil was produced close to the point of sale and needed no piping (Standard had long since built its refineries close to its markets). Nonetheless, Emery's pipelines for crude and refined oil permitted independents access to the ports of the east coast for products refined inland, and those with east coast refineries gained access to a flow of crude not controlled by Standard. Philip Poth, a major European oil distributor, handled exports for Emery's operations.

The logical final step for independents was a consolidation of Producers' Oil, Producers' and Refiners' Oil, and United States Pipeline. Each of the companies had been created through extraordinary legal efforts to prevent interference, purchase, or control by Standard Oil. Nevertheless, Standard and affiliates did manage to throw up obstacles to the development of a consolidated independent oil company through stock purchases and court suits designed to circumvent the precautions raised against them. The independents would be forced to create yet another company if they were to attain their goal of an integrated competitive independent. Pure Oil was the company they formed.

Pure Oil received a New Jersey charter in 1895 (a majority of the stock was placed with a trustee to guard against a Standard takeover). In the United States, Pure would use the facilities owned by Producers' Oil, Producers' and Refiners' Oil, and United States Pipeline, and in Europe it would use Poth's facilities. Actual consolidation was thwarted, but the combined employment of the component firms' machinery began in 1896. Plans in Europe were upset when Standard's representatives on the Continent bought out Poth, forcing Pure Oil to establish its own European outlet. Pure gained controlling ownership of its component companies in 1900. Further integration was attained over the next few years as Pure entered direct production and refining, then purchased a tanker to haul products to the European market, the center of Pure's activities. Pure Oil was not a threat to Standard Oil in either foreign or domestic markets but was rather a surviving competitor and exemplar for future oil firms that would compete with the titan Standard Oil.

While Pure Oil was establishing itself as an integrated competitor that could survive side by side with the great Standard Oil Company, Standard was extending its integrated status. Standard began as a refining company and gained strength and power in further gaining control of strategic trunk pipelines. Production of crude oil had been left to the well owners and drillers. Because Standard could influence the prices it paid for crude, it had little incentive to risk drilling wells. The development of the Lima fields, however, positioned Standard to seize a grand windfall in the production of oil. The company moved quickly and decisively to attain the advantage attached to extended integration.

Crude oil pumped from the Lima fields of Ohio could not be refined like the Appalachian crude, and its high sulphur content and foul odor limited its usefulness. The principle market for the Lima crude was a newly developing one for fuel oil. The crude was sold untreated to be burned in furnaces in place of coal, which was an attractive use if the price remained low enough to undersell coal. At 15 cents a barrel, the market price in the late 1880s, the oil was sold for fuel either directly from the wellhead or after some treatment to remove the heavy fractions and to deodorize. Standard Oil was well placed to capitalize on the low-priced oil—oil usually selling for less than 20 percent of the price of Appalachian crude.

Standard had the money to underwrite research into industrially feasible techniques of refining to produce oil products from Lima crude that were competitive with those from Appalachian crude. In late 1888, after more than two years of work, Standard developed refining techniques for sulphur crude. The company immediately altered its policy of eschewing production and began the purchase of oil properties large and small. Although alternative means of refining sulphur crude had already been developed, only Standard had the resources with which to build and operate a refinery of scale sufficient to make the use of Lima crude profitable. A massive refinery for Lima crude was constructed at Whiting, Indiana (near Chicago), and Standard Oil began refining products competitive with those from Appalachian crude while using as an input a crude oil marketed at a fraction of the cost of Appalachian crude. Standard eventually owned over half the Lima crude holdings—purchased at prices depressed by the limited market—and at once increased its profit position and extended its integration backward into production.

Once Standard began backward integration with the purchase of Lima producing properties, it undertook to acquire holdings in the Appalachian fields. By 1891 Standard held properties producing about 25 percent of all U.S. crude. Changes were also made in the refining segment of Standard. Because the company owned considerable quantities of Lima crude and could charge a refinery with it at a fraction of the cost of Appalachian crude, Standard converted many of its refineries to production from Lima. Cleveland refineries were changed to Lima crude, as were those in Philadelphia; Olean, New York; and Bayonne, New Jersey. The Ohio-Indiana oil discoveries (Lima field) had not only proved lucrative, but had also prepared the company for future shifts in the U.S. oil industry.

At the end of the nineteenth century, Standard had a firm grasp on the oil industry. Over 90 percent of American oil was produced in the Appalachian and Lima fields, and Standard held a substantial portion of these two producing areas. But within five years the Appalachian-Lima areas were pumping less than 50 percent of the national oil output. New fields in California and on the Gulf of Mexico were, by 1904, accounting for slightly less of the U.S. output than that from the Appalachian-Lima fields. The rise of these fields was accompanied by the rise of new oil companies that were able to integrate sufficiently to be competitive with Standard. By 1914 the Appalachian-Lima fields accounted for about 11 percent of output: Fields being opened in Kansas and Oklahoma produced about 37 percent; California itself produced over 37 percent that year. Although Standard was a competitor in these newer regions, it was facing giants in the firms of Gulf Oil, Texaco, Shell, Phillips, Cities Service, Sun Oil, and, of course, the first of its integrated competitors, Pure Oil Company.[5]

Coincident with the rise of integrated competitors was the rise of public sentiment against Standard Oil in particular and trusts in general. In the 1870s and 1880s, when Standard was acquiring stock in complementary and competitive enterprises in a bid for the security of integration, new ground had to be broken in the area of organization. The holding company device had not been developed and legalized for ready use; many states even had laws against the ownership of one corporation by another. Standard began to use the trust device as early as 1872, when stock in a New York firm was placed in the hands of Standard Oil executive Henry M. Flagler. Flagler held the stock in a trust for Standard's stockholders. Standard was thus able to own and control another corporation without violating the letter of state laws against such practices. As Standard acquired stock in other companies over the 1870s, trusteeships were extended to other top executives in the company. Secrecy was a bonus of the trust system—a bonus held in high regard by a management interested in maintaining a facade of independent companies when in fact no competition existed. Several apparently competitive firms might all belong to Standard. Had the public known of the arrangement, changes might have been demanded.

In 1879 Standard altered its provisions for holding stocks in trust. Stocks were taken from the top managers and placed with three employees in the Cleveland office. The new trustees were charged with managing the stocks for the benefit of Standard stockholders. In 1882 the trust arrangement was formalized in the Standard Oil Trust Agreement. Under the formal agreement, Standard Oil of Ohio was joined by several new companies: Standard Oil of New York and Standard Oil companies in other states. The new firms were formed to manage Standard holdings better within the various states. The actual management of Standard was directed by its top executives, John D. and William Rockefeller, Flagler, Stephen Harkness, and Oliver H. Payne, with the support of committees of managers from the different operating divisions. The trust device provided the required flexibility for operating a multimillion-dollar multinational business.[6]

The secrecy allowed by a trust arrangement fueled Americans' fear of giant firms at the turn of the twentieth century. Firms with assets larger than those of many nations and enough employees to be a state were viewed with anxiety and concern. Might not management in firms so large and so powerful set prices very low for raw materials and very high for finished products? Ignorance of market operation led many in the public to conclude that a firm as large as Standard Oil must be a monopoly, and a monopoly could charge whatever its management decreed without regard for consumer demand. In fact, Standard Oil was not a monopoly. At the peak of Standard's power, the trust controlled over 90 percent of crude oil production and refining capacity. By the time the firm was dismembered under court order—the manifestation of the public's fear and ignorance— Standard controlled less than 70 percent of production and refining, and the percentages were falling.

In 1899 Standard reorganized as a holding company under New Jersey law: Standard Oil of New Jersey. The holding company device settled the legality of organizational form and eliminated both the specter and the advantage of secrecy. Management techniques did not have to be drastically altered in the shift from trust to holding company, although allowances had to be made for increased public exposure. Regardless of these measures, the public's fear of Standard was not abated. The Sherman Antitrust Act of 1890 had exacerbated the fear of trusts and evoked calls for trust-busting. Standard was no longer a trust, but public fervor for its dissolution remained.

Once Standard Oil had demonstrated the advantages of vertical integration and Pure Oil had demonstrated the possibility of entry and operation as a small-scale firm with vertical integration, other firms seized opportunities in new oil fields to compete in the industry. By the time of Standard's demise in 1909, the industry was shifting toward oligopoly. Nevertheless, courts at the state level—and eventually at the federal level—undertook to change the titan Standard Oil. Legal efforts culminated in a decision rendered in 1909 by the U.S. Circuit Court for the Eastern District of Missouri. The court found Standard guilty of restraint of trade with intent to monopolize the oil industry. Standard was ordered to divest itself of the stock of thirty-seven affiliates, an order upheld by the U.S. Supreme Court in 1911.[7]

The near monopoly of the oil industry was already evolving into oligopoly when Standard cut loose its thirty-seven affiliates. The dissolution of Standard Oil reinforced the oligopolistic tendency that had already begun, for most of the newly freed firms were not integrated. To survive, the dissociated affiliates had to either maintain established ties with Standard of New Jersey or expand vertically into firms better able to compete. Although there is little doubt that Standard Oil was large—indeed was at one time a near monopoly—and its executives were guided by questionable ethics, by the time the courts divided the company, the market was already acting to curb Standard's power. Standard of New Jersey lost its standing as a titan but remained a giant amidst giants. Despite the breakup of Standard and the decades that have since passed, the name remains synonymous with monopoly, great size, and power.

NOTES

1. Harold F. Williamson and Arnold R. Daum, *The Age of Illumination, 1859–1899*, vol. 1 of *The American Petroleum Industry*, Northwestern University Studies in Business History (Evanston, IL: Northwestern University Press, 1959), 69.

2. Ibid., 103.

3. Ibid., chart 6.1, 118.

4. *Horizontal integration*: bringing together in one company the functions of two or more firms doing the same business; the combination of two refineries into one company, for example. *Vertical integration*: bringing together in one company the functions of two or more firms performing different stages of production; the combination into one company of an oil refinery and an oil well, for example. Complete vertical integration comprises firms providing all stages of production from raw materials and transportation through storage, manufacturing, and distribution.

5. Williamson and Daum, *Age of Illumination*, table 2.2, 17.

6. For an analysis of the management of Standard Oil, see Alfred D. Chandler Jr., *The Visible Hand: The Managerial Revolution in American Business* (Cambridge, MA: Harvard University Press, Belknap Press, 1977), 418–26.

7. See Allan Nevins, *John D. Rockefeller: The Heroic Age of American Enterprise*, vol. 2 (New York: Scribner's Sons, 1940), 586–613.

CHAPTER 12

United States Steel Corporation

Standard Oil was the most notorious of the titans among American business giants of the period from 1860 to 1914, but United States Steel was the largest. It was the first company incorporated at a figure above a billion dollars—in 1901 the firm boasted a capitalization of $1,402.85 million. Competing steel companies, although giants in their own right, were dwarfed by U.S. Steel. Republic Steel, with the second-largest capitalization, was valued at $55 million in 1899, a mere 3.9 percent of the U.S. Steel total. The other leading competitors, their capitalizations, and percentages of U.S. Steel's capitalization, respectively, were: Jones and Laughlin Steel Corporation (1902), $30 million, 2.1 percent; Bethlehem Steel Corporation (1905), $29.7 million, 2.1 percent; Youngstown Sheet and Tube Company (1900), $0.6 million, 0.04 percent; Inland Steel Corporation (1899), $0.26 million, 0.018 percent; Armco Steel Corporation (1899), $0.2 million, 0.014 percent; National Steel Corporation (1900), $0.2 million, 0.014 percent.[1]

The capitalization of U.S. Steel reflected complete vertical integration and some water.[2] The corporation, a merger of eighteen established companies, owned mineral rights for iron ore, coal, and flux, as well as the equipment to mine these raw materials, ships and barges to move them, and docking facilities for loading and unloading. In addition, the corporation owned 77 blast furnaces; 110 open-hearth furnaces; 35 Bessemer converters; 60 blooming, slabbing, billet, and sheet bar mills; 6 rail mills; 13 plate mills; 21 rod mills; 22 wire works; 444 sheet and tin mills (in 45 plants); 23 tube mills; and 11 structural steel mills.[3]

Despite such holdings, this titan of steel did not control the percentage of production ithat Standard Oil controlled in the petroleum industry. At the peak of its power, Standard held over 90 percent of the production and refining facilities of the domestic oil industry. In 1902 U.S. Steel produced 74 percent of domestic Bessemer steel, 73 percent of the tin plate, and 65 percent of the rails manufactured in the United States. Its control of other markets was less impressive: 55 percent of open-hearth steel, 45 percent of the ore mined, 41 percent of the coke produced, and only 33 percent of the structural steel manufactured in America.[4] The steel industry manufactured too many products in too many places to be effectively monopolized by a single firm, even a firm whose capitalization was twenty-five times larger than its nearest competitor's.

Although capitalization figures offer insights into the comparative size of U.S. Steel, production and capacity data focus the total picture. In 1901 the U.S. domestic steel industry had an estimated ingot (processed steel not yet turned into wire, rails, or other products) capacity of slightly over 24 million tons: U.S. Steel held 10.56 million tons, or 44 percent of that capacity. The percentage of national ingot capacity owned by U.S. Steel reached its half-century peak (1901–50) in 1907, when the firm's 16.55 million ton capacity equaled almost 52 percent. U.S. Steel had doubled its 1901 ingot capacity by 1914; nevertheless, it held only 48 percent of that year's industry total. U.S. Steel was growing in the years between its founding and the 1914 end of this study period (as indeed it would continue to grow, although at a slower rate, until the Depression years), but competing firms were also expanding and at a faster pace.[5]

When capacity data are compared with production figures, the advantages accruing to U.S. Steel's vertical integration are revealed. In 1901, for example, U.S. Steel had an ingot capacity of 10.56 million tons. The industry produced at 62.8 percent of capacity that year, but U.S. Steel's production of 9.9 million tons was almost 94 percent of capacity. The industry, including U.S. Steel, operated at 41 to 85 percent of capacity over the years 1901 to 1914 inclusive, with an average of almost 69 percent. U.S. Steel, by comparison, operated at a low of 50 percent to a high of over 100 percent of capacity, with a fourteen-year average of 82 percent. The advantages of large size and complete integration enabled the titan steel firm to operate during industry lags when competitors could not.[6]

U.S. Steel represented the final stage in a process of development in the ferrous metals industries in America. It was the largest iron and steel producer in the country and was completely integrated. Yet other firms were able to compete, survive, and prosper. One firm—even one as large as U.S. Steel—was incapable of throttling competitive growth and development. The industry had a history of unfettered growth in opposition to regulative attempts by Great Britain during the colonial epoch. The iron and steel industries consequently took root and grew in the United States almost as naturally as farming, fishing, and lumbering.

Iron had been an essential ingredient in Western civilization for more than twenty-five centuries when English colonies were established in North America. Colonists needed iron products if they were to re-create in America the civilization they had left behind in Europe. It was natural they would seek out indigenous ore and produce for local-demand items that would be expensive to import from abroad. Iron was expensive to import, necessary for economic development, and readily available for local manufacture.

By the middle of the seventeenth century, colonial Americans were producing iron nails, tools, and other simple products basic to life in Western civilization. Iron ore was ubiquitous, and trees as a source of charcoal were no less available. Furnaces were essentially unchanged from ancient times. A stone stack was charged at the top with charcoal, ore, and lime. Air to hasten combustion was forced in from the bottom, and iron was drawn off from below and run into sand forms to produce pigs—pig iron.[7] Castings were made directly with iron from the furnace, and iron products requiring more resilience than found in castings were made from wrought iron.

The process used to turn pig iron into wrought iron, or bar iron, was simple but labor-intensive: the pig was heated at a forge, then pounded, reheated, and pounded again. The cycle was repeated until the metal had been freed of enough carbon to make it suitable for its intended use. If the pigs were processed for sale as wrought iron in no particular form, the product was bar iron. Bar iron was usually manufactured in large quantities at forges equipped with trip-hammers powered by water.

The manufacture of iron—pig and bar—and iron products was an issue in the mercantilistic policymaking of the British. Interests in the home country tended to cancel one another during debates for a regulatory policy on iron. British furnace operators wanted limitations on the importation of pig iron, whereas the forge operators sought increased imports of pig iron and a reduction in bar iron and finished iron goods. Finally, after decades of debate, the Iron Act of 1750 was passed, with the intention of encouraging the flow of pig iron from America to stem that coming from the European mainland. The law permitted free entry of pig iron (at first into London only, but eventually other ports were added) but prohibited the construction of new forges and mills in the colonies. The sale of pig iron to England increased as expected; Americans, however, ignored the restrictions on new construction. In 1762 pig iron was placed on the enumerated list as another colonial product that had to be exported to England exclusively.

The colonial iron industry produced weapons and munitions for the Revolutionary forces and became the foundation for the industry in the new United States. Immediate postwar development of the industry was based on the geographic expansion of the charcoal-fuel technological base. Although British ironmakers were adopting new technology based on coke made from coal, their American counterparts continued using the charcoal technology. Why Americans were slow to adopt newer technology has been a matter for scholastic debate.[8] Until the middle of the nineteenth century, the American iron industry centered around the iron plantation, a rural operation similar to agrarian plantations.

Iron plantations were established in forested areas near iron ore deposits. They were large, ranging from 3,000 to 10,000 acres. Extensive landholdings guaranteed a fuel supply: About 150 acres were necessary to provide enough charcoal for a year of operations. Given a twenty-year regeneration period, 3,000 acres could keep a furnace in business almost indefinitely. Because of the need for proximity to fuel and the large amount of fuel necessary to run a furnace, there were no advantages to locating many furnaces in one place—no economies of large scale.[9] Dependence on wood for fuel also made forward integration unattractive. A forge was ordinarily located in its own forested preserve rather than near a furnace that burned the well-placed wood. The ironmaster generally owned the plantation land and closely controlled the operation. Yet plantation iron production began to give way to a different arrangement in the 1830s, and by the 1870s the change was nearly complete.[10]

Ironmakers introduced a heated blast blown at a higher pressure than they could use in a charcoal furnace and shifted to coke for fuel after 1830. They heated the blast with a separate furnace fueled by gases released at the top of the stack and increased power for the blower by substituting steam engines for water power. The steam was also generated by the otherwise wasted stacktop gases. As furnaces were constructed on a larger scale, the steam power was harnessed to lifts to haul the ore and fuel charges to the top of the stack. This shift from charcoal to coal for fuel unleashed both motive power and scale economies.

When blast furnaces were liberated from the restraints of a fuel taken from the forest, ironmasters constructed their furnaces in central locations. So long as charcoal fueled the furnace, operations were restricted to the vicinity of the forest and were therefore spread throughout the forest. The coal necessary to fuel a furnace was more concentrated than the trees necessary to fuel the furnace. It was an accepted practice to ship coal even over great distances, but charcoal was not easily shipped (producers feared the disintegration of charcoal shipped over any distance—modern producers process charcoal into more durable blocks sized by planned use). Concentration of the fuel source and shipability of the fuel combined to permit the construction of multiple furnaces in a single location to profit from the spread of the costs of skilled labor and administration over a large output.

When ironmasters adopted mineral fuel in place of organic, they changed the character of integration within the industry. Although ironmasters had to buy woodlands to secure timber for burning into charcoal, they did not have to buy coal mines to guarantee a supply of coal to be cooked into coke. But market production of charcoal was limited by the shipping problems. Pressures for backward integration—expansion of the production organization toward raw materials—were reduced by the shift to mineral fuel. Forward integration—expansion of the production organization toward final consumers of the product—was stimulated by the shift of the refined iron industry from wood fuel to mineral fuel and the puddling technology that could be applied to ore and scrap as well as to pig iron.

Furnace operators did not shift to the new technology simultaneously. Peter Temin devotes considerable space in *Iron and Steel in Nineteenth-Century America* to the furnaces east of the Allegheny Mountains, which adopted the new methods several decades ahead of those to the west. The pivotal factor was that anthracite coal was commercially available in the East after 1840. Eastern ironmongers found a hot blast essential to ignite and burn the hard anthracite coal. Western ironmasters, however, continued to employ charcoal even with a hot blast.

Variations in the quality of the iron produced by the two techniques and the market demand for iron in the two regions explain the different timetable for shifts to a mineral fuel. In the last decades of the nineteenth century the hot blast was combined with coke for blast furnace production in both regions, when a high-quality coking coal all but eliminated the differences in quality of the final product.

The last decades of the eighteenth century had found the British refined iron (bar iron) industry altering both technology and fuel for production. The British were not generously endowed with trees for charcoal, but they did have an abundance of coal. The puddling process separated fuel from the furnace charge in a reverberatory furnace, so ironmakers who used the puddling process could use coke for heating. Puddling, or stirring, of the molten metal burned away many of the impurities in the iron charge. This method was simultaneously adopted by American ironmakers on both sides of the Allegheny Mountains. Temin estimates that by the mid-1850s about 90 percent of the refined iron was produced with puddling.[11] Contact between fuel and furnace charge explains the use of coke in refined ironmaking before its use in blast furnaces was accepted: In the blast furnace the fuel is in direct contact with the ore charge and contributes its impurities, if any, to the pig iron, whereas the puddling furnace separates fuel and iron and reduces contamination. Although Western blast furnace operators had to be concerned with their coke reducing the quality of their pig iron (in the years before superior coking coal was available), refiners did not.

After the Civil War ironmakers turned to better and more efficient ways to make and shape steel. The Bessemer process, open-hearth manufacturing, the electric furnace, and rolling mill technology were the leading innovations, although many related developments played strong supporting roles that were not so well publicized. Along with the major technical changes came scale economies in production and pressures for integration that combined to create the oligopolistic industry that existed at the beginning of World War I.

The Bessemer process was the first of the technological developments to measurably alter the interrelationship between the various components of the iron and steel industry. Pig iron was pounded or puddled into wrought iron by carefully leaving in the metal just the right amount of carbon necessary for strength and flexibility. In steelmaking the puddling process cooked off all carbon in the charge and then the desired trace was added with the blister or crucible processes. An alternative, the Bessemer converter blew a blast of compressed air through the molten iron charge to burn off the carbon. As early as 1856 Henry Bessemer claimed to be able to stop the process short of removing all carbon, but there was no way to accurately determine how much carbon remained in a charge until Robert Mushet developed a process for replacing the necessary carbon to a charge blown clean in a Bessemer converter. William Kelly secured the American patent on what became known as the Bessemer process; Bessemer, the patents for the converter (the equipment); and Mushet, those for the carbon process for making Bessemer steel. All three patents were in force by 1857.

The Bessemer process was not immediately adopted in the United States. Steelmakers were reluctant to invest in the process until it proved feasible and patent rights were pooled for easy access. The process had limitations: ores containing phosphorous were unsuitable for the Bessemer converters because phosphorous was not removed by the oxygen that took off the carbon. Once the Bessemer process came into regular use, it was restricted to ores with phosphorus levels low enough to be ignored.

A patent pool was a decade in the making. In 1866 John F. Winslow and John A. Griswold, both of Troy, New York, and Daniel J. Morrell of Johnstown, Pennsylvania, brought together the three Bessemer patents. They eventually vested the patent rights in the Pneumatic Steel Association (of New York). The Bessemer Steel Company Limited (1877, Pennsylvania) held the patents until 1890, when the Steel Patents Company took them over. As the original patents expired, the company holding the pool continued as a clearinghouse for newer patents for processes and equipment that supported the original process. The role of the patent pool owners was that of selling their processes to the iron and steel industry.

Selling the industry on the Bessemer technique was facilitated by the increased demand for steel rails from the ever-expanding railroads and the cost advantage of rolling rails with Bessemer steel. The expense of fuel, labor, and machinery for Bessemer production was less than 20 percent of the cost of steelmaking by either the crucible or the blister process. A license to use the patents in the pool cost the buyer $5,000 for the necessary plans and processes, and about $5 for every ton of iron processed. The licensee also received regular briefings on advances in steelmaking technology.[12]

Firms joining the Bessemer pool could send two employees for training in a plant already using the patented equipment and processes. Moreover, technical personnel moved about within the membership of the pool, sharing their experience as they shifted employment. Forming an elite of professionals, the Bessemer personnel communicated technical developments through mailings and meetings within the boundaries of the larger association. One result of the patent pool and the information sharing associated with it was a high degree of uniformity among the eleven Bessemer firms in operation by 1880. Such technology sharing was simple because Bessemer firms concentrated on the production of steel rails.

To be economically feasible, Bessemer firms had to develop large-scale operations. The converters did their cleansing work in less than twenty minutes per charge. A charge ranged from five to twenty tons and was determined by the size of the converter. Auxiliary equipment was necessary to melt the pig iron (unless an integrated operation provided molten iron from the blast furnace for the Bessemer charge), heat the converter, and process the molten steel discharged into ingot molds. Most Bessemer operations employed two converters: one was in use while the other was being prepared (or repaired) for another charge. The two-converter Bessemer plant of 1880 turned out about ten times more processed iron than the puddling operation it replaced—an efficient plant had to be large enough to take advantage of the scale economies associated with Bessemer steel production.

Economies of scale and integration went hand in hand for Bessemer firms. The converters were installed to supply rolling mills for rails. The Bessemer ingots were held in soaking pits until they were needed in the rolling mill. Soaking equalized the temperature of the ingots, cooling them to the best rolling temperature. Bessemer plants integrated backward into blast furnaces to guarantee the quantity and quality of pig iron necessary to keep the converters operating. Producers found it simpler to provide their own raw materials than to depend on the market for a large quantity of low-phosphorous pig iron on demand. To guarantee pig iron for the converters, the Bessemer firms built or purchased their own blast furnaces. The backward integration encouraged technological developments to increase the efficiency of the linkages between the furnaces and the steel plants. Bessemer plants with the capacity to charge their converters directly from the blast furnaces saved the expense of melting pig iron before using it in the steelmaking process.

Blast furnace performance was improved with the growing demand for pig iron to feed Bessemer converters. The American branch of the Western iron and steel industry developed the concept of increasing the output of a blast furnace beyond the rated capacity of the furnace. The concept was labeled "hard driving" and involved a stepped-up production schedule supported with increases in the temperature and the pressure of the blast, the results of which included greater outputs and rapid deterioration of the furnace linings. From the beginnings of hard driving—frequently dated at 1870, when Andrew Carnegie built the Lucy furnace in Pittsburgh and set his crews about outstripping the Isabella, the furnace of a rival firm—new American furnaces were constructed to overcome problems discovered while hard driving existing ones. The Lucy furnace that produced 13,000 tons a year in the early 1870s (the largest furnaces of the 1860s produced about half as much per year) reflected the various improvements in design and operations when it produced over 100,000 tons annually in the late 1890s.

Two hard-driving furnaces were constructed by Carnegie at the Edgar Thomson Steel Works in Pittsburgh: the first in 1879, the second in 1880. The second furnace, the Edgar Thomson B, was built to reflect the changes designed to avoid defects discovered while hard driving the early plants.[13] The best furnaces were, by the 1890s, producing from ten to fifteen times the output of the best furnaces of the early 1870s. These high-output furnaces were parts of integrated Bessemer steel operations that included Edgar Thomson, South Chicago, Cambria, and the Pennsylvania Steel Company. Typical furnaces produced well below the hard-driving operations of the Bessemer connection; nevertheless, individual blast furnace production rose from the era of the Civil War to the beginning of World War I. The 681 furnaces of 1880 had dwindled to 559 by 1890, but the output of pig iron had risen from 3.8 million tons to 9.2 million tons. The number of furnaces declined to 451 in 1914, but pig iron production that year was 23.3 million tons—an increase of over 150 percent in output (between 1890 and 1914) and nearly a 20 percent reduction in the number of furnaces.[14]

Because hard driving produced large outputs of pig iron, firms employing the high heat–high pressure techniques could introduce ancillary improvements made affordable by the large output over which their costs could be spread. Power hoists that hauled fuel, ore, and fluxing materials to the top of the furnace stack for charging were too expensive for firms unable to drive down their per-unit costs with extraordinary output levels. Casting machinery for making pigs was similarly unique to the hard-driving furnaces.

Over the years 1860 to 1913, the U.S. total annual pig iron production increased from 0.82 million tons to a peak of 30.97 million tons (in the last year of the period under study here, 1914, pig production was 23.33 million tons). Accompanying the increase in output was a change in fuels used to charge the furnaces. In 1860 anthracite coal produced 56 percent of the pig iron, while coke cooked from bituminous coal produced 13 percent and charcoal 30 percent. By 1913 anthracite coal and charcoal combined fueled about 2 percent of American-made pig iron: bituminous coal, in the form of coke, provided the heat force for 98 percent. Pig iron made in electric furnaces was credited to the bituminous account.[15]

The Bessemer process gained a dominant position in the U.S. steel industry because of the demand for steel rails. About 36 percent of the rails used in the United States in 1875 were of domestically rolled steel: Approximately 62 percent were domestically produced iron, and the remainder were net imports. In 1880 the American steel industry produced about 55 percent of all rails used in the country. Within five years domestic steel accounted for 99 percent of the rails used in the United States, iron rail production had fallen to less than 2 percent, and exports of rails exceeded imports. After 1890 the domestic steel industry rolled enough steel rails every year to provide the entire amount consumed in the United States (1892, 1902, and 1903 were exceptions) and produced extra for net exports. Iron rails were no longer rolled after 1911.[16]

Bessemer steel dominated the industry in quantity of steel produced, almost from its introduction until 1908. In 1879, 0.83 million gross tons of ingots and castings were produced with Bessemer converters. Bessemer production accounted for 89 percent of ingot and casting production that year. Bessemer output reached its peak in 1906 with 12.28 million tons, an increase of 1380 percent over almost three decades. The peak year output, however, represented only 52 percent of total steel production in 1906; in 1879 the output was 89 percent. During the years of domination by Bessemer, another steelmaking process was developing into the technique for the future: open-hearth production. In 1907 Bessemer steel accounted for 50 percent of total production and open-hearth steel for 49 percent. In 1879 open-hearth production made up only 5 percent of ingots and castings; but starting in 1908, when it accounted for 56 percent, it permanently displaced Bessemer steel as the leader in production. By 1914 open-hearth furnaces produced 73 percent of the domestic output and Bessemer furnaces only 26 percent. And by 1924 open-hearth production accounted for 83 percent against 16 percent for Bessemer.[17]

The open-hearth furnace uses from the puddling furnace. In its essentials, the open-hearth process uses a puddling furnace operated at very high temperatures attained by blowing superheated air into the burner. The high temperatures replace the puddling action as the molten metal is permitted to cook off impurities. The process can be closely monitored because samples of the molten mass can be drawn through an opening on the furnace, the open hearth. Although some open-hearth furnaces were built to process extremely large charges, the process did not demand the scale economies of the Bessemer system. Small furnaces operated at slow speeds permitted steel producers to compete without massive investments. Nevertheless, the scale economies and vertical integration associated with Bessemer production had shaped the industry by the time open-hearth methods began to replace Bessemer techniques. Many of the firms making the shift to open hearth were already large and integrated.

Several advantages accrued to open-hearth production. A leading inducement to employ open-hearth techniques was the possibility of charging the furnaces with large amounts of scrap, a considerably larger percentage of the charge than was possible for Bessemer production. Another advantage of the open-hearth furnace was its capacity for using ores that could not be used in Bessemer converters: phosphorus ores not suitable for Bessemer production were suitable for open-hearth production. Perhaps the most important of the open-hearth advantages, however, was the reliability of the steel for structural shapes. Bessemer steel was introduced to meet the demand for steel rails. When American railroads stopped their pell-mell expansion, the market for rails declined. In 1887, for example, 41 percent of domestically rolled steel went into rails, but only 11 percent was used in 1914. The market for other steel products, including structural shapes, was developing to fill the gap left by declining rail demand. Nonetheless, Bessemer steel was not well received for many of the new uses because of unexplained splitting and cracking and general failure under loads. The problem was eventually traced to nitrogen that did not burn off in the rapid Bessemer process. The slower open-hearth process with its close quality control produced a superior steel that eventually drove Bessemer steel out of most markets.

Additional technological changes reinforced the direction taken by the steel industry in the last decades of the period from 1860 to 1914. By 1900 the industry was dominated by large, vertically integrated firms, and open-hearth facilities were rapidly replacing Bessemer converters. The integrated operations adopted hard driving as the rule for pig iron production, and coke made from bituminous coal was increasingly the standard fuel. Within this changing industrial framework, the by-product oven was altering the fuel-production arrangements of the industry in a way that not only reinforced hard driving and was linked with open-hearth production but created a new industrial chemicals component to the industry. An innovation that fit neatly into the evolving framework was the electric furnace.

When coke first began to replace charcoal in the blast furnace, the coal was processed in a simple device called a beehive oven. The beehives were constructed and operated at the coal mines: The coal was baked, and the gases were released into the atmosphere. A beehive oven cost $700 to $800 to construct in 1912. In 1893 a by-product oven was introduced that was considerably more expensive to construct, $12,000 to $18,000 in 1912,[18] but yielded a higher percentage of coke (60 to 65 percent for a beehive and 75 to 80 percent for the by-product oven) and collected the gases and chemicals cooked off the coal in the coking process. The by-product coke met with prejudice from steelmakers, who were satisfied with the quality of beehive coke and preferred the lower cost of beehive construction. The development of industrial markets for ammonium sulfate, gas, and tar (tar provided, among other products, benzol, toluol, naphtha, and naphthalene)—all produced with by-product ovens—spurred the acceptance of by-product coke. Moreover, the surplus gas and tar produced in the ovens served well in the open-hearth steel furnaces. The surplus gas and tar gave integrated steel firms an incentive to shift from beehives to by-product ovens and, in so doing, to move coke production from the coal mines to the location of the furnaces. In 1895 the first by-product ovens were built at the Cambria works.[19]

By-product coke remained secondary to beehive coke until 1919. Ninety-five percent of the coke manufactured in the United States in 1900 was produced in beehive ovens. Even at the end of 1914, the period employed for this study, beehives were still responsible for 67 percent of domestic coke. By 1919, however, by-product coke accounted for 57 percent of U.S. coke production, taking the lead from beehive ovens.[20]

The ascendancy of by-product coking and its role in the integrated steel firm's rise to dominance was exemplified at United States Steel. When the first billion-dollar corporation was formed, there were 1,085 by-product ovens in the United States, yet none belonged to U.S. Steel. That changed in 1918 when U.S. Steel built 640 ovens at the Clairton Works, the largest single by-product coke operation. Monongahela River barges brought 1,250 tons of coal a day to the ovens. Gas was produced for plants in Pittsburgh and the Monongahela Valley and, via nines miles of forty-inch piping, to Clairton, Homestead, and the Edgar Thomson works.[21]

The electric furnace was developed in Europe in the last decades of the nineteenth century and first produced steel in the United States in 1906 at the Halcomb Steel Company of Syracuse, New York. Electric furnaces can be constructed for small or large charges and are frequently used with an open-hearth furnace, taking a hot charge from the open hearth for further refinement. The electric furnace can be closely regulated to precisely refine its charge. Electric furnaces were more expensive to build and operate than Bessemer units in the period before World War 1, but they were only slightly more expensive than open-hearth furnaces. The additional expense for electric steel was more than compensated by its superior quality. By the end of the Civil War–World War I period the electric furnace was an established component of the U.S. steel industry.

Despite the high costs of establishing and operating steel plants, steel manufacturing has historically been a competitive industry in the United States. As capacity passed consumption of iron and steel products, industry leaders merged to integrate both horizontally and vertically. They also tried pooling, especially for uniform products like rails, but their pools were no more successful than any others. Horizontal mergers in steel—like horizontal mergers in oil, sugar, and hundreds of other products—did not reduce competitive pressures but did create large firms that were vulnerable to new entrants. Vertical integration, however, provided protection and insulation from the vicissitudes of supply; steel firms might integrate from ore and coal through final products, but they did not usually own firms that would use the rails, nails, or industrial shapes they manufactured.

A rash of mergers in the 1890s left the iron and steel industry no more stable than it had been the decade before. Andrew Carnegie was a giant among the oligopolists battling for the leadership of the industry, but even he was unable to bring order to iron and steel.[22] In 1901 Charles M. Schwab (who became the first president of U.S. Steel and later rebuilt Bethlehem Steel)[23] proposed a merger of the most powerful steel firms into a superfirm. His suggestion became a reality on April 1, 1901, when United States Steel Corporation began operations.

Schwab's superfirm was to bring order to the industry by eliminating competition between the larger competitors. U.S. Steel would be large enough to rationalize the extensive holdings of its component firms, holdings that had been accumulated over several decades of competition. Duplication of facilities could be eliminated and obsolete plants closed and scrapped. U.S. Steel in the ideal could have been the model of efficiency for the remainder of the industry, but it absorbed so much of the iron and steel industry that observers were concerned lest it become the industry itself, a monopoly. American Sugar, American Tobacco, and Standard Oil had been divided under the antitrust statutes. U.S. Steel also had to stand the test applied to these and other titans.

The decade-long antitrust war began in October of 1911, when the United States Circuit Court in Trenton, New Jersey, received a government request for a dissolution order against U.S. Steel. The case was brought to court on the issues of monopoly and restraint of trade. Testimony from U.S. Steel executives and competitors convinced the court that the defendant was not a monopoly and did not operate to restrain trade. In 1915 the court unanimously agreed that U.S. Steel should not be dissolved. The appeal to the Supreme Court was answered in 1920 with a decision to uphold the circuit court decree.[24] U.S. Steel was the first of the titans to avoid prosecution under the antitrust laws. It has continued as a giant firm into the twenty-first century, altering structure over the years to address competition for American markets from a mushrooming international steel industry.

NOTES

1. William T. Hogan, *The Reorganization of the Iron and Steel Industry, 1900–1920*, vol. 2, part 3, of *Economic History of the Iron and Steel Industry in the United States* (Lexington, MA: D.C. Heath, Lexington Books, 1971), table 21-1, 478–79; 559; 592; table 21-16, 557; 629; 602; 615; 576.

2. See ibid., 476–77, for a discussion of estimates of the overcapitalization of United States Steel. Iron and steel firms were often overcapitalized in the late nineteenth century—one of the reasons for forming U.S. Steel.

3. Ibid., 481–84.

4. Ibid., table 21-2, 480.

5. Data are from United States Steel Corporation, *Business . . . Big and Small . . . Built America: Statements by Officials of United States Steel Before the Subcommittee on the Study of Monopoly Power of the House Committee on the Judiciary, Washington, DC, April 26–28, 1950* (New York: United States Steel Corporation, 1950), 154.

6. Ibid., 158, 164.

7. The ancients did not stimulate burning with forced air, so their stacks produced a bloom, a spongy mass of iron that could be shaped by hammering. To raise stack temperatures enough to melt the iron and allow casting, colonial Americans added a forced air flow generated by a bellows driven by a water wheel. Heating the air to produce a hot blast was a nineteenth-century innovation. Shepard B. Clough and Richard T. Rapp, *European Economic History: The Economic Development of Western Civilization* (New York: McGraw-Hill, 1975), 27–33; Hogan, *Reorganization of Iron and Steel*, 1–8; Arthur C. Bining, *Pennsylvania Iron Manufacture in the Eighteenth Century* (Harrisburg: Pennsylvania Historical Commission Publications, 1938; reprint, New York: Kelly, 1970); and Peter Temin, *Iron and Steel in Nineteenth-Century America: An Economic Inquiry*, MIT Monographs in Economics, no. 2 (Cambridge, MA: MIT Press, 1964), 13–19.

8. Temin, *Iron and Steel*, ch. 3.

9. *Economies of large scale*: falling average cost of production associated with increasing output.

10. Temin, *Iron and Steel*, 81–90.

11. Ibid., 99.

12. Ibid., 131.

13. For a study of the location of the steel industry, see Kenneth Warren, *The American Steel Industry, 1850–1970: A Geographical Interpretation*, Oxford Research Studies in Geography (Oxford: Clarendon Press, 1973; reprint, Pittsburgh, PA: University of Pittsburgh Press, 1988).

14. Figures for blast furnaces in 1880 and 1890 are from Hogan, *Reorganization of Iron and Steel*, 211. Production data and number of furnaces in 1914 are from *Annual Statistical Report of the American Iron and Steel Institute for 1924* (New York: Iron and Steel Institute, 1925), 9–10, 18.

15. *Annual Statistical Report of the American Iron and Steel Institute for 1924*, 9–10.

16. Ibid., 36.

17. Ibid., 24.

18. Hogan, *Reorganization of Iron and Steel*, 378–79.

19. Warren, *American Steel Industry*, 113.

20. Hogan, *Reorganization of Iron and Steel*, 383–85.

21. Warren, *American Steel Industry*, 115; and Hogan, *Reorganization of Iron and Steel*, 384.

22. For a biography of Andrew Carnegie, see Harold C. Livesay, *Andrew Carnegie and the Rise of Big Business*, ed. Oscar Handlin (Boston: Little, Brown, 1975).

23. For short biographies of several men important to the steel industry, see Arundel Cotter, *United States Steel: A Corporation with a Soul* (Garden City, NY: Doubleday, Page, 1921), ch. 5.

24. For details of the court proceedings, see Hogan, *Reorganization of Iron and Steel*, 529–37.

CHAPTER 13

The Meat Packers

The petroleum and steel industries have competitive origins and histories almost as old as man. Both industries became oligopolistic: petroleum spurred by a court order and steel by competitive evolution. Standard Oil dominated petroleum and U.S. Steel dominated the iron and steel industry. The meat industry, however, is as old as mankind, dating from the hunting cultures of prehistory. As a modern industry, meat is oligopolistic at the national level, but unlike petroleum and steel, it did not develop around a dominant member. Modern refrigeration stimulated the growth of five competitive firms in meat packing, four of which continue, after a century of operation, to influence the industry.

In the years before refrigeration, meat packers preserved cut meats. Provisions, the product of the packer or farmer, included salted, smoked, sugar-cured, and dried meat, as well as barreled meat and brine. Once canning technology was available in the United States, circa 1818, meats were packed in jars and tin cans (an important market after about 1880). Fresh, or dressed, meat was available locally. Farm families slaughtered animals during the cold months, consumed fresh meat, and preserved what they did not sell. The non-farm population purchased fresh meat from area farmers until the local market grew large enough to support a butcher.

The community abattoir held slaughter stock that had been purchased from neighboring farms or had been driven into town from more distant farms. Frequency of kills was determined by local demand. A small-town butcher held regular kill days for different animals. Buyers knew what would be available on particular days and purchased accordingly. The meat had to be consumed or cured immediately. Killing and packing were restricted to cold weather: low temperatures extended the time fresh meat could be stored before consumption and kept treated meat fresh while the cure penetrated to preserve it.

Farmers and butchers knew the by-product potential of their livestock kills but were limited in their ability to capitalize on it. About 40 percent of an animal goes into dressed meat, and the remainder is raw material for products ranging from brushes to glue. Extensive labor and capital are necessary to process raw material into usable products before spoilage sets in. Although farmers and butchers historically processed some of the inedible portions of the slaughtered animals, the bulk of the raw materials went to waste for want of equipment and manpower to process it. In the 1820s, market demand for pork was limited to hams, shoulders, sides, and lard. Demand for offal, heads, spare ribs, neck pieces, and backbones was not strong enough to support processing, so packers routinely disposed of that waste by tossing it into rivers or burying it. Large-scale production was prerequisite to economical by-products manufacturing and, in turn, demanded a large market for the output and a heavy capital investment.[1]

In the early decades of the nineteenth century, livestock producers west of the Appalachians sought access to the markets of the east coast. Although some farmers drove their livestock to the Eastern population centers, the drive was arduous and expensive, and the animals that survived the journey were not attractive for meat. By 1820 packing centers were emerging along the major river systems of the Old Northwest. Cincinnati became famous as the pork-packing capital of the world. Hogs were slaughtered and packed in numbers large enough to permit economies of scale in some by-products manufacturing. During the winter of 1832–33, some 85,000 hogs were slaughtered at Cincinnati packing-houses.[2] Other packing centers were Louisville, Kentucky, and the Illinois towns of Alton, Beardstown, Chicago, Peoria, and Quincy. Cincinnati packers slaughtered nearly 500,000 head of cattle and hogs in 1847–48.[3] The output of the Western packing centers was shipped down the Ohio and Mississippi rivers and sold in towns and plantations along the rivers, in New Orleans, on Caribbean islands (especially to provide cheap cuts of meat to feed slaves), in the ports of the Southeast (again, for slave food), in the Northeast (via coastal shipping), and in Europe (some direct from New Orleans, some trans-shipped from the Northeast).

By 1861 and the beginning of the Civil War, the American meat industry was developing into a vertically integrated business. Packing and slaughtering had begun merging in the late 1830s. Packers with growing investments in space and equipment could not afford to rely on farmers and butchers for cut meat. Just as sawmill owners were forced into lumbering to guarantee a flow of timber to their mills and Bessemer steelmakers into building their own blast furnaces to supply their converters with molten iron, packers were compelled to buy livestock at the stockyards and provide butchering facilities to keep operating at near-capacity.

Stockyards replaced on-the-farm buying for all but local meat markets. Before organized stockyards facilitated livestock transactions, buyers sent agents to farms and maintained a watch on roads that drovers might use to enter town. Sellers either waited for buyers to seek them out or drove their animals from town to town looking for the best price. That haphazard arrangement did not satisfy the needs of buyers or sellers. Gradually, de facto marketing points emerged in areas

outside packing towns, where drovers and rail shippers pulled their herds together before looking for buyers. The construction of railroads spurred the
growth of physical facilities to accommodate livestock shipped by rail.

Sellers left their stock at the railroad yards while seeking or waiting for buyers,
and buyers went from stockyard to stockyard evaluating market supply conditions. The yards were an improvement over the farm buying and primitive
herding points, but neither buyers nor sellers were well served. The answer was a
consolidation of all stockyards in a city. The leading example of consolidation was
Chicago's Union Stockyards. Union replaced the yards of nine railroads with 100
acres of pens and chutes that went into operation on Christmas Day, 1865. Meat-
packing centers either consolidated or surrendered their share of the market to
those that did.[4]

The pre–Civil War developments in stockyard organization and the merger of
butchering and packing were reinforced by an expansion of the foreign market for
American meats and the introduction of artificial refrigeration. The industry
progressed like others that gave rise to titan firms: an expanded market allowed
vertical integration and economies of scale to firms quick to exploit the profitable
atmosphere. The English market for the highest quality American meats

TABLE 13.1 Value of Meat and Meat Products Exported from
the United States, 1855–81 (millions of current dollars and
millions of constant dollars of 1910–14[a])

Year	Current Dollars	1910–14 Dollars
1855	16	16.3
1860	14	18.2
1865	35	23.6
1870	21	18.8
1871	30	29.4
1872	55	50.9
1873	71	68.9
1874	71	69.6
1875	68	68.7
1876	79	88.8
1877	101	113.5
1878	107	148.6
1879	102	141.7
1880	114	142.5
1881	134	150.6

The current value of exports was adjusted with the Warren and Pearson food
products index series to allow for the changing value of dollars and the
changing prices of food products.

Source: Historical Statistics of the United States, Colonial Times to 1957, ser. U 84,
p. 547 and ser. E 2, p. 115.

burgeoned after changes in the British tariff code in 1843. The high standards demanded by the British encouraged the introduction of inspection systems and generally forced American producers to upgrade their processing operations. The drive for high standards consequently stimulated integration in the processing stages: packers could more easily control quality in their own butchering and packing plants than find it in the market. The figures in table 13.1 evidence the extent of the foreign market for American meat and meat products from 1855 to 1881.

In the years after the Civil War, east coast cities grew into metropolitan centers. The demand for fresh meat that grew with the population stimulated the range-cattle industry, but growing populations also drove up market prices of land around cities and made it too expensive for profitable ranching. Grasslands in the trans-Mississippi West attracted entrepreneurs who invested in feeder stock for fattening on public domain at no cost to themselves for the feed. Grass-fed cattle were herded to railheads, shipped to Chicago, and sold in the organized market there. From Chicago, beef cattle were shipped by rail to the abattoirs of east coast cities and communities.

Change was afoot by 1880, but the new technology of rail transport and the organized large-scale marketing of cattle were still part of the long-established small-scale community and city slaughterhouse system for distributing fresh meat. Meat intended for provisions was processed in specialized packing centers, and only the final product was shipped to the market area. To be thus distributed, fresh meat had to be kept cool enough to retard spoilage. Midwest meat dealers were aware of the potential of the Eastern urban markets; they were equally aware of the conditions governing shipments and sales of dressed meat in those markets. As early as 1869 George H. Hammond had used the protection of winter cold to ship dressed beef from Detroit to Boston. Although Hammond continued to ship a few carloads of beef a year, more manageable refrigeration was necessary to support a large business in Western dressed beef for sale in the eastern United States.[5]

In the years before 1890 people refrigerated with natural ice. They continued to use ice after 1890 but turned increasingly to machinery to lower temperatures and to make the ice. Though ice had been harvested on a small scale in America before 1825, the principles of refrigeration were not widely known. A few people stored ice for household use in specially constructed bunkers (Thomas Jefferson had two at Monticello), but commercial operations were incipient. Ice was stored for sale in Boston at least as early as 1806, and in Southern cities retail ice establishments dated from 1799. New England shippers sailing South for cotton found in ice an inexpensive ballast with a market in the warm regions of the cotton South.[6]

The public had little understanding of how best to use ice. Ice boxes were designed as much to preserve ice as to chill other items. Ice was scarce, but to use it efficiently was to allow it to reduce the temperature of food and drink as it melted. The scarcity of commercial ice was tied to harvesting technology. Natural ice was chopped and sawed with tools designed for other uses. Irregular chunks were difficult to handle, did not store well (the air space between pieces accelerated melting), and required special care to transport (melting chunks could shift the load in a wagon or a ship's hold). These problems were solved in the mid-1820s by the inventions of Nathaniel Jarvis Wyeth of Cambridge, Massachusetts.

Wyeth devised a system for cutting ice in blocks. Cutters pulled by horses scored the surface of an ice field and eased the task of breaking the ice into regular blocks that could be floated to the icehouse. Wyeth also designed a hoist, powered by steam or horses, that lifted the ice from the water and dropped it into a shaping machine above a chute leading into a bunker. Inside the bunker, workers stacked the uniform blocks close together. Insulated by layers of straw or sawdust, block ice would keep for as long as three years. Shaped blocks loaded onto a wagon or into a ship's hold would not shift. Wyeth's inventions reduced the cost of harvesting a ton of ice from 30 cents to 10 cents, a cost reduction that encouraged the change in sales from size to weight.[7] Wyeth produced ice for Frederic Tudor, who sold it in Southern cities, in Havana, Cuba, and as far distant as Calcutta.[8]

Wyeth's inventions spread rapidly. Tudor, consequently, could not achieve the monopoly of ice he had envisioned; instead, heavy competition pushed the price of ice so low that it became attractive for widespread use in businesses and households. Ice consumption in New Orleans increased from 365 tons in 1827 to 3,600 tons in 1838 and to 24,000 tons in 1860.[9] The meat-packing industry made use of the increasing volume of cheap ice first to extend the packing season for provisions from the cold months to the entire year and then to build a system for transporting fresh meat. These changes were effected with natural ice until 1890. Although the market for natural ice continued into the twentieth century, after 1890 refrigeration depended increasingly on mechanical equipment or manufactured ice. In 1869 there had been four ice plants in the United States; there were 222 by 1889 and by 1919, 2,687.[10]

The use of snow, ice, and winter temperatures to retard deterioration of untreated meat is as old as humankind's appetite for meat. Nature's low temperatures are beyond control, so ice is a given—but its efficient use requires an understanding of the behavior of air and ice and the reactions of ice to various chemicals. In 1855 John C. Schooley of Cincinnati patented a system for chilling a room in which pork products could be cured year-round. Schooley's work, reinforced by that of Benjamin M. Nyce of Indiana (Nyce received a patent in 1858), made summer packing practical. The high prices paid for pork products in the warm seasons encouraged packers to use ice to extend their work beyond the cool months. (Enterprising packers stored ice above the meat so that cooled air fell and pushed warmer air up and into contact with the ice. The warm air surrendered its moisture to the ice, chilled, and fell.) Competition forced firms to either adopt all-season packing or leave the industry.[11]

Chill rooms cooled with ice preceded commercially feasible mechanical refrigeration equipment. By the 1880s chilling carcasses to keep them fresh over extended periods was an accepted innovation in the industry (not all packers used chill rooms by then, but most recognized their value), and in Chicago packers were investing in mechanical equipment to guarantee desired temperatures in their chill rooms. Carl Linde of Munich received a U.S. patent in 1880 on a practical compressor that used ammonia as a refrigerant. Although Linde's refrigeration equipment competed with a wide range of machines, it set the standard for efficient (and, compared to the large steam-powered machinery of the nineteenth century, small), dependable cooling and freezing devices for use in the packing industry.[12] Refrigeration equipment in the 1880s and for about a half century afterwards served well to manufacture ice and reduce the temperature in chill rooms, but it was too cumbersome to provide refrigeration for perishable goods in transit.[13]

After his initial (1869) success with shipping dressed beef from Detroit to Boston, George Hammond gradually built a monopoly on dressed beef for sale in New England. His efforts broke new ground. By contracting with established distributors in his markets, he encountered little or no resistance to his products. (The refrigerated Davis car Hammond employed was not particularly efficient, however, forcing Hammond to preserve his meat more with winter temperatures than with artificial refrigeration.) And Hammond continued his livestock shipping business, skirting conflict with livestock shippers and railroads, who feared losing markets to dressed beef: Railroads, especially the trunk lines—the Erie, the Pennsylvania, and the New York Central—had substantial investments in stockyards and livestock cars. Perhaps he avoided conflict principally by keeping his dressed-beef business small. Although livestock shipping dominated the beef business in the early 1870s, Hammond's growing market attracted competitors. Nelson Morris of Chicago, a successful livestock shipper and packer, began shipping dressed beef to Boston in 1874. Morris used winter cold to preserve his beef, and he offered no innovations for the new industry. Nofsinger & Company of Kansas City shipped beef to Philadelphia and Boston in 1875 but was repeatedly frustrated by the established system that favored shipments of live animals.[14]

Slow but steady growth in the western dressed-beef trade within the United States stimulated export trade. British demand for American dressed beef attracted livestock shippers into the overseas business. The costs and risks of shipping live animals to Europe (special shipping decks, damage to animals, weight losses) encouraged innovations in shipping dressed meat. Timothy C. Eastman began exporting dressed beef to England on a commercial scale in October of 1875. Eastman, a successful packer who shipped live cattle to his New York facilities, built a transoceanic business on the experience of others. Nelson Morris and John T. Bate had experimented with dressed-beef shipments to Europe in 1874 and 1875. Morris attempted—unsuccessfully—to ship in winter temperatures without refrigeration; Bate, however, innovated a refrigeration system: an insulated meat locker constructed between decks was cooled with the draft from a steam-driven fan directed through a bunker holding thirty tons of ice.

Bate sold his process to Eastman, who used it on several vessels to ship dressed beef to England.[15]

The export trade in western dressed-beef expanded rapidly in the 1870s—from less than 110 thousand pounds of refrigerated meat to Britain in 1874 to more than 72 million pounds in 1880.[16] Competition drove prices down and put some dressed-beef shippers out of business. While supply was not excessive for the British market as a whole, it exceeded the functional market. Shippers concentrated on gathering livestock at their slaughterhouses on the east coast of the United States. Refrigerated transport was available for their dressed meat en route to England, but these novice exporters failed to provide cold-storage facilities in the ports of sale. British butcher shops were not equipped to store refrigerated meat, and the butchers, opposed to imported competition, refused to install cooling equipment. Shippers were able to keep their products fresh aboard ship until a sale could be made in the port cities, but the interior market was out of reach for want of refrigerated railcars to take the meat to buyers. Solutions to the marketing standoff facing American dressed-beef exporters would be gradually worked out in the 1880s and 1890s, after similar problems had been solved in America's internal market.

Social critics of the late nineteenth century argued that well-financed packing companies were taking advantage of their control of refrigerated plants, ships, and railroad cars to destroy competitors and build a monopoly—an interpretation of events that reinforced muckraking revelations but hardly holds up to close scrutiny.[17] The interstate shippers of dressed meat did become big packers, if they were not already large concerns. Morris and Armour and Company were wealthy, well-established livestock shippers and packers before they became interstate shippers of dressed beef, but Gustavus F. Swift began with modest resources and became wealthy by succeeding in the dressed-beef trade. Economic strength in dressed beef was based on control of refrigeration equipment and refrigerated railcars. The big packers did not, however, seize upon refrigerated cars and distribution plants until Swift, a small independent packer, led the way to a profitable industry. Control of refrigeration equipment was a matter of private ownership: Competition was stifled by the necessity of large investments and large markets to justify the investments, and oligopoly (a few large competitors)—not monopoly—became the market form in the interstate packing business. Local packing, not interstate, was better characterized as monopolistically competitive (many small competitors, each with minute market influence).

Swift was a partner in the Boston wholesale meat business of Hathaway and Swift when he moved to Chicago in 1875. He worked as a cattle buyer while investigating the possibilities of shipping dressed beef to the east coast. Following George Hammond's example, Swift shipped fresh beef to his partner and others he had contacts with by using winter temperatures and standard boxcars with open doors for ventilation. Dissatisfied with the seasonal limitations of weather-protected shipments, Swift rented refrigerated railroad cars. The railroads did not provide refrigerated cars and, as Swift learned, had no interest in changing their policy of building only general-purpose cars. The rented equipment was hired from fast-freight companies that were experimenting with year-round shipments of fruits and vegetables. Swift could not assemble and schedule enough suitable equipment to establish a regular dressed-beef business on the east coast. The choice was Swift's: surrender his idea of building a new industry to replace livestock shipments and local slaughterhouses, or construct his own fleet of refrigerated railroad cars.

In 1878 Swift entreated the railroads to supply him with the railcars he and engineer Andrew Chase had designed. Railroad executives were neither interested in investing in refrigerator cars nor committed to hauling dressed beef. The roads were committed to the livestock traffic and had considerable sums tied up in livestock cars and stockyards. Their executives were farsighted enough to recognize the impact that dressed-beef shipments would have on the livestock traffic, but not so farsighted as to see that dressed-beef shipments were going to materialize with or without the railroads' investment in refrigerated cars. Their decision to force investment in equipment onto the shippers helped create the oligopolistic structure of the evolving dressed-beef industry. The meat packers' ownership of refrigerator cars would parallel the oil companies' ownership of pipelines: only those firms large enough to build and efficiently employ their own refrigerated railcars could compete for a share of the interstate market in dressed beef.

Although American railroads refused to construct or haul Swift and Chase's refrigerator cars, the Grand Trunk of Canada agreed to haul whatever cars Swift could secure. The Grand Trunk thus played a strategic role in the creation of interstate traffic in dressed beef. American trunk lines had a greater number of and the more direct routes into New England and controlled most of the traffic in livestock. The Grand Trunk's northerly route was often too cold for live cattle, a competitive disadvantage that had kept it largely out of the main flow of livestock to the East. Grand Trunk stood to gain by hauling dressed beef; American trunks stood to lose livestock traffic if the fresh meat from Chicago displaced locally slaughtered meat.

Swift contracted later in 1878 with the Michigan Car Company of Detroit to build ten refrigerator cars. Superior in design, they carried more meat than other cars in use and were cooled with ice loaded from the outside into top-mounted bunkers. As cool air fell to the floor of the car, warmer air pushed up and out of the car through roof-mounted vents. Swift planned to take advantage of the cooling efficiency of his cars to carry fruits and vegetables from the east coast back to Chicago; in contrast, livestock cars were returned to Chicago stockyards empty.

While awaiting delivery of his special equipment, Swift began shipping beef during the autumn of 1878 in whatever cars he could rent. To provide logistical support for effective operations, he bought ice harvesting rights at selected points on the Great Lakes and arranged to have his cars re-iced at intervals dictated by weather conditions along the routes. One of Swift's most important innovations was the branch plant. Selling dressed beef required cooling facilities at major market points. Americans shipping cooled beef to other countries were limited to what they could sell from the coolers aboard ship because facilities for keeping meat refrigerated were unavailable abroad. Swift, however, was not to suffer that shortfall. He built refrigerated facilities at railheads from Chicago to Boston, and these branch houses supplied the markets around them. Markets beyond the reach of the branch plant were served by beef sales made directly from refrigerated cars. Undaunted by an Atlantic crossing, Swift broached foreign markets, employing his proven approach to shipping, keeping, and selling dressed beef.

For distribution in local markets, Swift cooperated with established firms. Leading dealers were offered the opportunity of selling a minority share in their businesses to Swift; in return, these dealers became local distributors of Swift's Western dressed beef. If targeted firms refused to cooperate, Swift entered the local markets with his own branch plants. The cost advantage in dressed beef allowed Swift to either drive competitors from the market or force them to join him. And distributing through established local dealers reduced consumers' reluctance to buy beef slaughtered a thousand miles away. Dealers who resisted the dressed-beef shippers used distance as an argument against these incursions into their markets; but as they succumbed to the economies of shipped beef, so did consumers, for Swift passed along lower costs to his buyers. By 1890 the market in dressed beef was in place, and Swift was sharing it with competitors who used his success as a guide for their own operations.

Philip Armour was Swift's first, and major, competitor. Unlike Swift, Armour had ample financial resources at his disposal. Trade in grain, cured pork, and provisions and speculation in provisions were the source of funds Armour used to enter the interstate trade in refrigerated dressed beef. Having four brothers in the meat business (pork and provisions) extended his business connections. When Armour entered the dressed-beef trade in 1882, Swift was a formidable competitor, shipping over 3,000 carcasses a week in 200 refrigerator cars to 43 branch plants. Armour had to match Swift's scale if he was to compete. Within two years Armour was operating 300 refrigerator cars and was responsible for 22 percent of the total Chicago beef slaughter. Swift held 34 percent of that total. By 1889 Armour's share of the kill had surpassed Swift's: Armour accounted for 28 percent that year; Swift, 24 percent.[18]

Nelson Morris, a wealthy livestock shipper with experience in the export market for dressed beef, became a serious competitor in the interstate market in 1884. Morris's share of the market did not rise as quickly as Armour's had risen, but he assumed a respectable third place. In 1890, when Armour's slaughter facilities butchered 27 percent of the Chicago cattle and Swift's 26 percent, Morris's processed 2 percent.[19] Twelve percent of the 1890 total slaughter can be traced to George Hammond's firm. His had been the first of the original four firms to ship dressed beef, but Hammond had not reacted quickly enough to Swift's innovations to maintain his firm's lead. He did, however, follow Swift's example of integrated, large-scale operations. By the time Armour bought Hammond's firm in 1901, Hammond owned approximately 1,200 refrigerator cars; the value of his cars, slaughter plants, and branch houses totaled to nearly $5 million.[20]

Swift, Armour, Morris, and Hammond saturated the markets of the northeastern United States and began pooling as early as 1886, only eight years after Swift had made the interstate dressed-beef trade a viable avenue to profits. Samuel Allerton, a livestock shipper and hog packer, joined the big four in a pooling agreement to coordinate the flow of meat into markets in the Northeast. The pool was directed from Allerton's offices and, for that reason, is known as the Allerton pool. Competition was not impeded in the other markets. Packers were forced into a cooperative agreement in the Northeast but were not prepared to establish pools for other regional markets until conditions of oversupply and depressed prices forced them to do so. A second pool was established to coordinate the flow of dressed beef into the South in 1891. The following year the pools collapsed from outside pressure brought to bear by a new entry, the Cudahy Packing Company.

A pooling agreement had two deadly enemies: the members of the pool and nonmembers of the pool. The danger from members grew out of the ease of cheating (selling more than the quantity agreed upon or selling at a lower price than agreed upon—reverse sides of the same coin) and the difficulty of verifying it. Pooling agreements could not be legally enforced. Nonmember firms could enter a pooled market with prices below those agreed upon by the members. Survival demanded that members of the pool retaliate against the outsider (or insider, for that matter) by reducing prices below those established to maximize profits for the pool. Such price retaliation marked the end of the pool.

The Cudahy brothers destroyed the Allerton pool from the outside. Michael and Edward Cudahy entered the meat-packing business in the 1870s as executives for Armour & Company. With Armour's backing, the Cudahys established a packing operation in south Omaha in 1887. In 1890 Armour sold his share of the new business to the Cudahy brothers, who quickly became fierce competitors in the interstate meat trade. A measure of their success is the collapse of the Allerton pool in 1892. New cooperative agreements had to include the Cudahys.

The Cudahys' entrance into the interstate dressed-beef trade paralleled the chartering of the Pure Oil Company (1895) in the petroleum industry. Pure Oil was proof that a large and powerful firm with almost a monopoly of the petroleum industry—Standard Oil—could not prevent the rise of competitors. The key to survival was vertical integration. Pure Oil was not large, but it held its own sources of crude oil and facilities for transportation, refining, and marketing. The giant Standard was not slain, only forced to accept competition. The Cudahys, and eventually Wilson & Company, forced their way into the interstate dressed-beef trade much as Pure forced its way into the oil industry. The Cudahys faced not a monopoly but four well-established oligopolies engaged in pooling (Allerton's holdings were absorbed by Morris & Company). Vertical integration from livestock yards to branch houses and car routes allowed the Cudahys to shove their way into an already crowded market. The crowd was pooling to preserve profits, but success demanded including the newcomer.

The collapse of the Allerton pool coincided with the panic of 1893. Depressed business conditions combined with unbridled competition in the dressed-beef industry to press the packers into another pool. The first Veeder pool functioned from 1893 to 1896. Henry Veeder served as secretary of the pool. His father, Albert H. Veeder, was the attorney for Swift & Company. Henry, a law clerk in his father's office in the Counselman Building in Chicago, rented the sixth floor of the building to house the two o'clock Tuesday afternoon meetings of the pool members. Armour & Company, Swift & Company, and Morris & Company were regular participants. The G. H. Hammond Company and Cudahy Packing Company were occasionally represented.

The Veeder pool divided the national market into territories. Territory A, the major market area, included those states east of the Mississippi River and north of the Ohio and the Potomac rivers, excluding Illinois but including West Virginia. The percentages of beef each participant had shipped into territory A during some specified earlier period served as a basis for dividing the market. Veeder maintained a statistical service for the pool. Participants submitted information to Veeder on Monday, and he processed the data in time for the regular Tuesday meeting. Each packing company offered two reports: One declared the quantity of beef shipped into territory A during the previous week; the other revealed the closed selling price received in territory A. Veeder prepared reports on shipments and prices, assessing packers who exceeded their quota 40 cents for every 100 pounds they shipped over and above their share. To those who shipped less than their share, he gave the receipts of his collections.[21]

The participants in the Veeder pool stopped meeting after May of 1896. The pool had once again been disrupted from the outside by a newcomer determined to break into the market with a vertically integrated organization. The New York firm Schwarzschild & Sulzberger was new in the interstate dressed-beef trade but was well established in livestock exports and local slaughtering for the kosher meat business. Schwarzschild & Sulzberger was run by experienced businessmen who could see the advantage of backward integration in a market increasingly controlled by the big packers. They had bought a slaughtering plant in Kansas City in 1893 and were using it as a base for expanding into Western markets. The firm used Eastern capital to fund a rapid expansion into areas already dominated by the pool members. Oligopolists selling a homogeneous product at a mutually determined price are vulnerable to underselling by a competitor who does not abide by their price agreement.[22] By 1895 Schwarzschild & Sulzberger was disrupting the Veeder pool and received an invitation to join, but the invitation was rejected in favor of continued expansion at the expense of the pool members. A year later Schwarzschild & Sulzberger had expanded to over fifty branch houses, and the pool closed until the newcomer could be thwarted.

Henry Veeder and his staff operated a statistical bureau during 1897 for the members of the then-defunct pool—the bureau worked with data only for territory A. The pool was instituted anew in 1898 and included Schwarzschild & Sulzberger. The penalty for overshipment was increased from 40 cents per 100 pounds to 75 cents, towns in territory A with more than one shipper were given allotments, and auditors were employed to check shipments. In all other ways, the second Veeder pool operated much like the first. Together, the pool members established costs so that compatible figures on margins of profit could be computed for all firms. They set a kill cost to be added to the purchase cost of the animal. They then subtracted allowances (mutually determined) for hides and fat and other nonmeat products to reach a carcass cost and divided that by the number of pounds of meat produced by the animal (a mutually established percentage of original weight) to derive the test cost. To the test cost an agreed-upon margin of profit was added. Meat was sold at various prices, but if the test cost and margin arrangements were applied properly, each firm earned the same margin of profit.[23]

The pool existed to regulate the supply of meat entering selected markets and to maintain prices sufficient to guarantee the profit margins sought by pool members. Over time, members came to recognize capacity figures for their operations. But neither the size of capacity nor its precise meaning was as important as their establishing base figures around which supply could be regulated. If a particular market showed signs of glut, the branch houses there might be assigned a percentage below capacity—perhaps 80 percent; if a market could be expected to absorb more meat, the houses might be permitted shipments above capacity—perhaps 120 percent of capacity. Margins and capacity were used together to regulate pooled markets.[24]

The second Veeder pool operated from 1898 to 1902 for the benefit of the six giant competitors in the interstate dressed-beef trade: Armour, Swift, Morris, Hammond, Cudahy, and Schwarzschild & Sulzberger. Competition in territory A was dampened by pooling, but expansion continued apace in the remainder of the nation and competition heightened in by-products like oleomargarine. The pool members included new territories for regulation of meat shipments and erected new pools in several by-product industries. By 1902 the industry had outgrown the pooling device and was ready to move into a more controlled, stable arrangement. At the same time, the federal government began responding to two decades of public reaction against the growing size and strength of the meat packers and their ancillary operations.

The meeting of April 13, 1902, was the last for the Veeder pool. Its members agreed to liquidate and ordered the destruction of all records of the meetings held between 1893 and 1902. On May 10, 1902, the U.S. Department of Justice asked for an injunction to stop the monopolization of the livestock and meat business. A temporary injunction was issued on May 27, and, following arguments on both sides and a preliminary injunction in 1903, the Supreme Court affirmed on April 11, 1905, a perpetual injunction.[25] The cumbersome, inefficient pooling agreements were now illegal.

Judges and lawyers argued the legality of the packers' actions while the packers themselves moved toward a more efficient collusive arrangement. Following the example of U.S. Steel, three of the five major interstate meat firms planned a merger that would create a packing superbusiness. Armour, Swift, and Morris began arrangements to merge by agreeing on a division of the stock of the proposed firm (46.70 percent for Swift, 40.11 percent for Armour, and 13.19 percent for Morris)[26] and establishing an advance security deposit of $1 million from each participant. To purchase smaller competitors, the three firms collectively borrowed $8 million from the First National Bank of the City of New York. One of the purchases would be the packing operations of Hammond, previously one of the big six interstate meat shippers.

Two of the five big packers remained outside the merger agreement until midsummer 1902. In July the Cudahy interests joined directly into the merger arrangements, and in August Schwarzschild & Sulzberger agreed to be absorbed by the merging parties in exchange for stock and cash. In October a preliminary financial agreement for a $60 million loan was written between the packers and Jacob Schiff, representing Kuhn, Loeb & Company (the initial sum was $90 million, but negotiation had reduced that amount). The loan was to finance the merger; so in late November when Schiff decided against completing the arrangements (he anticipated the financial crisis of 1903), the merger failed. Cudahy and Schwarzschild & Sulzberger consequently withdrew from the packers' proceedings. Armour, Swift, and Morris arranged to coordinate the firms they had agreed to purchase in preparation for merger. They negotiated a $15 million loan with James Stillman (Kuhn, Loeb & Company) and Edward H. Harriman to finance the purchase of the properties by a newly formed firm, the National Packing Company. National's stock was divided at 40.11 percent to Armour, 46.70 percent to Swift, and 13.19 percent to Morris. Title to stock in other firms held by National Packing was held by Swift, Armour, and Morris in the same proportions as they held National stock.[27]

National Packing Company was officially formed in March 1903 as a New Jersey corporation. In July of 1912, seven months shy of its tenth anniversary, the company was dissolved under the direction of the Justice Department. The dissolution was voluntary but, at the packers' request, would be directed by the Justice Department. While it operated, the National stabilized the interstate meat-packing industry, something the pools had not been able to do. National's directors met in Veeder's office, just as the members of the pools had done earlier. Armour, Swift, and Morris—joint owners of National—met regularly to manage their firm. In the process, they coordinated the operations of their individual firms and regulated a large share of the American meat-packing industry.[28]

Under the auspices of National Packing, the big packers learned to coordinate their businesses for mutual benefit and survival. They did so under fire, as the target of welfare reformers, the U.S. Justice Department, Congress, President Theodore Roosevelt, and the general public. Publication of Upton Sinclair's *Jungle* in 1905 was probably the single most explosive event in that torrid decade. In the novel, Sinclair had attacked the industry for insalubrious production conditions and the sale of tainted meats. Already angry with the packers over rising meat prices, the American public was ready to believe the worst about the conditions under which meat was prepared. The *Report of the Commissioner of Corporations on the Beef Industry* (March 3, 1905) did not free the packers of public ire, despite its objective conclusion that "these companies do a smaller proportion of the beef business of the country than is ordinarily supposed, and comparatively narrow limits are placed upon the control which they could, even if they acted in harmony, exercise over the prices of cattle and beef" (p. xxi).

The packers had been under attack almost from the beginning of interstate shipments of dressed beef. During those years when the refrigerated railroad car combined with centralized slaughtering were rationalizing the industry, the market for beef was changing. Beef prices did not fall, because buyers shifted to higher quality beef: consumers could spend what they had become accustomed to spending on beef and get better cuts and overall higher quality beef. The demand for higher cost, higher priced cornfed beef rose while that for lower cost, lower priced grass-fed beef declined. The surplus of cattle, therefore, was a surplus of meat the market did not want. Market changes coincided with and spurred the decline in the open-range grass-fed cattle industry. Cattlemen found the packers a convenient scapegoat for their distress. Consumers were also ready to join the army of malcontents, for they saw a contradiction in a market that was oversupplied with cattle yet was maintaining stable beef prices. It was not difficult for local butchers to build a following of partisans convinced that the market price of beef was stable despite the surplus of cattle because the packers were operating a monopoly. The 1905 *Report of the Commissioner of Corporations* had spelled out the market for beef, but the buying public and the financially distressed ranchers and local butchers—whose markets were being taken away by the packers—were not interested in reason: they were already convinced that the packers were market-controlling monopolists responsible for the problems in the meat industry.

The first federal response to alarm over changes in the beef industry had been a resolution adopted by the Senate in May of 1888, calling for an investigation of the meat industry in the United States. A committee headed by Senator George Vest of Kansas City examined the industry and, after hearing testimony from butchers, cattlemen, and packers, offered findings in the Vest Report. Their conclusion: the packers exerted monopolistic control over the market and used it to keep cattle prices low and beef prices high and stable. The committee did not recommend drastic action by the government because the market was viewed as a mechanism able to right its own wrongs if given the opportunity. One such opportunity the Vest Committee encouraged was increased trade in foreign markets. Foreign governments had reacted to the disruptions in their meat trade by banning American products, for unlike European nations, the United States did not require inspection of meat and meat products. The strongest action suggested by the committee was the establishment of a federal meat inspection system to help American packers sell more meat abroad.[29]

The first meat inspection law, enacted in 1890, was a mild response to public concern over the concentration of production in the interstate meat trade. The act provided for voluntary inspection of meat products intended for foreign markets.

Packers used the service at no cost. The inspection system did not regulate or control the big packers, and it failed to open the foreign markets substantially. European governments interested in restricting the importation of American meats and in protecting domestic meat products simply adjusted their strictures. In 1891 Congress expanded the law to include meat entering interstate trade, and in 1895 it authorized inspectors to prevent the sale of condemned carcasses for meat.[30]

The second wave of attacks on the packers, 1905–06, broke on an established inspection system that was functioning inadequately. The system neither offered Americans any protection against tainted products (apparently many believed they were being protected by federal inspection although the law was never intended to protect consumers) nor satisfactorily inspected all exports because of shortages of trained meat inspectors. *The Jungle* alerted the American public: meat inspection was not working for them.

Dissatisfied with the *Report of the Commissioner of Corporations* and spurred by the public outcry following publication of Sinclair's polemical novel, President Roosevelt appointed a special team to investigate conditions in the packing industry. The investigation report was to be made directly to the president. Charles P. Neill and James B. Reynolds made their preliminary findings known to Roosevelt in early 1906. Neill and Reynolds concentrated not on the earnings and oligopolistic organization of the industry but on working conditions and sanitation. Roosevelt used the report as a lever to strengthen his position against the packers. He delayed releasing the report but threatened to release it without letting the packers know its exact contents. The president's strategy frustrated the packing companies: Roosevelt had neither declared his intentions nor formulated his own congressional bills to alter the industry.

While the packers waited for a clue to the president's intent, the Senate passed a meat inspection bill prepared by Senator Albert Beverage. The new bill established a strict inspection system and levied the cost on the packers. The bill went to the House, and the Neill-Reynolds report was leaked almost simultaneously: the president's trump card had been played for him. The battle shifted to Congress, where the packers used their strength in the House to counter the president's strength in the Senate. The outcome was the Meat-Inspection Law of June 30, 1906. Although the new law regulated sanitary conditions and expanded meat inspection, the cost was shifted back to the taxpayers—$3 million had been allocated for meat inspection.

Neither Roosevelt nor the packers could claim a clear victory. Meat inspection, though still an imperfect system, improved. A higher level of funding put more inspectors on the scene and allowed examination of more animals. Sanitary conditions in packinghouses improved, but federal legislation covered only meat-packing facilities engaged in interstate commerce. All in all, the new inspection system fell short of the goals expressed by reformers, including the president, and the problem associated with the fresh-beef market that was most visible to consumers had not changed: meat prices continued to rise as the supply of high-quality cuts of beef declined.

The Justice Department remained satisfied that illegal combinations among the packers were responsible for changes in the industry. Nevertheless, a case was difficult to make. The statute of limitations restricted prosecutors to the three years prior to the indictment. The Justice Department's arguments lost strength as they encompassed the relevant three years. A civil indictment was brought against the packers immediately before the 1910 criminal indictment, but however strong the government's evidence was for earlier years, it was weak for the three years subject to prosecution. That case was dropped in favor of the criminal charges, since the Justice Department considered the criminal evidence the stronger. Although the prosecution spent months presenting their allegation that the individual packers had used the meetings at National Meat Packing to control the industry, the defense made no argument. Legal counsel for the packers recommended allowing the prosecution to sink itself with insufficient evidence of illegal activity. The advice was sound: the jury found the packers not guilty.

The Justice Department continued its assault on National, and the packers decided to stop defending it. Voluntary dissolution settled the matter. Before the conclusion of the criminal trial, counselors for the defense informed the Justice Department of the packers' intent to dissolve National and requested guidelines for its dissolution. Armour, Swift, and Morris retained ownership of the physical facilities of National (a forced sale to bidders excluding the big three was not a financially attractive alternative), but the constituent companies and facilities were to be separated and parceled out between them. In dividing the property, the Justice Department sought a balance: A plant was awarded according to ownership; if Morris alone owned nothing in city X, National property there went to Morris.

The dissolution, completed in mid-1912, did little to change the oligopolistic structure of the packing industry. By 1912 Armour, Swift, and Morris had jointly operated National for a decade; the competitive mold of the industry was set. Armour, Swift, Morris, Cudahy, and Schwarzschild & Sulzberger continued to dominate the interstate meat trade. Their dominance was not unchallenged (in 1919 the Federal Trade Commission would investigate the industry and recommend socialization of refrigerated cars and plants to increase competition in the meat trade) but remained intact until technological changes after World War II—especially the reduced size and cost of refrigeration equipment—gave small operators a competitive footing almost on par with the packing giants.

NOTES

1. Rudolf Alexander Clemen, *The American Livestock and Meat Industry* (New York: Ronald Press, 1923), 96.

2. Willard F. Williams and Thomas T. Stout, *Economics of the Livestock-Meat Industry* (New York: Macmillan, 1964), 10.

3. Margaret Walsh, *The Rise of the Midwestern Meat Packing Industry* (Lexington: University Press of Kentucky, 1982), 20.

4. Institute of American Meat Packers, *The Packing Industry* (Chicago, IL: University of Chicago Press and Institute of American Meat Packers, 1924; reprint, *America in Two Centuries, An Inventory*, New York: Arno Press, 1976), 73–74; and Clemen, *American Livestock and Meat Industry*, 86–87.

5. Oscar E. Anderson Jr., *Refrigeration in America: A History of a New Technology and Its Impact* (Princeton, NJ: Princeton University Press, 1953), 49.

6. Richard O. Cummings, *The American Ice Harvests: A Historical Study in Technology, 1800–1918* (Berkeley: University of California Press, 1949), 3 and 6.

7. Ibid., 22.

8. Ibid., 30.

9. Anderson, *Refrigeration in America*, 26.

10. Cummings, *American Ice Harvests*, app. F, 171.

11. Anderson, *Refrigeration in America*, 23–26.

12. Clemen, *American Livestock and Meat Industry*, 212–17; and Anderson, *Refrigeration in America*, 83–85.

13. Clemen, *American Livestock and Meat Industry*, 217–18.

14. Mary Yeager, *Competition and Regulation: The Development of Oligopoly in the Meat Packing Industry*, Industrial Development and the Social Fabric, vol. 2 (Greenwich, CT: JAI Press, 1981), 54–55.

15. Anderson, *Refrigeration in America*, 60–61; Clemen, *American Livestock and Meat Industry*, 269–84; and Yeager, *Competition and Regulation*, 55.

16. Anderson, *Refrigeration in America*, 61.

17. Lewis Corey, *Meat and Man: A Study of Monopoly, Unionism, and Food Policy*, (New York: Viking Press, 1950), 39. Although the packers did not attain a monopoly, they did attempt to build one.

18. Yeager, *Competition and Regulation*, 65 and 67.

19. Ibid., 67.

20. Ibid., 5.

21. *Report of the Federal Trade Commission on the Meat-Packing Industry: Part II, Evidence of Combination among Packers* (Washington, DC: U.S. Government Printing Office, 1918), 14–15.

22. Meat products were not differentiated at the consumer level to the extent found in the modern period. Moreover, interstate dressed-beef merchants sold their products wholesale, and butchers are immune to brand names—they select by price and quality without regard to the name of the firm doing the selling (unless, of course, the butcher is contractually tied to the seller, in which case the market is not operating freely). See David O. Whitten, "A Flat-Kinked Demand Function for Oligopolistic Sellers of Homogeneous Products," *Review of Industrial Organization* 1, no. 3 (Fall 1984): 206–15.

23. *Report of the Federal Trade Commission*, 16–17.

24. Ibid., 15–17.

25. Ibid., 17–19.

26. Ibid., 20.

27. Ibid., 21–23.

28. Ibid., 24–25.

29. Yeager, *Competition and Regulation*, 172–78.

30. A. D. Melvin, "The Federal Meat-Inspection Service," in *Twenty-third Annual Report of the Bureau of Animal Industry for the Year 1906* (Washington, DC: U.S. Department of Agriculture, 1908), 65–100.

Selected Bibliography

Adams, Frederick Upham. *Conquest of the Tropics: The Story of the Creative Enterprises Conducted by the United Fruit Company*. Romance of Big Business, vol. 1. Garden City, NY: Doubleday, Page, 1914.

Adams, Kramer A. *Logging Railroads of the West*. Seattle, WA: Superior, 1961.

Akin, Edward N. *Flagler: Rockefeller Partner and Florida Baron*. Kent, Ohio: Kent State University Press, 1988. Reprint. Gainesville: University Press of Florida, A Florida Sand Dollar Book, 1992.

Alvarez, Eugene. *Travel on Southern Antebellum Railroads, 1828–1860*. University, AL: University of Alabama Press, 1974.

American Lumberman. *American Lumbermen: The Personal History and Public and Business Achievements of ... Eminent Lumbermen of the United States*. 3 vols. Chicago, IL: American Lumberman, 1905–1906.

Anderson, Oscar E., Jr. *Refrigeration in America: A History of a New Technology and Its Impact*. Princeton, NJ: Princeton University Press, 1953.

Andreano, Ralph L., ed. *The Economic Impact of the American Civil War*. Cambridge, MA: Schenkman, 1962.

Apelt, Brian. *The Corporation: A Centennial Biography of United States Steel Corporation, 1901–2001*. Edited by Warren Hull. Pittsburgh, PA: University of Pittsburgh, Cathedral Publishing, 2000.

Athearn, Robert G. *Union Pacific Country*. Chicago, IL: Rand McNally, 1971. Reprint. Lincoln: University of Nebraska Press, A Bison Book, 1976.

Atherton, Lewis E. *The Cattle Kings*. Bloomington: Indiana University Press, 1961.

Aurand, Harold W. *From the Molly Maguires to the United Mine Workers: The Social Ecology of an Industrial Union, 1869–1897*. Philadelphia, PA: Temple University Press, 1971.

Baldwin, Leland D. *The Keelboat Age on Western Waters*. Ph.D. diss., University of Michigan, 1932. Pittsburgh, PA: University of Pittsburgh Press, 1941.

Barrett, James R. *Work and Community in the Jungle: Chicago's Packinghouse Workers, 1894–1922*. The Working Class in American History. Urbana: University of Illinois Press, 1987.

Beachley, Charles E., comp. *History of the Consolidation Coal Company, 1864–1934.* New York: Consolidation Coal Company, 1934.

Bell, Mary T. *Cutting across Time: Logging, Rafting, and Milling the Forests of Lake Superior.* Schroeder, MN: Schroeder Area Historical Society; distributed by the Dry Store, 1999.

Berglund, Abraham. *The United States Steel Corporation: A Study of the Growth and Influence of Combination in the Iron and Steel Industry.* Studies in History, Economics and Public Law, vol. 27, no. 2. New York: Columbia University Press, 1907.

Bigelow, P. "Bonanza Farms of the West." *Atlantic Monthly* 45 (January 1880): 33–44.

Bining, Arthur C. *Pennsylvania Iron Manufacture in the Eighteenth Century.* Harrisburg: Pennsylvania Historical Commission Publications, 1938. Library of Early American Business and Industry, 39. Reprints of Economic Classics. New York: Kelly, 1970.

Bissell, Don. *The First Conglomerate: 145 Years of the Singer Sewing Machine Company.* Brunswick, ME: Audenreed Press, 1999.

Black, Robert C. *The Railroads of the Confederacy.* Chapel Hill: University of North Carolina Press, 1952.

Blatz, Perry K. *Democratic Miners: Work and Labor Relations in the Anthracite Coal Industry, 1875–1925.* Albany: State University of New York Press, 1994.

Bogen, Jules Irwin. *The Anthracite Railroads: A Study in American Railroad Enterprise.* New York: Ronald Press, 1927.

Bradley, Lenore K. *Robert Alexander Long: A Lumberman of the Gilded Age.* Durham, NC: Forest History Society; distributed by Duke University Press, 1989.

Brandon, Ruth. *A Capitalist Romance: Singer and the Sewing Machine.* Philadelphia, PA: Lippincott, 1977.

Brann, W. L. *The Romance of Montgomery Ward and Company.* New York: N.p., 1929.

Briggs, Harold E. "Early Bonanza Farming in the Red River Valley of the North." *Agricultural History* 6 (January 1932): 26–37.

Bringhurst, Bruce. *Antitrust and the Oil Monopoly: The Standard Oil Cases, 1890–1911.* Contributions in Legal Studies, no. 8. Westport, CT: Greenwood Press, 1979.

Broehl, Wayne G. *The Molly Maguires.* Cambridge, MA: Harvard University Press, 1964.

Brooks, John. *Telephone: The First Hundred Years.* New York: Harper & Row, 1976.

Brown, Nelson C. *The American Lumber Industry, Embracing the Principal Features of the Resources, Production, Distribution, and Utilization of Lumber in the United States.* New York: J. Wiley & Sons, 1923.

Bruchey, Stuart W. *The Roots of American Economic Growth, 1607–1861: An Essay in Social Causation.* New York: Harper & Row, Harper Torchbooks, 1968.

Burt, Jesse C. "Sherman, Railroad General." *Civil War History* 11 (March 1956): 45–54.

Bushnell, Charles Joseph. *The Social Problem at the Chicago Stockyards.* Chicago, IL: University of Chicago Press, 1902.

Casey, Robert J., and William A. S. Douglas. *The Lackawanna Story: The First Hundred Years of the Delaware, Lackawanna and Western Railroad.* New York: McGraw-Hill, 1951.

Chamberlain, John. *The Enterprising Americans: A Business History of the United States.* New York: Harper & Row, 1974.

Chandler, Alfred D., Jr. "The Beginnings of 'Big Business' in American Industry." *Business History Review* 33 (Spring 1959): 1–31.

———. "The Railroads: Pioneers in Modern Corporate Management." *Business History Review* 39 (Winter 1965): 16–40.

————. "Anthracite Coal and the Beginnings of the Industrial Revolution in the United States." *Business History Review* 46 (Summer 1972): 141–81.

————. *The Visible Hand: The Managerial Revolution in American Business.* Cambridge, MA: Harvard University Press, Belknap Press, 1977.

————. *Scale and Scope: The Dynamics of Industrial Capitalism.* Cambridge, MA: Harvard University Press, Belknap Press, 1990.

————. *Strategy and Structure: Chapters in the History of the Industrial Enterprise.* Cambridge, MA: MIT Press, 1990.

Chaput, Donald. *The Cliff: America's First Great Copper Mine.* Kalamazoo, MI: Sequoia Press, 1971.

Christenson, Carroll L. *Economic Redevelopment in Bituminous Coal: The Special Case of Technological Advance in United States Coal Mines, 1930–1960.* Wertheim Publications in Industrial Relations. Cambridge, MA: Harvard University Press, 1962.

Clark, Victor C. *History of Manufactures in the United States.* 3 vols. New York: McGraw-Hill for the Carnegie Institution of Washington, DC, 1929.

Cleland, Robert Glass. *A History of Phelps Dodge, 1834–1950.* New York: Knopf, 1952.

Clemen, Rudolf Alexander. *The American Livestock and Meat Industry.* New York: Ronald Press, 1923.

Clough, Shepard B., and Richard T. Rapp. *European Economic History: The Economic Development of Western Civilization.* 3d ed. New York: McGraw-Hill, 1975.

Coffin, C. C. "Dakota Wheat Fields." *Harper's New Monthly Magazine* 60 (March 1880): 529–35.

Cole, Arthur Charles. *The Era of the Civil War, 1848–1870.* Springfield, IL: Springfield Centennial Commission, 1919.

Cole, Arthur H. "The American Rice-Growing Industry: A Study of Comparative Advantage." *Quarterly Journal of Economics* 41 (August 1927): 595–643.

Compton, Wilson M. *The Organization of the Lumber Industry, with Special Reference to the Influences Determining the Prices of Lumber in the United States.* Princeton, NJ: Princeton University Press, 1916.

Conley, Philip M. *History of the West Virginia Coal Industry.* Charleston, WV: Education Foundation, 1960.

Conrad, Alfred H., and John R. Meyer. *The Economics of Slavery and Other Studies in Econometric History.* Chicago, IL: Aldine, 1964.

Cooke, Jacob E., ed. *The Reports of Alexander Hamilton.* American Perspectives. New York: Harper & Row, 1964.

Corey, Lewis. *Meat and Man: A Study of Monopoly, Unionism, and Food Policy.* New York: Viking Press, 1950.

Corina, Maurice. *Trust in Tobacco: The Anglo-American Struggle for Power.* New York: St. Martin's Press, 1975.

Cotter, Arundel. *United States Steel: A Corporation with a Soul.* Enl. ed., *Authentic History of the United States Steel Corporation.* New York: Moody Magazine and Book Company, 1916. Garden City, NY: Doubleday, Page, 1921.

Cox, Thomas R. *Mills and Markets: A History of the Pacific Coast Lumber Industry to 1900.* Emil and Kathleen Sick Lecture-Book Series in Western History and Biography. Seattle: University of Washington Press, 1974.

Crowley, John E. *The Privileges of Independence: Neomercantilism and the American Revolution.* Early America. Baltimore, MD: Johns Hopkins University Press, 1993.

Cummings, Richard O. *The American Ice Harvests: A Historical Study in Technology, 1800–1918*. Berkeley: University of California Press, 1949.

Cunningham, Bill. *On Bended Knees: The Night Rider Story*. Nashville, TN: McClanahan, 1983.

Curry, Mary Elizabeth. *Creating an American Institution: The Merchandising Genius of J. C. Penney*. Garland Studies in Entrepreneurship. New York: Garland, 1993.

Davies, Robert Bruce. *Peacefully Working to Conquer the World: Singer Sewing Machines in Foreign Markets, 1854–1920*. American Business Abroad. New York: Arno Press, 1976.

Davis, Richard C., ed. *Encyclopedia of American Forest and Conservation History*. 2 vols. New York: Macmillan, 1983.

Depew, Chauncey M., ed. *One Hundred Years of American Commerce*. New York: D. O. Haynes, 1895.

Dickerson, Oliver M. *The Navigation Acts and the American Revolution*. Philadelphia: University of Pennsylvania Press, 1951.

Dilts, James D. *The Great Road: The Building of the Baltimore and Ohio, the Nation's First Railroad, 1828–1853*. Stanford, CA: Stanford University Press, 1993.

Dragon, Andrea C. "Zinc." In *Infrastructure and Services: A Historiographical and Bibliographical Guide*. Vol. 3 of *Handbook of American Business History*, edited by David O. Whitten and Bessie E. Whitten, 15–28. Westport, CT: Greenwood Press, 2000.

Du Boff, Richard B. "Business Demand and the Development of the Telegraph in the United States, 1844–1860." *Business History Review* (Winter 1980): 459–79.

Eastley, Charles M. *The Singer Saga*. Braunton, Devon: Merlin Books, 1983.

Eavenson, Howard Nicholas. *Coal Through the Ages*. New York: American Institute of Mining and Metallurgical Engineers, 1935.

———. *The First Century and a Quarter of American Coal Industry*. Pittsburgh, PA: Baltimore Weekly Press, 1942.

Eichner, Alfred S. *The Emergence of Oligopoly: Sugar Refining as a Case Study*. Baltimore, MD: Johns Hopkins Press, 1969.

Elias, Stephen N. *Alexander T. Stewart: The Forgotten Merchant Prince*. Westport, CT: Praeger, 1992.

Engerman, Stanley. "The Economic Impact of the Civil War." *Explorations in Economic History* 3 (Spring 1966): 176–99.

Ershkowitz, Herbert. *John Wanamaker: Philadelphia Merchant*. Conshohocren, PA: Combined Pub., 1999.

Eyle, Alexandra. *Charles Lathrop Pack: Timberman, Forest Conservationist, and Pioneer in Forest Education*. Syracuse, NY: State University of New York, College of Environmental Science and Forestry, ESF College Foundation, 1994.

Fairbanks, William L., and William S. Hamill. *The Coal-Mining Industry of Maryland*. Baltimore: Baltimore Association of Commerce, Maryland Development Bureau, 1932.

Ferry, John William. *A History of the Department Store*. New York: Macmillan, 1960.

Ficken, Robert E. *The Forested Land: A History of Lumbering in Western Washington*. Durham, NC: Forest History Society; Seattle: University of Washington Press, 1987.

Fishlow, Albert. *American Railroads and the Transformation of the Antebellum Economy*. Harvard Economic Studies, vol. 127. Cambridge, MA: Harvard University Press, 1965.

Fite, Emerson D. *Social and Industrial Conditions in the North During the Civil War*. New York: Macmillan, 1910. Reprint. New York: P. Smith, 1930.

Fogel, Robert W. *The Union Pacific Railroad: A Case in Premature Enterprise.* Johns Hopkins University Studies in Historical and Political Science, vol. 78, no. 2. Baltimore, MD: Johns Hopkins Press, 1960.

————. *Railroads and American Economic Growth: Essays in Econometric History.* Baltimore, MD: Johns Hopkins Press, 1964.

Forbes, Robert James. *Studies in Early Petroleum History.* Leiden, Netherlands: E. J. Brill, 1958. Reprint. History and Politics of Oil. Westport, CT: Hyperion Press, 1976.

Fraginals, Manuel Moreno. *The Sugarmill: The Socioeconomic Complex of Sugar in Cuba, 1760–1860.* New York: Monthly Review Press, 1976.

Fries, Robert F. "The Mississippi River Logging Company and the Struggle for the Free Navigation of Logs, 1865–1900." *Mississippi Valley Historical Review* 35 (June 1948–March 1949): 429–48.

————. *Empire in Pine: The Story of Lumbering in Wisconsin, 1830–1900.* Madison: State Historical Society of Wisconsin, 1951.

Frink, Maurice, W. Turrentine Jackson, and Agnes Wright Spring. *When Grass Was King: Contributions to the Western Range Cattle Industry Study.* Boulder: University of Colorado Press, 1956.

Gagnon, John G., with photography by Don Waatti and drawings by Sandy Slater. *Hard Maple, Hard Work.* Marquette: Northern Michigan University Press in cooperation with the College of Arts and Sciences, 1996.

Gallman, Robert E., ed. *Recent Developments in the Study of Business and Economic History: Essays in Memory of Herman E. Krooss.* Greenwich, CT: JAI Press, 1977.

Gates, Paul Wallace. "Large Scale Farming in Illinois, 1850–1870." *Agricultural History* 6 (January 1932): 14–25.

————. *Agriculture and the Civil War.* The Impact of the Civil War. New York: Knopf, 1965.

————. *The Farmer's Age: Agriculture, 1815–1860.* Economic History of the United States, vol. 3. New York: Holt, Rinehart & Winston, 1960; New York: Harper Torchbooks, 1968.

————. *Jeffersonian Dream: Studies in the History of American Land Policy and Development.* Edited by Allan G. Bogue and Margaret Beattie Bogue. Historians of the Frontier and American West. Albuquerque: University of New Mexico Press, 1996.

Gerrell, Pete. *Old Trees: The Illustrated History of Logging the Virgin Timber in the Southeastern United States.* Crawfordville, FL: Southern Yellow Pine Pub., 2000.

Gibb, George S., and E. H. Knowlton. *The Resurgent Years, 1911–1927.* Vol. 2 of *History of Standard Oil Company (New Jersey).* New York: Harper, 1956. Reprint. Companies and Men. Arno Press, 1976.

Giebelhaus, August W. *Business and Government in the Oil Industry: A Case Study of Sun Oil, 1876–1945.* Industrial Development and the Social Fabric, vol. 5. Greenwich, CT: JAI Press, 1980.

Gilchrist, David T., and W. David Lewis, eds. *Economic Change in the Civil War Era.* Greenville, DE: Eleutherian Mills-Hagley Foundation, 1965.

Goodrich, Carter. *Government Promotion of American Canals and Railroads, 1800–1890.* New York: Columbia University Press, 1960.

————. *The Government and the Economy, 1783–1861.* American Heritage Series, AHS 65. Indianapolis, IN: Bobbs-Merrill, 1967.

Gove, Bill. *J. E. Henry's Logging Railroads: The History of the East Branch & Lincoln and the Zealand Valley Railroads*. Littleton, NH: Bondcliff Books, 1998.

Greely, William B. *Some Public and Economic Aspects of the Lumber Industry*. Washington, DC: U.S. Government Printing Office, 1917.

Hacker, Louis M. *The Triumph of American Capitalism: The Development of Forces in American History to the End of the Nineteenth Century*. New York: Simon & Schuster, 1940.

Haites, Erik F., and James Mak. "Ohio and Mississippi River Transportation 1810–1860." *Explorations in Economic History* 8 (Winter 1970): 153–80.

———. "The Decline of Steamboating on the Antebellum Western Rivers: Some New Evidence and an Alternative Hypothesis." *Explorations in Economic History* 11 (Fall 1973): 25–36.

Haites, Erik F., James Mak, and Gary M. Walton. *Western River Transportation: The Era of Early Internal Development, 1810–1860*. Johns Hopkins University Studies in Historical and Political Science, ser. 93, no. 2. Baltimore, MD: Johns Hopkins University Press, 1975.

Hamilton, Neil A. *American Business Leaders: From Colonial Times to the Present*. Santa Barbara, CA: ABC-CLIO, 1999.

Hamilton, Walton H., and Helen R. Wright. *The Case of Bituminous Coal*. Investigations in Industry and Labor. New York: Macmillan in association with the Brookings Institution, Institute of Economics, 1926.

———. *A Way of Order for Bituminous Coal*. Investigations in Industry and Labor. New York: Macmillan in association with the Brookings Institution, Institute of Economics, 1928.

Hammond, Matthew B. *The Cotton Culture and the Cotton Trade*. Part 1, *The Cotton Industry: An Essay in American Economic History*. Publications of the American Economic Association, n.s., no. 1. New York: Macmillan for the American Economic Association, 1897.

Hanlon, Howard A. *The Bull-Hunchers: A Saga of the Three and a Half Centuries of Harvesting the Forest Crops of the Tidewater Low Country*. Parsons, WV: McClain Printing, 1970.

Harper, Ann K. *The Location of the United States Steel Industry, 1879–1919*. Ph.D. diss., Johns Hopkins University, 1976. Dissertations in American Economic History. New York: Arno Press, 1977.

Harvey, Katherine A. *The Best-Dressed Miners: Life and Labor in the Maryland Coal Region, 1835–1910*. Ithaca, NY: Cornell University Press, 1969.

Hazard, Rowland G. *Our Resources*. New York: Wynkoop, Hallenbeck, & Thomas, 1864.

Hessen, Robert. *Steel Titan: The Life of Charles M. Schwab*. New York: Oxford University Press, 1975. Reprint. Pittsburgh, PA: University of Pittsburgh Press, 1990.

Hickman, Nollie. *Mississippi Harvest: Lumbering in the Longleaf Pine Belt, 1840–1915*. University, MS: University of Mississippi, 1962.

Hidy, Ralph W., and M. E. Hidy. *Pioneering in Big Business, 1882–1911*. Vol. 1 of *History of Standard Oil Company (New Jersey)*. New York: Harper, 1955. Reprint. Companies and Men. New York: Arno Press, 1976.

Hilton, George W., and John F. Due. *The Electric Interurban Railways in America*. Stanford, CA: Stanford University Press, 1960.

Hogan, William T. *The Reorganization of the Iron and Steel Industry, 1900–1920.* Vol. 2, part 3, of *Economic History of the Iron and Steel Industry in the United States.* Lexington, MA: D. C. Heath, Lexington Books, 1971.

Hoge, Cecil C., Sr. *The First Hundred Years Are the Toughest: What We Can Learn from the Century of Competition between Sears and Wards.* Berkeley, CA: Ten Speed Press, 1988.

Horn, Norbert, and Jürgen Kocka. *Law and the Formation of the Big Enterprises in the 19th and Early 20th Centuries.* Göttingen: Vandenhoeck & Ruprecht, 1979.

Hudson Coal Company. *The Story of Anthracite.* New York: Hudson Coal Company, 1932.

Hungerford, Edward. *The Romance of a Great Store* [Macy's]. New York: R. M. McBride, 1922.

Hurst, James W. *Law and Economic Growth: The Legal History of the Lumber Industry in Wisconsin, 1836–1915.* Cambridge, MA: Harvard University Press, Belknap Press, 1964. Reprint. Madison: University of Wisconsin Press, 1984.

Hyde, Charles K. "Metal Mining." In *Extractives, Manufacturing, and Services: A Historiographical and Bibliographical Guide.* Vol. 2 of *Handbook of American Business History,* edited by David O. Whitten and Bessie E. Whitten, 69–90. Westport, CT: Greenwood Press, 1997.

———. *Copper for America: The United States Copper Industry from Colonial Times to the 1990s.* Tucson: University of Arizona Press, 1998.

Igler, David. *Industrial Cowboys: Miller & Lux and the Transformation of the Far West, 1850–1920.* Berkeley: University of California Press, 2001.

Institute of American Meat Packers. *The Story of Meat: A Brief History of the Live Stock and Meat Industry and the Story of Meat from the Farm to the Table.* Chicago, IL: Institute of American Meat Packers, 1930.

———. *The Packing Industry.* Chicago, IL: University of Chicago Press and Institute of American Meat Packers, 1924. Reprint. America in Two Centuries, An Inventory. New York: Arno Press, 1976.

Jack, Andrew B. "The Channels of Distribution for an Innovation: The Sewing Machine Industry in America, 1860–1865." *Explorations in Entrepreneurial History* 9 (February 1957): 113–41.

Jacobstein, Meyer. *The Tobacco Industry in the United States.* Studies in History, Economics and Public Law, vol. 26, no. 3. New York: Columbia University Press, 1907.

———. "The Conditions of Tobacco Culture in the South." In *Economic History, 1865–1909.* Vol. 6 of *The South in the Building of the Nation,* edited by James Curtis Ballagh, 66–72. Richmond, VA: Southern Historical Publication Society, 1909.

Jensen, Merrill. *The New Nation: A History of the United States During the Confederation, 1781–1789.* New York: Knopf, 1950. Reprint. Boston: Northeastern University Press, 1981.

John, Richard R. *Spreading the News: The American Postal System from Franklin to Morse.* Cambridge, MA: Harvard University Press, 1995.

Jones, Chester Lloyd. *The Economic History of the Anthracite-Tidewater Canals.* Series in Political Economy and Public Law, no. 22. Philadelphia: University of Pennsylvania, 1908.

Jones, Eliot. *The Anthracite Coal Combination in the United States: With Some Account of the Early Development of the Anthracite Industry.* Harvard Economic Studies, vol. 11. Cambridge, MA: Harvard University, 1914.

Katz, Donald R. *The Big Store: Inside the Crisis and Revolution at Sears, Roebuck.* New York: Viking, 1987.

Kellar, Herbert Anthony, ed. *Solon Robinson: Pioneer and Agriculturalist.* Indianapolis: Indiana Historical Bureau, 1936.

Keller, Charles L. *The Lady in the Ore Bucket: A History of Settlement and Industry in the Tri-Canyon Area of the Wasatch Mountains.* Salt Lake City: University of Utah Press, 2001.

Kelly, Alfred H., Winfred A. Harbison, and Herman Belz. *The American Constitution: Its Origins and Development.* 2 vols. 7th ed. New York: Norton, 1991.

Kolko, Gabriel. *Railroads and Regulation, 1877–1916.* Princeton, NJ: Princeton University Press, 1965.

Krass, Peter. *Carnegie.* New York: John Wiley & Sons, 2002.

Kroll, Harry H. *Riders in the Night.* Philadelphia: University of Pennsylvania Press, 1965.

Labbe, John T., and Vernon Goe. *Railroads in the Woods.* Berkeley, CA: Howell-North, 1961.

Lane, Winthrop D., with introduction by John R. Commons. *Civil War in West Virginia: A Story of the Industrial Conflict in the Coal Mines.* Freeman Pamphlets. New York: B. W. Huebsch, 1921. Reprint. American Labor. New York: Arno Press, 1969.

Larson, Agnes M. *History of the White Pine Industry in Minnesota.* Minneapolis: University of Minnesota Press, 1949.

Latham, Frank B. *1872–1972: A Century of Serving Consumers; The Story of Montgomery Ward.* 2d ed. Chicago, IL: Montgomery Ward, 1972.

Lebhar, Godfrey M. *Chain Stores in America, 1859–1950.* New York: Chain Store Publishing Corporation, 1952.

Leech, Harper, and John Charles Carroll. *Armour and His Times* [Philip Danforth Armour]. New York: D. Appleton-Century, 1938. Reprint. Freeport, NY: Books for Libraries Press, 1971.

Lewis, Ronald L. *Coal, Iron, and Slaves: Industrial Slavery in Maryland and Virginia, 1715–1865.* Contributions in Labor History, no. 6. Westport, CT: Greenwood Press, 1979.

Lief, Alfred. *A Century in the Life and Times of Strawbridge & Clothier, 1868–1968.* Vol. 1 of *Family Business.* New York: McGraw-Hill, 1968.

Lindley, Lester G. *The Constitution Faces Technology: The Relationship of the National Government to the Telegraph, 1866–1884.* Ph.D. diss., Rice University, 1971. Dissertations in American Economic History. New York: Arno Press, 1975.

Livesay, Harold C. *Andrew Carnegie and the Rise of Big Business.* Edited by Oscar Handlin. Library of American Biography. Boston: Little, Brown, 1975.

Long, Priscilla. *Where the Sun Never Shines: A History of America's Bloody Coal Industry.* New York: Paragon House, 1989.

Lucia, Ellis, with introduction by Arthur W. Priaulx. *Head Rig: Story of the West Coast Lumber Industry.* Portland, OR: Overland West Press, 1965.

———. *The Big Woods: Logging and Lumbering, From Bull Teams to Helicopters, in the Pacific Northwest.* Garden City, NY: Doubleday, 1975.

Magnusson, Lars. *Mercantilism: The Shaping of an Economic Language.* New York: Routledge, 1994.

Malone, Laurence J. *Opening the West: Federal Internal Improvements Before 1860.* Contributions in Economics and Economic History, no. 196. Westport, CT: Greenwood Press, 1998.

Mann, Charles K. *Tobacco: The Ants and the Elephants*. Salt Lake City, UT: Olympus in cooperation with the Southern Regional Council, 1975.

Manning, Richard. *One Round River: The Curse of Gold and the Fight for the Big Blackfoot*. New York: Henry Holt, 1998.

Marshall, Jennings B. "Bituminous Coal Mining." In *Extractives, Manufacturing, and Services: A Historiographical and Bibliographical Guide*. Vol. 2 of *Handbook of American Business History*, edited by David O. Whitten and Bessie F. Whitten, 93–103. Westport, CT: Greenwood Press, 1997.

Maxwell, Robert S., and Robert D. Baker. *Sawdust Empire: The Texas Lumber Industry, 1830–1940*. College Station: Texas A&M University Press, 1983.

May, Stacy, and Galo Plaza. *The United Fruit Company in Latin America*. Case Study, NPA Series on United States Business Performance Abroad, no. 7. Washington, DC: National Planning Association, 1958.

McDonald, Forrest. *We the People: The Economic Origins of the Constitution*. Chicago, IL: University of Chicago Press, 1958.

Melville, John H. *The Great White Fleet*. New York: Vantage Press, 1976.

Melvin, A. D. "The Federal Meat-Inspection Service." In *Twenty-third Annual Report of the Bureau of Animal Industry for the Year 1906*. Washington, DC: U.S. Department of Agriculture, 1908.

Meneely, Alexander H. *The War Department, 1861: A Study in Mobilization and Administration*. Studies in History, Economics and Public Law, no. 300. New York: Columbia University Press, 1928. Reprint. New York: AMS Press, 1970.

Mercer, Lloyd J. "Railroad Transportation." In *Extractives, Manufacturing, and Services: A Historiographical and Bibliographical Guide*. Vol. 2 of *Handbook of American Business History*, edited by David O. Whitten and Bessie E. Whitten, 313–53. Westport, CT: Greenwood Press, 1997.

Miller, Carol J. "Tobacco Manufacturing." In *Manufacturing: A Historiographical and Bibliographical Guide*. Vol. 1 of *Handbook of American Business History*, edited by David O. Whitten and Bessie E. Whitten, 65–86. Westport, CT: Greenwood Press, 1990.

Miller, John Chester. *The Federalist Era, 1789–1801*. The New American Nation. New York: Harper & Row, 1963.

Miller, William. "American Historians and the Business Elite." *Journal of Economic History* 9 (November 1949): 184–208.

Mills, C. Wright. "The American Business Elite: A Collective Portrait." *Journal of Economic History* 5 (December 1945): 20–44.

Misa, Thomas J. *A Nation of Steel: The Making of Modern America, 1865–1925*. Johns Hopkins Studies in the History of Technology. Baltimore, MD: Johns Hopkins University Press, 1995.

Mothershead, Harmon Ross. *The Swan Land and Cattle Company, Ltd.* Norman: University of Oklahoma Press, 1971.

Mumford, John K. *Anthracite*. Romance of Industry Series. New York: Industries Publishing, 1925.

Munn, Robert F. *The Coal Industry in America: A Bibliography and Guide to Studies*. Morgantown: West Virginia University Library, 1965.

Murray, Stanley N. "Railroads and the Agricultural Development of the Red River Valley of the North, 1870–1890." *Agricultural History* 31 (October 1957): 57–66.

Myers, Margaret G. *A Financial History of the United States*. New York: Columbia University Press, 1970.

Nall, James O. *The Tobacco Night Riders of Kentucky and Tennessee, 1905–1909*. Louisville, KY: Standard Press, 1939. Reprint. Kuttawa, KY: McClanahan, 1991.

Nevins, Allan. *The Emergence of Modern America, 1865–1878*. A History of American Life, vol. 8. New York: Macmillan, 1927.

———. *John D. Rockefeller: The Heroic Age of American Enterprise*. Vol. 2. New York: C. Scribner's Sons, 1940.

———. *Study in Power: John D. Rockefeller, Industrialist and Philanthropist*. 2 vols. New York: Scribner, 1953.

———. *The War for the Union*. 4 vols. New York: Scribner, 1959–71.

Neyhart, Louise Albright. *Giant of the Yards* [Gustavus Franklin Swift]. Boston, MA: Houghton Mifflin, 1952.

Nordyke, Lewis. *Cattle Empire: The Fabulous Story of the 3,000,000 Acre XIT*. New York: W. Morrow, 1949. Reprint. New York: Arno Press, 1977.

North, Douglass C. *Growth and Welfare in the American Past: A New Economic History*. Englewood Cliffs, NJ: Prentice-Hall, 1966.

Oberholtzer, Ellis Paxson. *Jay Cooke: Financier of the Civil War*. 2 vols. Philadelphia, PA: G. W. Jacobs, 1907.

O'Connell, William E., Jr. "The Development of the Private Railroad Freight Car, 1830–1966." *Business History Review* 44 (Summer 1970): 190–209.

O'Connor, Richard. *Iron Wheels and Broken Men: The Railroad Barons and the Plunder of the West*. New York: Putnam, 1973.

Olmsted, Frederick Law. *A Journey in the Back Country, 1853–1854*. New York: Mason Brothers, 1860.

Oppedisano, Jeannette M. *Historical Encyclopedia of American Women Entrepreneurs: 1776 to the Present*. Westport, CT: Greenwood Press, 2000.

Otter, Floyd Leslie. *The Men of Mammoth Forest: A Hundred-Year History of a Sequoia Forest and Its People in Tulare County, California*. Ann Arbor, MI: Edwards Bros., 1963.

Owens, Harry P. *Steamboats and the Cotton Economy: River Trade in the Yazoo-Mississippi Delta*. Jackson: University of Mississippi Press, 1990.

Palladino, Grace. *Another Civil War: Labor, Capital, and the State in the Anthracite Regions of Pennsylvania, 1840–68*. The Working Class in American History. Urbana: University of Illinois Press, 1990.

Pate, J'Nell L. *Livestock Legacy: The Fort Worth Stockyards, 1887–1987*. Centennial Series of the Association of Former Students, Texas A&M University, no. 27. College Station: Texas A&M University Press, 1988.

Patton, Spiro G. "Local and Suburban Transit." In *Extractives, Manufacturing, and Services: A Historiographical and Bibliographical Guide*. Vol. 2 of *Handbook of American Business History*, edited by David O. Whitten and Bessie E. Whitten, 357–74. Westport, CT: Greenwood Press, 1997.

Perkins, Edwin J. *The Economy of Colonial America*. 2d ed. New York: Columbia University Press, 1988.

———. *American Public Finance and Financial Services, 1700–1815*. Historical Perspectives on Business Enterprise. Columbus: Ohio State University Press, 1994.

Perkins, Edwin, and Gary M. Walton. *A Prosperous People: The Growth of the American Economy*. Englewood Cliffs, NJ: Prentice-Hall, 1985.

Peto, S. Morton. *The Resources and Prospects of America, Ascertained During a Visit to the States in the Autumn of 1865*. London: A. Strahan, 1866.

Pettengill, Robert B. "The United States Copper Industry and the Tariff." *Quarterly Journal of Economics* 46 (November 1931): 141–57.

Phillips, Charles F. "A History of the F. W. Woolworth Company." *Harvard Business Review* 14 (January 1935): 225–36.

Phillips, Edward K. "The Gulf Coast Rice Industry." *Agricultural History* 25 (April 1951): 91–96.

Presbrey, Frank. *The History and Development of Advertising*. Garden City, NY: Doubleday, 1929. Reprint. New York: Greenwood Press, 1968.

Price, Andrew, Jr. *Port Blakely: The Community Captain Renton Built*. Seattle, WA: Port Blakely Books, 1990.

Prichard, Walter. "The Effects of the Civil War on the Louisiana Sugar Industry." *Journal of Southern History* 5 (August 1939): 315–32.

Puter, Stephen A. Douglas, and Horace Stevens. *Looters of the Public Domain*. Portland, OR: Portland Printing House, 1908.

Ransom, Roger. "British Policy and Colonial Growth: Some Implications of the Burden from the Navigation Acts." *Journal of Economic History* 28, no. 3 (September 1968): 427–35.

Report of the Federal Trade Commission on the Meat-Packing Industry: Part II, Evidence of Combination among Packers. Washington, DC: U.S. Government Printing Office, 1918.

Resseguie, Harry E. "Alexander Turney Stewart and the Development of the Department Store, 1823–1876." *Business History Review* 39 (Autumn 1965): 301–22.

Richter, F. Ernest. "The Amalgamated Copper Company: A Closed Chapter in Corporation Finance." *Quarterly Journal of Economics* 30 (February 1916): 387–407.

———. "The Copper Mining Industry in the United States, 1845–1925." *Quarterly Journal of Economics* 41 (1926–27): 236–91 and 684–717.

Robert, Joseph C. *The Story of Tobacco in America*. Chapel Hill: University of North Carolina Press, 1967.

Roberts, B. W. C., and Snow L. Roberts. *Bull Durham Business Bonanza, 1866–1940*. Durham, NC: Genuine Durham Press, 2002.

Roberts, Peter. *The Anthracite Coal Industry*. New York: Macmillan, 1901.

———. *Anthracite Coal Communities: A Study of the Demography, the Social, Educational and Moral Life of the Anthracite Regions*. New York: Macmillan, 1904.

Rothstein, Morton. "A British Investment in Bonanza Farming, 1879–1910." *Agricultural History* 33 (April 1959): 72–78.

———. "The Big Farm: Abundance and Scale in American Agriculture." *Agricultural History* 49 (October 1975): 583–97.

Rudolf, Paul O. *History of the Lake States Forest Experiment Station*. St. Paul, MN: U.S. Department of Agriculture, Forest Service, North Central Forest Experiment Station, 1985.

Saggus, James. "Old Bond Default Haunts Mississippi: 145-Year-Old Debt Surfaces," *Washington Post*, September 16, 1986, C1, C2.

Schaefer, Donald F. *A Quantitative Description and Analysis of the Growth of the Pennsylvania Anthracite Coal Industry, 1820 to 1865*. Dissertations in American Economic History. New York: Arno Press, 1977.

Scott, Carole E. "Radio and Television Broadcasting." In *Infrastructure and Services: A Historiographical and Bibliographical Guide*. Vol. 3 of *Handbook of American Business History*, edited by David O. Whitten and Bessie E. Whitten, 55–101. Westport, CT: Greenwood Press, 2000.

Scott, Roy V. "American Railroads and Agricultural Extension, 1900–1914: A Study in Railway Developmental Techniques." *Business History Review* 39 (Winter (1965): 74–98.

Seltzer, Curtis. *Fire in the Hole: Miners and Managers in the American Coal Industry*. Lexington: University Press of Kentucky, 1985.

Sensel, Joni. *Traditions Through the Trees: Weyerhaeuser's First 100 Years*. Seattle, WA: Documentary Book Publishers, 1999.

Sherman, Simon Augustus, and Ceylon Childs Lincoln. *Wisconsin River Lumber Rafting*. Madison: Wisconsin State Historical Society, 1911.

Shoebotham, H. Minar. *Anaconda: Life of Marcus Daly, the Copper King*. Harrisburg, PA: Stackpole, 1956.

Shugg, Roger Wallace. "Survival of the Plantation System in Louisiana." *Journal of Southern History* 3 (Summer 1937): 311–25.

Shurick, Adam T. *The Coal Industry*. Boston, MA: Little, Brown, 1924.

Sitterson, J. Carlyle. "The McCollams: A Planter Family of the Old and New South." *Journal of Southern History* 6 (Summer 1940): 346–67.

―――. "The Transition from Slave to Free Economy on the William J. Minor Plantations." *Agricultural History* 17 (October 1943): 216–24.

―――. *Sugar Country: The Cane Sugar Industry in the South, 1753–1950*. Lexington: University of Kentucky Press, 1953.

Skaggs, Jimmy M. *Prime Cut: Livestock Raising and Meatpacking in the United States, 1607–1983*. College Station: Texas A&M University Press, 1986.

Smith, David C. *A History of Lumbering in Maine, 1861–1960*. University of Maine Studies, no. 93. Orono: University of Maine Press, 1972.

Smith, Walker C. *The Everett Massacre: A History of the Class Struggle in the Lumber Industry*. Chicago, IL: I.W.W. Publishing Bureau, 1918. Reprint. New York: Da Capo Press, 1971.

Sobel, Robert. *The Age of Giant Corporations: A Microeconomic History of American Business, 1914–1970*. Contributions in Economics and Economic History, no. 7. Westport, CT: Greenwood Press, 1972.

―――. *The Entrepreneurs: Explorations within the American Business Tradition*. New York: Weybright & Talley, 1974.

―――. *They Satisfy: The Cigarette in American Life*. New York: Doubleday, Anchor Press, 1978.

Spence, Clark C. *British Investments and the American Mining Frontier, 1860–1901*. Ithaca, NY: Cornell University Press for the American Historical Association, 1958.

Spicer, Michael W. *The Founders, the Constitution, and Public Administration: A Conflict in Worldviews*. Washington, DC: Georgetown University Press, 1995.

Stabile, Donald R. *The Origins of American Public Finance: Debates over Money, Debt, and Taxes in the Constitutional Era, 1776–1836*. Contributions in Economics and Economic History, no. 198. Westport, CT: Greenwood Press, 1998.

Starling, Robert B. "The Plank Road Movement in North Carolina." *North Carolina Historical Review* 16 (1939): 1–22.

Steer, Henry B., comp. *Lumber Production in the United States, 1799–1946*. U.S. Department of Agriculture Miscellaneous Publication no. 669. Washington, DC: U.S. Government Printing Office, 1948.

Stein, Harry. *Rooted in the Past, Growing for the Future: Pope Resources* [Pope & Talbot Lumber Co.]. Seattle, WA: Sasquatch Books, 2003.

Stover, John F. *The Railroads of the South, 1865–1900: A Study in Finance and Control*. Chapel Hill: University of North Carolina Press, 1955.

———. *The Life and Decline of the American Railroad*. New York: Oxford University Press, 1970.

———. *Iron Road to the West: American Railroads in the 1850s*. New York: Columbia University Press, 1978.

———. *History of the Baltimore and Ohio Railroad*. West Lafayette, IN: Purdue University Press, 1986.

———. *American Railroads*. 2d ed. Chicago History of American Civilization. Chicago, IL: University of Chicago Press, 1997.

Sullivan, Timothy E. "Water Transportation." In *Extractives, Manufacturing, and Services: A Historiographical and Bibliographical Guide*. Vol. 2 of *Handbook of American Business History*, edited by David O. Whitten and Bessie E. Whitten, 409–36. Westport, CT: Greenwood Press, 1997.

Swan, Dale Evans. *The Structure and Profitability of the Antebellum Rice Industry, 1859*. Ann Arbor, MI: University Microfilms, 1972.

Swift, Louis Franklin, in collaboration with Arthur Van Vlissingen Jr. *The Yankee of the Yards: The Biography of Gustavus Franklin Swift*. 1927. Reprint. New York: AMS Press, 1970.

Tarbell, Ida M. *The History of the Standard Oil Company*. 2 vols. New York: McClure, Phillips, 1904.

———. *The Life of Elbert H. Gary: A Story of Steel*. 1925. Reprint. New York: Greenwood Press, 1969.

Taylor, Edith Wharton. *Money on the Hoof, Sometimes*. Fort Collins, CO: Old Army Press, 1974.

Taylor, George Rogers. *The Transportation Revolution 1815–1860*. Economic History of the United States, vol. 4. New York: Rinehart, 1951.

Taylor, George Rogers, and Irene D. Neu. *The American Railroad Network, 1861–1890*. Studies in Economic History. Cambridge, MA: Harvard University Press, 1956.

Temin, Peter. *Iron and Steel in Nineteenth-Century America: An Economic Inquiry*. MIT Monographs in Economics, no. 2. Cambridge, MA: MIT Press, 1964.

Tennant, Richard B. *The American Cigarette Industry: A Study in Economic Analysis and Public Policy*. Hamden, CT: Archon Books, 1971.

Thompson, Robert Luther. *Wiring a Continent: The History of the Telegraph Industry in the United States, 1832–1866*. Princeton, NJ: Princeton University Press, 1947.

Turner, Charles W. "Railroad Service to Virginia Farmers, 1828–1860." *Agricultural History* 22 (1948): 239–48.

Turner, Frederick Jackson. *The Frontier in American History*. New York: H. Holt, 1920.

Twinning, Charles E. *George S. Long, Timber Statesman*. Seattle: University of Washington Press, 1994.

———. *F. K. Weyerhaeuser: A Biography*. St. Paul: Minnesota Historical Society Press, 1997.

United States Steel Corporation. *Business . . . Big and Small . . . Built America: Statements by Officials of United States Steel Before the Subcommittee on the Study of Monopoly Power of the House Committee on the Judiciary, Washington, DC, April 26–28, 1950.* New York: United States Steel Corporation, 1950.

U.S. Bureau of the Census. *Census of Electric Industries: 1917 Electric Railways.* Washington, DC: U.S. Government Printing Office, 1920.

———. *Historical Statistics of the United States, Colonial Times to 1957.* Washington, DC: U.S. Government Printing Office, 1960.

U.S. Federal Trade Commission. *The American Tobacco Company and the Imperial Tobacco Company.* Washington, DC: U.S. Government Printing Office, 1926.

Virtue, George O. "The Anthracite Combinations." *Quarterly Journal of Economics* 10 (April 1896): 296–323.

Wade, Louise Carroll. *Chicago's Pride: The Stockyards, Packingtown, and Environs in the Nineteenth Century.* Urbana: University of Illinois Press, 1987.

Walker, Laurence C. *The Southern Forest: A Chronicle.* Austin: University of Texas Press, 1991.

Wallis, George A. *Cattle Kings of the Staked Plains.* Dallas, TX: American Guild Press, 1957.

Walsh, Margaret. *The Rise of the Midwestern Meat Packing Industry.* Lexington: University Press of Kentucky, 1982.

Walsh, William I. *The Rise and Decline of the Great Atlantic and Pacific Tea Company.* Secaucus, NJ: L. Stuart, 1986.

Ward, James A. *Railroads and the Character of America, 1820–1887.* Knoxville: University of Tennessee Press, 1986.

Warren, Kenneth. *The American Steel Industry, 1850–1970: A Geographical Interpretation.* Oxford Research Studies in Geography. Oxford: Clarendon Press, 1973. Reprint. Pittsburgh, PA: University of Pittsburgh Press, 1988.

———. *Triumphant Capitalism: Henry Clay Frick and the Industrial Transformation of America.* Pittsburgh, PA: University of Pittsburgh Press, 1996.

———. *Big Steel: The First Century of the United States Steel Corporation, 1901–2001.* Pittsburgh, PA: University of Pittsburgh Press, 2001.

Weals, Vic. *Last Train to Elkmont: A Look Back at Life on Little River in the Great Smoky Mountains.* Knoxville, TN: Olden Press, 1991.

Weigley, Russell F. *Quartermaster General of the Union Army: A Biography of M. C. Meigs.* New York: Columbia University Press, 1959.

Weiss, Harry B., and Grace M. Weiss. *Rafting on the Delaware River.* Trenton: New Jersey Agricultural Society, 1967.

Wells, David A. *The Recent Financial, Industrial and Commercial Experiences of the United States: A Curious Chapter in Politico-Economic History.* New York: J. H. and C. M. Goodsell, 1872.

Wendel, Susan DuBrock. "Telegraph Communications." In *Infrastructure and Services: A Historiographical and Bibliographical Guide.* Vol. 3 of *Handbook of American Business History,* edited by David O. Whitten and Bessie E. Whitten, 31–53. Westport, CT: Greenwood Press, 2000.

White, John H. *The Great Yellow Fleet: A History of American Railroad Refrigerator Cars.* San Marino, CA: Golden West Books, 1986.

Whitten, David O. *Antebellum Sugar and Rice Plantations, Louisiana and South Carolina: A Profitability Study.* Ann Arbor, MI: University Microfilms, 1970.

———. "Tariff and Profit in the Antebellum Louisiana Sugar Industry." *Business History Review* 44 (Summer 1970): 226–33.

———. "An Economic Inquiry into the Whiskey Rebellion of 1794." *Agricultural History* 49, no. 3 (July 1975): 491–504.

———. "American Rice Cultivation, 1680–1980: A Tercentenary Critique." *Southern Studies* 21 (Spring 1982): 5–26.

———. "A Flat-Kinked Demand Function for Oligopolistic Sellers of Homogeneous Products." *Review of Industrial Organization* 1, no. 3 (Fall 1984): 206–15.

———. "On the Road with King Cotton, 1926–1940." *Essays in Economic and Business History* 10 (1992): 240–56.

———. *Andrew Durnford: A Black Sugar Planter in the Antebellum South.* New Brunswick, NJ: Transaction Publishers, 1995.

———. "Anthracite Coal." In *Extractives, Manufacturing, and Services: A Historiographical and Bibliographical Guide.* Vol. 2 of *Handbook of American Business History*, edited by David O. Whitten and Bessie E. Whitten, 105–21. Westport, CT: Greenwood Press, 1997.

———. "Alternate Routes: Exceptional Road Building Materials." *Essays in Economic and Business History* 17 (1999): 229–43.

———. "Earth Roads Are Easy." *Essays in Economic and Business History* 18 (2000): 197–210.

Wiley, B. I. "Salient Changes in Southern Agriculture Since the Civil War." *Agricultural History* 13 (April 1939): 65–96.

Williams, Richard L. *The Loggers.* Old West. New York: Time-Life Books, 1976.

Williams, Willard F., and Thomas T. Stout. *Economics of the Livestock-Meat Industry.* New York: Macmillan, 1964.

Williamson, Harold F., and Arnold R. Daum. *The Age of Illumination, 1859–1899.* Vol. 1 of *The American Petroleum Industry.* Northwestern University Studies in Business History. Evanston, IL: Northwestern University Press, 1959.

Williamson, Harold F., Ralph L. Andreano, Arnold R. Daum, and Gilbert C. Klose. *The Age of Energy, 1899–1959.* Vol. 2 of *The American Petroleum Industry.* Northwestern University Studies in Business History. Evanston, IL: Northwestern University Press, 1963.

Wilson, Charles Morrow. *Empire in Green and Gold: The Story of the American Banana Trade.* New York: H. Holt, 1947.

Winkler, John K. *Tobacco Tycoon, The Story of James Buchanan Duke.* New York: Random House, 1942.

Wolff, David A. *Industrializing the Rockies: Growth, Competition, and Turmoil in the Coalfields of Colorado and Wyoming.* Mining the American West. Boulder: University Press of Colorado, 2003.

Wood, Virginia S., with drawings by Walter E. Channing. *Live Oaking: Southern Timber for Tall Ships.* Boston: Northeastern University Press, 1981. Reprint. Annapolis, MD: Naval Institute Press, 1995.

Wright, Gavin. *The Political Economy of the Cotton South: Households, Markets, and Wealth in the Nineteenth Century.* New York: Norton, 1978.

Yeager, Mary. *Competition and Regulation: The Development of Oligopoly in the Meat Packing Industry.* Industrial Development and the Social Fabric, vol. 2. Greenwich, CT: JAI Press, 1981.

Yearley, Clifton K., Jr. *Enterprise and Anthracite: Economics and Democracy in Schuylkill County, 1820–1875.* Johns Hopkins University Studies in Historical and Political Science, ser. 79, no. 1. Baltimore, MD: Johns Hopkins Press, 1961.

Young, James A., and Jerry Budy. *Endless Tracks in the Woods.* Crestline Agricultural Series. Sarasota, FL: Crestline, 1989. Reprint. Osceola, WI: Motorbooks International, 1993.

Zulker, William Allen. *John Wanamaker: King of Merchants.* Wayne, PA: Eaglecrest Press, 1993.

Index

About the Authors

DAVID O. WHITTEN is Professor of Economics at Auburn University. He is the author of *A History of Economics and Business at Auburn University* (1992) and *Andrew Durnford: A Black Sugar Planter in the Antebellum South* (1995); coauthor, with Douglas Steeples, of *Democracy in Desperation: The Depression of 1893* (1998); and editor of *Eli Whitney's Cotton Gin, 1793–1993* and *Essays in Economic and Business History*, the journal of the Economic and Business Historical Society.

BESSIE E. WHITTEN is editor (with David O. Whitten) of *Manufacturing: A Historiographical and Bibliographical Guide* (1990), *Extractives, Manufacturing, and Services: A Historiographical and Bibliographical Guide* (1997), and *Infrastructure and Services: A Historiographical and Bibliographical Guide* (2000), volumes 1–3 of the *Handbook of American Business History*; and of *Business Library Review International*, a journal of refereed articles, book review articles, and book notes (1988–2001).